Social Security

What Role for the Future?

Edited by

Peter A. Diamond

David C. Lindeman

Howard Young

NATIONAL ACADEMY OF SOCIAL INSURANCE
Washington, D.C.

Copyright © 1996
NATIONAL ACADEMY OF SOCIAL INSURANCE
1776 Massachusetts Avenue, N.W., Washington, D.C. 20036
Distributed worldwide by THE BROOKINGS INSTITUTION
1775 Massachusetts Avenue, N.W., Washington, D.C. 20036-2188, U.S.A.

Library of Congress Cataloging-in-Publication Data

Social security : what role for the future? / Peter Diamond,
    David C. Lindeman, Howard Young, eds.
      p. cm.
      Includes bibliographical references and index.
      ISBN 0-8157-1835-7 (pbk.)
      1. Social security — United States.   I. Diamond, Peter A.
      II. Lindeman, David C., 1944–   .   III. Young, Howard, 1932–   .
HD7125.S5996   1996   95-41812
368.4′3′00973 — dc20   CIP

9 8 7 6 5 4 3 2 1

Typeset in Times Roman

Composition by AlphaTechnologies/mps, Inc.
  Charlotte Hall, Maryland

Printed by R. R. Donnelley and Sons Co.
  Harrisonburg, Virginia

Acknowledgments

The National Academy of Social Insurance is a nonprofit, nonpartisan organization devoted to furthering knowledge and understanding of Social Security and related programs. The Academy provides a forum in which to explore challenges and opportunities facing the field of social insurance; assesses social insurance programs and their relationships to other public and private programs; helps develop future scholars and administrative leaders; supports basic study, policy analysis, and research; and promotes public understanding of social insurance principles and programs.

This book is based primarily on papers delivered at the seventh annual conference of the Academy.[1] The conference, "Social Security: What Role for the Future?," was held on January 25–26, 1995, in Washington. Sessions and speakers took a fresh look at questions that are key to understanding the future of the cash benefits portion of old-age protection under Social Security.

As with all activities organized under its auspices, the Academy takes responsibility for assuring the independence of this book. Participants in the conference were chosen for their recognized expertise and with due consideration of the balance of disciplines appropriate to the program. The resulting chapters represent the views of those who presented the papers and are not necessarily the views of the officers, board, staff, or members of the Academy.

We would like to thank all the conference participants for sparking a lively discussion of ideas and the Academy staff for making the conference run as smoothly as it did. We also appreciate the efforts of all the people who have made this book possible: the authors for their timely attention to the huge task

1. The exceptions are the introduction by David C. Lindeman, which was produced after the conference; the commentary in chapter 6 by Peter Diamond, which is a revised version of a longer paper that appeared in *Revista de Analysis Económico,* no. 9, 21–34, 1994; and chapter 7 by Peter Diamond, which is a revised version of the Nemmers Prize lecture delivered at Northwestern University on April 19, 1995.

of turning their presentations into chapters; Nick Curraba, the student intern who collected the chapters and worked with the authors; the managing editor at the Brookings Institution, Deborah Styles, and the Brookings editors, Tanjam Jacobson and Steph Selice; and the Academy staff, especially Pamela J. Larson and Terry T. Nixon, who saw the project through to completion.

PETER A. DIAMOND
DAVID C. LINDEMAN
HOWARD YOUNG

Contents

Introduction   1
David C. Lindeman

1   Social Security and Retirees: Two Views of
    the Projections   21
    Robert L. Brown   21
    Diane J. Macunovich   43
        Comment by Stephen C. Goss   67
        Comment by Sylvester J. Schieber   78

2   Fund Accumulation: How Much? How Managed?   89
    Barry P. Bosworth
        Comment by Carolyn L. Weaver   115
        Comment by David W. Mullins Jr.   120

3   Reexamining the Three-Legged Stool   125
    David M. Cutler
        Comment by Edward Gramlich   149
        Comment by Margaret Simms   153
        Comment by Howard Young   154

4   Social Security Income and Taxation: Four Views
    on the Role of Means Testing   157
    Robert H. Binstock 157
    Martha Phillips 163
    C. Eugene Steuerle 167
    Gary Burtless 172

5   Social Security around the World   181
    Estelle James
        Comment by Alicia H. Munnell 197
        Comment by Dalmer Hoskins 198
        Comment by Robert P. Hagemann 201
        Comment by Jagadeesh Gokhale 204

6   Social Security Reform in Chile: Two Views   209
    Robert J. Myers 209
    Peter A. Diamond 213

7   The Future of Social Security   225
    Peter A. Diamond

Introduction

David C. Lindeman

RECENT REPORTS of the Old Age, Survivors', and Disability Insurance (OASDI) trustees note an increasing deficiency in the program's long-term financing. From the perspective of annual flow, the reports project that the deficiency will grow to between 3 and 5 percent of annual payroll after the year 2020 and will amount to approximately 15 percent of program spending over the next seventy-five years. More important, however, the reports project that unless corrective action is taken, the Social Security program will become insolvent—no longer be able to pay promised benefits in full—around the year 2030, well within the retirement years of the baby boom generation. And, equally critical, the date at which the trust fund stops being a net contributor and becomes a net claimant on the federal budget has been moved forward to the year 2013 in these projections.

These findings are disturbing to many people who believed that the 1983 Social Security amendments, which were largely based on the Greenspan commission's recommendations, had "fixed" the program through the period of the baby boom's retirement. In addition, the news media have begun to report increasing skepticism, especially among the young, of whether Social Security will be paying anything at all when they reach retirement age.

In November 1994, the American public elected a Republican majority in both houses of Congress, despite having elected a "New Democrat" president in 1992. Although it can be argued that the country had been tending to the right for more than two decades, these elections opened up explicit debates about the basic ends and means of government. The welfare state consensus forged in the prosperity of the period 1947–73 is now under strong challenge.

The notion of fundamental health care reform collapsed in 1994, and substantial cuts on spending for the elderly and disabled have come under active discussion in 1995, in a debate over Medicare that may presage a similar debate about Social Security in 1997. The Concord Coalition, led by former senators

1

Paul Tsongas and Warren Rudman and by Peter Peterson of the New York financial firm the Blackstone Group, has proposed a means-testing agenda that challenges traditional thinking about social insurance. The World Bank has published an extensive study that recommends substantially less reliance on government-run pay-as-you-go schemes in favor or greater (but not exclusive) reliance on funded retirement schemes that use private investment management. In other countries, rich and not so rich, major modifications in social insurance have been enacted or are under serious consideration.

The fix from the 1983 Social Security amendments has begun to unravel for several reasons. First, time has moved on. Given projections of ever-increasing longevity and holding everything else constant, a valuation period that stretches from 1995 through 2070 looks worse than one that stretches from 1983 through 2058. Second, because of many small changes in assumptions, Social Security actuaries have revised their understanding of current conditions such that projections for future are less robust—for example, it appears that the immigrant population is older than originally thought. Third, the trustees have adopted assumptions about the future that tend to increase costs relative to income.

Thinking about the Future

Assumptions about the future largely shape the debate over the role and size of social insurance, particularly pay-as-you-go systems. Assuming a future of rising fertility and robust productivity, pay-as-you-go systems can be managed without major controversy. If, however, zero population growth and relatively low productivity growth rates are projected—arguably, the condition in the United States since 1973—swings in cohort sizes and longevity increases pose some very painful choices. Although the question of how to think about the future permeates all the discussions in this book, it is the particular focus of chapter 1, "Social Security and Retirees: Two Views of the Projections."

In the first section of this chapter Robert Brown concentrates on the "inevitable surprises" inherent in what is known with some certainty about today's demographics. Brown does not seek any overarching theoretical framework into which he can fit demographic and economic phenomena. Rather, he discusses key assumptions sequentially, comparing and contrasting various theories in the literature.

Brown first draws the important distinction between the existing level of a country's aged dependency burden (consumption by the retired elderly and disabled relative to production by the working population) and the rate of change predicted in that level. He argues that by themselves, projected longevity increases do not pose major (or at least, not abrupt) transition problems. He postulates that for countries such as Sweden and the United Kingdom, where the proportion of aged persons is already large, future increases in that population will not pose a political problem, unless the public already finds the current contribution rate too burdensome. Interestingly, both of these countries have undertaken reforms to stabilize and even reduce their old age and disability pay-as-you-go programs, which suggests that their publics are reexamining the distributional preferences of earlier generations. As discussed below, in Sweden future mortality improvements will be internalized into the benefit formula. (Other countries, such as India and China, also are facing major changes in the percentage of their populations that are aged, but as they have no large, formal public or private schemes in place to address the problem, they may face a different sort of crisis in the next century.)

In a few countries, notably the United States and Canada, the phenomenon of a large baby boom followed by fertility rates at or below zero population growth presents a more difficult transition problem. Brown notes that this problem has been exacerbated because the baby boomers have accumulated a large explicit public debt, the burden of which is being passed on to lower birth cohorts.

He suggests that an increase in retirement age, including the initial age of eligibility, would accommodate the transition without further increasing the wealth transferred to a nonworking-aged population. An increase in retirement age of five years (or commensurate increases in actuarial decrements, if the initial age were not increased by a full five years) would be sufficient. Brown believes that labor markets can and probably will accommodate changes of this magnitude. Commentator Sylvester Schieber has studied the behavior of current employers and is less optimistic than Brown that older workers can be easily retained in labor markets where continual technological change is commonplace. He believes that much will depend on the relative demand for older workers, which in turn, will depend on the supply of the younger workers and capital.

Brown suggests that given the current age profile of the baby boom, which he defines in a somewhat lagged manner as compared to the conventional definition, countries such as the United States and Canada should be seeking to attract an educated immigrant group ages twenty-nine and younger. This would help to top up the low birth rates that have followed the baby boom; older immigrants only amplify the baby boom phenomenon. On the key issue of whether fertility rates will rebound in accordance with the thesis postulated by demographer Richard A. Easterlin, however, he is cautious. Brown sides with John F. Ermisch and Nathan Keyfitz in concluding that, given the increased entry of women into the full-time labor market, the opportunity costs of having many children have increased so greatly that long-term fertility rates are unlikely to rise above zero population growth.

On the supply of capital, Brown predicts an upturn in savings as baby boomers move toward and into retirement; lower real interest rates; an increase in capital to labor ratios; and generally lower unemployment rates, with an increasing demand for older workers. He notes, however, that demography is not necessarily destiny with respect to these economic effects. The demand for younger workers may be undercut if they are not sufficiently educated. It also is worth bearing in mind that the large debt overhang exacerbates the burden of the baby boom's retirement. Although Brown does not draw these implications, continued government dissaving can undercut any increases in household savings among middle-aged baby boomers, thereby keeping real interest rates relatively high. In addition, infusions of foreign capital cannot sustain or increase capital-to-labor ratios in the long term.

Both Brown and Schieber touch on an emerging issue: the extent to which the effects of the baby boom's retirement and future increases in longevity can be mitigated by moving to a more funded regime, either in the public Social Security program or in private supplementary plans. As Nicholas Barr has shown, in a closed economy funded and pay-as-you-go retirement regimes share the same transition adjustments when large birth cohorts are followed by smaller cohorts.[1] In a pay-as-you-go regime, smaller successive cohorts may refuse to pay the higher contributions or payroll taxes necessary to support larger previous cohorts at promised benefit levels, forcing the latter to work longer or accept lower consumption levels than they desire or expect. Assuming no major growth in the propensity to increase savings among smaller successive cohorts, in a funded regime larger previous cohorts may find themselves trying to cash in assets whose value cannot be preserved at the level needed to maintain desired, or expected, consumption in retirement. Either the nominal price of the assets will fall as supply outstrips demand (as may already have happened with the housing stock, for example), or demand-push inflation may erode the purchasing power of fixed price assets more than anticipated (meanwhile, younger workers are protected through inflation-adjusted wage increases). Brown presents a similar analysis, and Schieber references a paper that he prepared with John Shoven, outlining the problems that privately funded defined benefit plans may face during the baby boom's retirement.

Brown suggests two solutions: decreasing retirement periods and building up financial claims against countries whose populations have younger age

1. See Barr (1979).

profiles than those in the northern hemisphere. Selling U.S. financial assets to workers in other countries in an open economy at the time of the baby boom's retirement may also be a solution. Lest the virtues of increased domestic saving be forgotten, however, more saving and investment now can mean higher productivity and hence, a larger GDP by the time baby boomers retire. A larger GDP implies a higher base against which to impose payroll taxes in a pay-as-you-go regime and higher real incomes from which future workers will purchase the financial assets of baby boomer retirees.

Brown notes that higher productivity could help square the circle of demographic transition, but Schieber cautions that future workers may be unwilling to share enough of their increased output to fully protect baby boomer retirees. After all, few future workers are likely to understand that their incomes are higher by reason of increased antecedent saving by the baby boomers in the latter's late middle age. Accordingly, future younger workers may resist higher payroll taxes. In addition, their real incomes are unlikely to be so much larger that they can absorb all the baby boomers' retirement assets at the baby boomers' desired price levels. In the end, some combination of longer working lives and increased savings is necessary to accommodate the baby boomers' retirement and the subsequent plateau of a permanently higher aged dependency ratio.

On the issue of increased retirement savings, Schieber argues that over the past fifteen years U.S. public policy has discouraged pension funding, particularly in traditional final pay defined benefit plans. In effect, these now behave more like pay-as-you-go than funded plans. Thus they may face almost as acute demographic transitions as does Social Security.

In the second section of chapter 1, Diane Macunovich presents a carefully wrought exposition of the how Richard Easterlin's theory of relative cohort sizes can help to explain the bad news of the past twenty-five years. The same theory also suggests that the next decades may have better outcomes than now predicted. As Brown explains in his paper:

> Easterlin has postulated that fertility rates rise and fall in a wavelike pattern with a cycle length, from peak to peak or from trough to trough, of two generations.[2] He points out that couples from a small cohort, such as those born in the 1930s, find life relatively easy. Jobs are plentiful, advancement is fast, and wealth is accumulated relatively easily. Such couples will tend to have large families, as was the case in the 1950s. Conversely, couples from a large cohort, such as those born in the period

2. Easterlin (1978).

from 1951 to 1966, find life more difficult. Unemployment is high, advancement is slow, and wealth is more difficult to accumulate. These couples tend to have small families. If Easterlin is correct, then the recent upturn in fertility rates in the United States may continue.

Using econometrics, Macunovich takes the Easterlin theory of relative cohort size several steps forward, outlining first-order effects on male relative earnings, unemployment, inflation, interest, and savings rates; second-order effects on fertility, marriage and divorce, and female labor force participation; and third-order effects on industrial structure, GDP, productivity, and average wages. The comprehensiveness of her extension is captured in the following paragraph:

> In sum, increasing relative cohort size leads to declining male relative earnings, which leads to increasing female labor force participation, which leads to the increased commoditization of "low productivity" work, which leads to reduced measures of productivity growth simply because the measures of GDP and productivity are so imperfect. While it might be argued that these measures work acceptably when there is little change in market behavior, they fall apart completely in the face of dramatic changes in female labor force participation. But . . . the great increase in female labor force participation rates has ended. It was this increase which led to the increased desire to purchase replacements for home services, which, in turn, drove the shift toward growing proportions of low wage, low productivity service jobs in the U.S. economy. With the recent attenuation in female labor force participation rates, the momentum of the shift toward such low productivity jobs will also slow down. This assumption is supported by the recent announcement by the Bureau of Labor Statistics (BLS) that new job creation between spring of 1992 and the fall of 1994 occurred primarily in occupations earning above average wages.[3]

Within this analysis, Macunovich also incorporates a discussion of family wage theory and how family wage premium has been eroded by women entering the labor market as full-time career workers.[4]

Macunovich suggests that unless they consider all these effects of relative cohort size, analysts may not understand why some trends appear to be so

3. *New York Times,* October 17, 1994.

4. Family wage theory identifies the practice whereby an employer compensates a male worker on the basis of his marital status. The employer would pay a family premium to a married man in order to obtain both the worker's own production and the services of his spouse, whose domestic production presumably makes the worker more productive.

negative. Consequently, they may inappropriately project trends of low average real wage growth and low fertility into the future when, in fact, those trends
may be just turning around. Worse yet, they would project these negative
trends onto a future in which increasing female labor force participation—the
one positive trend for Social Security in the past decade—is estimated as
tapering off.

In contrast, Schieber notes that much of the increased labor force participation of women preceded the baby boom cohorts. Although this observation
hardly undermines Macunovich's framework, it suggests that factors other than
relative cohort size (for example, more competitive labor markets in an increasingly open world economy) may underlie the low rate of real average
wage growth. Likewise, fertility rates may not rebound among the smaller
cohorts following the baby boomers if factors other than relative cohort size are
affecting how women and their husbands weigh their desire for children
against the opportunity costs of having large families.

Schieber counsels policymakers to adopt Brown's somewhat pessimistic
perspective rather than Macunovich's more optimistic scenario because it is
not clear how relative cohort size will affect either real GDP growth in the
aggregate or future fertility decisions. Given these uncertainties, as well as the
question of how financial markets will handle the transition in funded plans,
Schieber argues for policies that would limit the size of the pay-as-you-go
commitment, such as increasing retirement ages. Should the situation look
better in the period 2010–30, retirement age increases could then be frozen, or
benefits increased.

Retirement Income Policy

The second and third chapters focus less on Social Security, in particular,
and more on the provision of retirement income in general. In chapter 2, "Fund
Accumulation: How Much? How Managed?" Barry Bosworth explores issues
related to the partial funding of the mandatory piece of retirement provision
and the macroeconomic implications of different levels of national retirement
saving. In chapter 3, "Reexamining the Three-Legged Stool," David Cutler
concentrates on microeconomic decisions within households about voluntary
retirement provision, which is, for the most part, funded.

Cutler concludes that today's elderly have reasonable levels of retirement
income from Social Security, pensions, and asset accumulations. The prospects
for future retirees are clouded, however, because of the long-term Social
Security imbalance and the decline in the relative importance of the traditional
employer-sponsored defined benefit plan.

Social Security and defined benefit plans offer forms of insurance that are not typical of other retirement accumulations. First, because Social Security and employer-sponsored defined benefit plans pool mortality risks through group annuities, individuals are immunized against outliving their assets. Second, in the absence of indexed bonds, Social Security is the only program that provides indexed annuities that will protect individuals from unexpected inflation. Third, in theory, Social Security and defined benefit plans offer protection against investment risk, particularly short-term fluctuations. Finally, Social Security and defined benefit plans offer firms and workers greater options for early retirement in the event of poor health, declining productivity among older workers, or economic retrenchment.

Cutler notes, however, that the insurance advantages of Social Security and defined benefit plans are not unconditional: "Not even the government can pool something that is common to everyone." Nor is it without a price. Inflation adjustments in Social Security may not happen during periods of negative wage growth if current contributors are unwilling to protect beneficiaries from inflation by more than the nominal wage growth they are experiencing. Similarly, the protection from investment risk is not immutable. If the implicit rate of return in Social Security plummets because of low fertility and real wage growth, lower future benefit levels may be legislated. It is not clear exactly how investment risk in private sector defined benefit plans is allocated between shareholders and workers, nor whether workers' total lifetime compensation reflects this investment risk insurance. The price of flexible early retirement is the moral hazard of inducing more lifetime leisure than is optimal, especially in a situation of growing life expectancies and less physically demanding work.

In contrast, individual savings and defined contribution plans (arguably, just a form of tax-advantaged individual savings) offer individuals choice in investment strategies and have few, if any, labor market distortions. Except for limited vesting requirements, defined contribution plans are more portable than most defined benefit plans—that is, workers do not lose potential pension wealth if they move from one place of employment to the other.

On balance, Cutler is not troubled by the growing dominance of defined contribution arrangements. In his comment, Howard Young takes exception to this point, noting that the other side of having less portability in the classic defined benefit plan is the greater allocation of contributions to individuals who make long-term commitments to one firm or industry over their work lives and who have a constantly increasing age-to-earnings profile in one location. Young quarrels with the notion that younger workers will make the necessary contributions to defined contribution plans. Although the payoff in retirement is greatest when contributions are made early in life, it is also during that time that competing demands on savings (housing, college loan payoffs, children) are the greatest. Further, he questions whether younger workers want, or can handle, the investment management decisions that defined contribution plans increasingly demand of their participants.

Cutler also reviews the evidence on whether individuals are saving enough for their retirement and concludes that, although aggregate savings roughly conform to the predictions of the life cycle model (about three times median income), too much savings is tied up in illiquid housing wealth, and a great many households appear to have suboptimal levels of wealth in retirement. In addition, recent data from the Congressional Budget Office suggest that current levels of retirement wealth will not persist into the baby boomers' retirement years, if only because those cohorts are unlikely to receive the very high real rates of return experienced by retirees today.[5] Finally, Cutler believes that at least some cutbacks in Social Security wealth will be legislated, which will further increase the retirement savings gap.

Edward Gramlich comments that the arguments of Cutler and Bosworth complement one another. Citing recent work by Schieber, he suggests that an analysis taking into account pre- and postretirement tax burdens, work expenses, and the purchase of durables before retirement could reveal individuals' consumption and wealth in retirement to be higher than Cutler indicates. Gramlich does not quarrel with Cutler's basic conclusion that baby boomers appear to be on a track toward inadequate retirement savings. He notes that Bosworth comes to a parallel conclusion by looking at national account data:

> National saving is the sum of saving in the private sector (household saving and the retained earnings of corporations) plus the saving of the public sector. In the period between the end of World War II and 1980 the national savings rate averaged about 8 percent of national income: a private saving rate of 8.5 to 9 percent, offset by the public dissaving of 0.5 to 1 percent. More recently the situation has deteriorated significantly. The private saving rate fell during the 1980s to reach an average of 6 percent in the period 1990–93, and public sector dissaving ballooned to nearly 4 percent, resulting in a national saving rate of only about 2 percent of national income.

5. Recall the argument discussed above that large birth cohorts face the risk of low rates of return on financial assets if subsequent cohorts are smaller.

Whereas Cutler, echoing Brown and Schieber, suggests that increasing early and normal retirement ages should be considered as a way to bring Social Security into balance, Bosworth recommends instead that Congress and the public consider changing Social Security to a partially funded system in which today's workers, and all future cohorts, pay for a portion of their mandatory retirement benefits in advance; and adopting a trust fund investment policy that increases the real rate of return on that advance funding.

Starting from a demographic analysis similar to Brown's, Bosworth demonstrates that pay-as-you-go financing implies that payroll taxes for Social Security cash benefits alone will climb to more than 16 percent by 2035, and to 18 percent by the end of the twenty-first century. One strategy might be to raise payroll taxes by 2 points now and invest these new infusions, along with those from the temporary surpluses now flowing from the 1983 Amendments, in Treasury bonds. This strategy, however, would have mixed results. Under certain constraints on federal budget policy, national saving would increase, and that increased saving would generate some combination of higher wage growth and returns on capital (various scenarios are possible, depending on how open the U.S. economy is assumed to be to global capital markets). Future workers would produce more and would thus be able to finance Social Security at current promised levels without sacrificing their own consumption.

As discussed earlier, however, these gains to future workers would not be very transparent. Under a Treasury bond–only strategy, the Social Security system would capture a relatively small portion of the increased national output that it had induced by raising national saving. In effect, a Treasury rate of return on the extra trust fund reserves would not be sufficient to offset the decline in system's implicit (or pay-as-you-go) rate of return flowing from declining fertility and increasing life spans. Under simulations produced for the Social Security Advisory Council, it would appear that an immediate 2 percentage point increase in the payroll tax, coupled with a Treasury-only investment policy, implies future payroll tax rates that are only about 1 percentage point below the pay-as-you-go rates outlined above.

Bosworth asks why the fund should only be credited with a 2 percent rate of return if its actions add closer to 6 percent in future income to the nation. Instead, he suggests that the portfolio strategy for Social Security be changed so that the trust funds receive a real rate of return that exceeds the Treasury-only return by 1 percent. For example, about 25 percent could be invested in a broad-based equity portfolio, and the remaining 75 percent held in Treasury bonds. In this scenario the small extra return, steadily compounding over the seventy-five-year forecast period, should eliminate any further need to raise payroll taxes during that period.

Commentator David Mullins agrees with Bosworth's conclusion that the trust funds could earn a higher return within the boundaries of acceptable risk, noting that they currently bear reinvestment risk because of the effects of interest rate fluctuations on the fund's long-term Treasury bonds. He suggests that a combination of shorter duration Treasury holdings and equity might have the same risk profile as today's long duration Treasury bonds, but would produce higher yields. Accordingly, Mullins supports revisions in what he regards as rigid and outmoded investment policies.

Bosworth does not advocate changing the trust fund portfolio policy under any and all circumstances. In the absence of substantial (and probably near-term) new infusions of income to Social Security, exchanging Treasury bonds for private sector investments in the trust funds would not increase the total return to society. As a consequence the exchange, pension funds and other financial intermediaries would hold more Treasury bonds (assuming government borrowing is constant). A higher return on the Social Security portfolio might be achieved, but only in exchange for a lower return on pensions or other savings. Bosworth wishes to raise national savings in order to increase future GDP and make trade-offs between future workers and baby boomer retirees less painful. Within this context, he asks that more of the extra marginal return to society be diverted so that it accrues within Social Security, rather than being allowed to accrue largely outside the program.

Bosworth also would like to see the portion of the trust funds that remains in Treasury bonds—about 75 percent—translate more clearly into national savings. Currently the president and Congress seem to take trust fund annual surpluses into account when deciding on other federal spending and revenues, despite the fact that the trust funds are "off-budget." Under these conditions, it is impossible to discern whether trust fund surpluses are holding down the public debt and thereby adding to national savings. Bosworth believes that Social Security should be treated as a distinct and separate entity in federal accounting, in the same way that individual states manage their own employee pension funds, and as Employee Retirement and Income Security Act (ERISA) and accounting standards require that businesses manage their workers' pension plans. With these institutional arrangements, Bosworth hopes that federal fiscal policy would change, and government dissaving would decrease through some combination of spending restraint or higher general taxes.

Bosworth shares Cutler's conclusion that Social Security must remain a key part of the national retirement system for the following reasons: first, only Social Security offers annuities and requires that mortality risk be pooled so that those annuities are affordable; second, only Social Security can redistribute the burden of retirement savings from those with high to those with low lifetime earnings in ways that largely preserve saving incentives; and third, only Social Security can offer some protection against unexpected inflation. Cutler would increase retirement ages and flatten the benefit schedule—that is, cut benefit levels even more among those with high lifetime earnings to maintain present levels for those with low lifetime earnings. Bosworth worries that the latter step would erode critical public support for the program and believes that it would be unnecessary, as long as people are sufficiently long-sighted to care both for their own retirement consumption and for the well-being of future generations:

> Many will believe that the solution presented here is overly simplified, and that such small changes in funding could not be sufficient to offset a near doubling of the future dependency rate. But these arguments fail to recognize that OASDI benefits will only increase by 2 percent of GDP between the mid-1990s and 2070, from 4.8 to 6.8 percent; and even in the trustees' high-cost projection, the increase is only 4 percent of GDP. The magnitude of these changes is less than the variations in the share of GDP devoted to defense over the past two decades. While Social Security represents a large proportion of the government budget as currently presented, it is a small element in the total economy. Given the high return from added capital formation and compounding growth rates, challenges of this magnitude can easily be met, as long as society is willing to act sufficiently far ahead of the need.

Bosworth does not argue for the complete transformation of Social Security into a funded scheme. In his view, this would require that one or two generations bear two liability burdens: satisfaction of the accumulated pay-as-you-go liability while simultaneously funding retirement accumulations with new savings. The most feasible option is a movement at the margin to a partially funded system, and even that would require some sacrifice in today's consumption. Although Bosworth mostly explores the concept of partial funding in the context of a unitary defined benefit system under current benefit rules, he acknowledges that an alternative design option exists. New funding could go into mandatory defined contribution accounts whose payout would be dovetailed with a modified pay-as-you-go defined benefit structure to produce outcomes similar to those that would result if funding were kept within a unitary defined benefit system. Bosworth suggests there are advantages and disadvantages to both approaches, but admits that creating a two-layer alternative presents many design challenges.

Commentator Carolyn Weaver suggests that Bosworth gives insufficient consideration to the notion of replacing, in whole or in part, the existing level of pay-as-you-go financing with a mandatory funded regime. She concurs with his analysis that the rate of return in the pay-as-you-go system has eroded support for the program, especially among younger workers, but believes that this may allow for greater flexibility in writing down what workers expect from the existing Social Security system. Younger workers might be more willing to bear a double burden during the transitional period, if they could trade the political uncertainties of the existing pay-as-you-go system for a funded system with distinct ownership rights.

Weaver also expresses considerable skepticism as to whether a large trust fund reserve could ever be immunized from political control, especially if it were as large as the 40 percent of GDP contemplated by Bosworth. First, she questions whether federal budget practices will truly be reformed to exclude the trust funds from other budgetary considerations, for example, to finance Medicare. And second, even if that were done, the temptation to direct private sector investments toward politically preferred targets would be high. According to Weaver, creating mandatory funded individual accounts would vitiate these problems. Once ownership rights in the accounts are lodged with the individual participants, the reserves axiomatically move off-budget. Once ownership and investment discretion is given to individuals, the risk of politicians channeling retirement savings would be no greater than for the investments of private pension plans.

The comments of Gramlich and Margaret Simms highlight the key policy questions raised by Cutler and Bosworth: How myopic are individuals in planning for retirement? How much retirement income provision should society mandate? Noting that the Social Security Administration will soon begin to send out benefit statements and that advice about retirement planning is generally becoming more available, Gramlich suggests that

> as long as consumers are properly forewarned about what they might expect from the public part of the system, and they can get further pension advice, there is not much public obligation to support private pension savings.
>
> It is also possible, though, that merely giving out the information will not be sufficient. However much information people receive, they often still do not get the point. Clearly it is time to open up the debate about the proper role of information, tax incentives, and related factors in encouraging more pension or retirement saving.

In effect, Cutler and Brown answer Gramlich's question with the proposition that information and incentives will be sufficient to compensate for downsizing mandatory Social Security. The answer given by Bosworth is that the public's myopia makes increased mandatory and funded savings necessary. However, none of these individuals propose increasing the pay-as-you-go burden on subsequent generations to support today's promised benefits.

How Much Redistribution, and How to Achieve It?

The fourth, fifth, and sixth chapters carry forward the two major issues raised by the earlier chapters: To what extent should the long-term Social Security financing deficit be closed by reducing program benefits in a manner that makes the program even more redistributional than at present, and how explicit should that redistribution be? And, what is the role of funding in Social Security reform in the United States and abroad?

Chapter 4, "Social Security, Income, and Taxation: The Roles of Means-Testing," focuses on proposals by the Concord Coalition and others that recipients of Social Security, Medicare, and other forms of federal entitlements be subject to a test of affluence. This test would reduce federal entitlement benefits as a function of increasing income, leaving the richest with only a residual fraction of the payments that legal formulas currently provide. In the case of Social Security, this would be 15 percent of benefits. Martha Phillips describes how the Concord Coalition developed its proposal in the context of its overall aim to bring the federal budget into balance and thereby reduce a growing debt burden for future generations.

Both Eugene Steuerle and Gary Burtless argue that explicit means-testing would distort incentives and undermine public confidence in the program. Steuerle believes that the existing Social Security system already contains too many poorly coordinated implicit taxes that distort older workers' decisions to work and save—the earnings test and the phase-in on benefit taxation in the federal income tax, for instance. Thus, any explicit means test must be carefully dovetailed with existing program provisions to avoid further distortion of incentives. Even then, an explicit means test based on income at the time of retirement would discourage supplementary savings in the years leading up to retirement. Steuerle suggests that if further redistribution is desired, it should be accomplished targeting the benefit formula (which is based on lifetime income) to produce even more redistribution from high to low lifetime earners than current law provides—in effect, the flattened benefit formula suggested by Cutler. In any event, Burtless believes that a contributory social insurance program must provide all contributors with noticeable and predictable returns.

Burtless takes Steuerle's economic analysis further by elaborating on the reason why means-testing would eviscerate political support among the upper-income population, whose political influence outweighs their numbers. It is precisely because Social Security combines individual equity and redistribution that it has been successful in helping those with low lifetime earnings. If the program becomes more explicitly a "safety net," those who, by design, will receive less benefits will turn on it, as happened with the ill-fated Medicare catastrophic care proposal. Burtless doubts that the program's benefit formula can be further tilted toward low lifetime earnings without breaking apart public consensus for the program.

Robert Binstock reinforces Burtless's analysis, suggesting that the country has moved from seeing the elderly as frail, poor, and deserving to viewing them as hedonistic, prosperous, and selfish. He believes that a "substantial trend of politically feasible incremental change has firmly established the practice of combining age and economic status as policy criteria in old age benefit programs." If that trend continues, Binstock thinks that the United States will eventually need to reestablish a safety net for the growing number of frail and homeless elderly (for example, almshouses). He suggests that it might be possible to avoid this outcome by replacing the generational equity paradigm with one that emphasizes the human capital investments that the elderly made in the past.

The differences between the Concord Coalition and its critics here may be smaller than they acknowledge. There is a shared concern about the total debt overhang on subsequent generation, whether it takes the form of explicit public debt or implicit social insurance debt. The Concord Coalition's proposal recognizes that all Social Security participants should receive some residual amount (however, because the proposed 15 percent residual is unrelated to lifetime earnings, it would result in effective replacement rates of 5 percent or less). If the Social Security program must be contained within the present payroll tax rate, higher-income individuals will receive 50 to 66 percent of present benefit levels. The quarrel over policies may be more about speed: how quickly such reductions could, or should, be made; and methods of implementation, especially how these might affect savings and other incentives.

Rethinking Old Age Pensions: International Developments

The question of methods and the formalities of program design also occupy much of the discussion in chapter 5, "Social Security Around the World." In this chapter, Estelle James presents an overview of the World Bank's recently released research report, *Averting the Old Age Crisis: Policies to Protect the Old and Promote Growth.*

I am indebted to Stanford Ross of the law firm Arnold and Porter, former Social Security Commissioner and former President of NASI, for the following fine summary of the report:

Basic data are presented to show that the world population is aging, in some areas very rapidly, and that increasing numbers of dependent older persons in all countries will be a major public policy issue that will have to be addressed continually over the next 50 years.

The problem is not only that governments are required to finance benefits for increasingly dependent populations . . . but also meeting the challenge of enabling individuals to provide for their own future support and well-being. The report makes clear that people most affected by these trends are the current workers, and particularly those who are at younger ages.

. . . Perhaps the most controversial conclusion is that traditional public pension systems of the defined benefits kind, financed by payroll taxes or general revenues, have generally operated perversely. They are said to have had unfortunate redistributional effects, adverse labor market impacts, and have often created financial, fiscal, and budgetary crises. The problems are attributed in part to political mismanagement, but the report suggests that the design of such programs is inherently flawed and would have likely produced bad experiences even if they were effectively managed.

The report indicates that occupational pension schemes are also generally deficient as the basis for a single pillar system, although it acknowledges that they may be valuable as a limited part of a multi-pillar system. The report emphasizes the need for strong, skillful regulation to allow occupational pension schemes to have any viable role.

The report suggests that mandatory savings schemes, with private management of funds, can have beneficial effects. It urges that fully funded, defined contribution plans can increase savings, develop capital markets, and make more secure provisions for retirement than traditional public pension system or occupational pension systems. The report here is heavily influenced—but not solely—by the Chilean developments.

The overarching conclusion of the report is that a so-called "multi-pillar system" will operate better than a single pillar system or any system that relies too heavily on any one pillar. The report holds out as a model a three-pillar system with first, a relatively small public pension system, optimally a minimum flat rate pension funded by general revenues; plus, second, a relatively large, funded, defined contribution plan with private management of the funds; plus, third, an opportunity for individuals to voluntarily contribute additional amounts to enhance their total retirement income.

While the report at points suggests pros and cons and variations, limitations, and constraints on its recommendations, it is overall quite blunt about its prescriptions. This may well be the most central and controversial aspect of the report. Its emphasis on the priority of theoretical economic analysis of design options, in contrast to pragmatic analysis of social, administrative, and political institutions in any given country, may well be seen as reflecting a fundamental tenet as to how this subject should be approached and debated.

As the report's principal author, James defends the construct of two mandatory pillars. In regard to its explicit separation of redistribution and equity, she notes that there is no reason why the willingness to redistribute would be greater in a nontransparent, messy public system. James argues that the lack of transparency has led to unintended redistribution to high-income individuals, if only because they tend to live longer. Moreover, she states that funding the second pillar would mean that "the costs would be clear from the outset and countries would not be tempted to start out by making unrealistic promises that they could not ultimately fulfill."

Although the World Bank's principal focus is to help developing countries increase their capital base through mandated retirement savings, James suggests that the report's prescriptions might apply to the United States as well. Because of demographics and a chronically low savings rate, she believes that this country inevitably faces a contribution rate of 15 to 20 percent for mandatory old age pensions, rather than 10 to 15 percent. Echoing Bosworth, she argues that putting extra monies into a funded second pillar would increase national savings, provided that various conditions are met. James also believes that an explicit second pillar would be more politically acceptable and less. distortionary than a partially funded unitary system. She questions, however, whether a second pillar of only 2 or 3 percent is sufficient to increase existing retirement savings, or would merely displace them.

Although all applaud the depth of information and accessibility of the World Bank report, many criticize its findings. Commentator Robert Hagemann agrees with its basic "three-pillar" framework but suggests that these pillars should be tailored to each country's traditions and circumstances. In particular, he suggests that for most countries, the second pillar (funded individual accounts and occupational pensions) would have to be smaller than the first, public, pillar. Their capital markets are often rudimentary; more significantly, they lack the necessary regulatory structures to protect funded schemes from mismanagement and fraud.

In his comment, Dalmer Hoskins also criticizes the report for not acknowledging that problems of governance are pervasive, not only in public pay-as-you-go and funded schemes, but *a fortiori* in regulated private arrangements. In addition, he takes issue with the notion that linking national saving with retirement income is easy or inevitable. Governments that have developed large provident funds to raise national savings, such as that of Singapore, are only now wrestling with how to translate those arrangements into annuitized retirement income. Hoskins also believes that the report gives too little weight to history. In his view, mandatory pensions in the developed world are largely pay-as-you-go systems for reasons grounded more in the ravages of war, economic depression, and hyperinflation than explicit policy choice.

Commentator Jagadeesh Gokhale faulted the study for not having developed a more comprehensive critique and noted that "analysis should be based on an internally consistent, analytical framework that takes the entire environment into account and generates a set of criteria for choosing between alternative policies." He believes that such generational accounting should examine the fiscal sustainability of all government spending, including the offsetting effects of public debt on mandated (and presumably voluntary) pension funding.

In the report's most pointed critique, Alicia Munnell makes the same argument: countries can handle old age crises without radical reform, and proposals for a clean separation of functions between the public pillar (pay-as-you-go and highly redistributional) and the private-but-regulated pillar (funded and individual return) are nice in theory, but dubious in practice. Along with Burtless and others, Munnell worries that the public pillar will collapse if too much weight is put on its redistributional function and that future low-income elderly will be the losers. She also questions whether the case for funding, as against pay-as-you-go, financing has been made. Like Gokhale, she suggests that a more comprehensive analysis of government and household behavior is needed before the effects of either financing method on national saving can be assessed.

In chapter 6, "Lessons from Chile's Social Security Reform: Two Views," Peter Diamond and Robert Myers examine the recent Chilean experience. They both point out that despite being hailed as a privatized pension scheme, the Chilean system is permeated with heavy state involvement, including mandates on the individual to save, substantive regulation of pension fund investments, and several backup guarantees (a minimum pension for those with twenty years of service, a floor on annual pension rates of return, and insolvency protection in the event of pension or insurance company failure).

The Chilean experience also suggests that transaction costs in a decentralized, privately managed scheme can be quite high, greatly exceeding the costs of a conventional unitary social insurance scheme. It is more troubling that the Chilean system has not yet found effective ways to handle mortality and inflation risks during the payout period. Although the problems in Chile are likely tractable, their presence indicates that privatized pension schemes require continual adjustments by the legislature just as do public social insurance systems.

Three Open Questions

The discussions in this book raise, but leave unanswered, three essential questions:

— Is it enough to have a social insurance program that provides a minimum floor, to give people information and the opportunity to save for retirement with little or no tax distortions, and then let events take their course? Or should policymakers target average replacement rates that exceed poverty alleviation because of the concern that individuals are too myopic?

— Are there limits on how much redistribution a public mandatory scheme can accomplish without eviscerating its support among influential elites? Or are the people who believe that such a limit exists fooling themselves that redistribution is more acceptable in one form than in another?

— Is a pay-as-you-go scheme preferable to a funded regime?

On the last question, the analytic consensus of the contributors to this book favors funding, at least at the margin. Those who would be satisfied with a minimal (and more redistributional) pay-as-you-go public pillar assume that individuals could, and would, save more for their retirement on their own. A number of those who recommend maintaining current benefit levels with current early retirement options would mandate marginal saving, both to raise national savings from the present inadequate levels and to hold down future contribution rates by garnering higher equity returns. At least one contributor argues that the present level of pay-as-you-go financing should gradually be shifted to a more funded regime.

But this consensus never broaches the gnawing doubt of whether funded regimes are more successful at bridging the demographic transition to higher dependency ratios. Greater savings may indeed lead to larger economies in the future. But what will happen when the holders of all those assets outnumber the buyers?

The third question can be addressed by further economic analysis. The other two are basic issues of political economy that go to each citizen's view of the duties and limits of government and how political consensus is, or should be, formed and maintained. These are not easy questions under any conditions; they are still harder in the context of limited growth and an aging population.

References

Barr, Nicholas. 1979. "Myths My Grandpa Taught Me." *Three Banks Review* 124 (December): 27–55.

Easterlin, Richard A. 1978. "What Will 1984 be Like? Socioeconomic Implications of Recent Twists in Age Structure." *Demography* 15(4): 397–432.

1

Social Security and Retirees:
Two Views of the Projections

IN THIS CHAPTER two experts, an actuary and an economist, thoroughly examine the relevant variables and arrangements that will affect the income needs and sources of future retirees. Another actuary and another economist comment on both papers.

An Actuary's Perspective
Robert L. Brown

THE ANNUAL REPORT of the Board of Trustees of the Federal Old-Age and Survivors' Insurance and Disability Insurance Trust Funds is dependent on a series of demographic and economic assumptions as to model variables. These include growth in wages and prices, unemployment rates, interest rates, fertility rates, mortality rates, and net immigration. This section reviews the likelihood of the assumptions used in the Trust Fund projection models in light of the important demographic shifts that have occurred in the United States over the past fifty years, and also summarizes some concerns about the security of retirement income systems in the next century. It concludes with certain recommendations for enhancing the format of the OASDI trustees' report.

Background

Articles are written almost daily outlining and analyzing the implications of population aging. Despite all that has been written, however, much misinformation still remains. What is meant by population aging? How dramatic will the demographic shifts that take place in the next half-century really be? Are existing retirement income security systems truly secure as a result of population aging?

One aspect of population aging is improved life expectancy. Table 1-1 indicates the significant improvement in life expectancies in the United States over the course of this century, especially among females. Obviously if every individual in the population is expected to live longer, then the population as a whole will age. Life expectancies have similarly improved in most parts of the world. However, if this were the only cause of population aging, there would be little need for discussion.

An alternative definition of the age of a population is that used by the United Nations, which looks at the percentage of the population that is age sixty-five or older. A young population has a small proportion of its population in this age range, while an older population has a relatively large percentage of its population in this range. With enhanced life expectancy, the proportion of the population age sixty-five or over (all else being stable) would increase. However, using this definition, the age of a population can also be affected by other changes in the age distribution of the population.

In particular, for Canada and the United States, a more compelling reason for the anticipated rise in the proportion of the population that is age sixty-five or over is the baby boom. Figure 1-1 shows fertility rates in Canada and the United States since 1922. Both countries experienced a sharp rise in fertility rates after World War II and a sudden drop in the late 1960s. This has become known as the baby boom tidal wave, followed by the baby bust. Only four countries in the world experienced a baby boom tidal wave worthy of note: Canada, the United States, Australia, and New Zealand. As figure 1-1 shows, the peak of the boom was higher in Canada than in the United States, while the Canadian trough was lower. Hence the impact of the tidal wave has been more significant in Canada than in the United States. The figure also indicates the beginning of an upturn in fertility rates in the United States in the late 1980s. This upturn has continued, and the fertility rate in the United States is now greater than 1.90. This is a measure of the number of children an average

Table 1-1. **Life Expectancy in the United States, 1930–90**

Year	At birth		At age 65	
	Male	Female	Male	Female
1930	59.8	61.1	11.7	12.8
1950	65.5	71.0	12.7	15.0
1970	67.1	74.7	13.0	16.7
1990	71.8	78.8	15.1	18.9

Source: U.S. life tables.

Figure 1-1. Total Fertility Rates, Canada and United States, 1922–88

Fertility rate

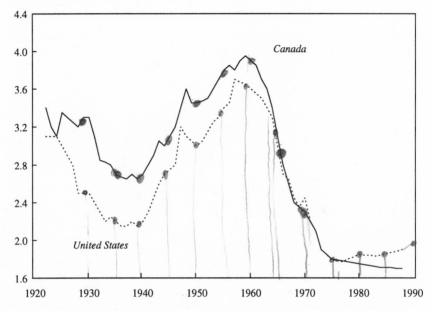

SOURCE: Robert L. Brown, *Introduction to the Mathematics of Demography*, 2d ed. (Winsted, Conn.: Actex Publications, 1993), p. 32.

female would have in her lifetime if today's age-specific fertility rates were to remain constant. Zero population growth (ignoring migration) requires a fertility rate of close to 2.10.

Figure 1-2 shows the number of live births in the United States during this century. Again the tidal wave of the baby boom and the baby bust is clearly evident. This demographic phenomenon has become known as the postwar baby boom. There are at least two problems with this description, however. First, the cause of the baby boom is often assumed to be the return of the soldiers from the war. In fact, the cause of the baby boom was the strong economy of the 1950s juxtaposed with the relatively low material expectations of those born and raised during the depression years. This combination made it possible to have one stay-at-home spouse and the resultant large families of the 1950s and early 1960s. Second, a postwar baby boom implies the cohort born in 1945 or very shortly thereafter. That is, baby boomers would be assumed to be age fifty in 1995. This also is not true. A careful study of the graph of live births in the United States indicates clearly that the baby boom can be measured as the births in the years from 1951 to 1966, and that the baby bust started

Figure 1-2. Live Births, United States, 1905–89

Millions of births

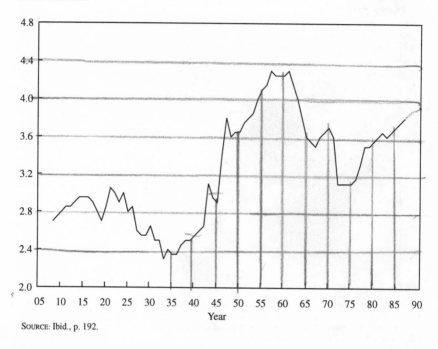

Year

SOURCE: Ibid., p. 192.

after 1966. The number of live births peaked in 1957. Therefore in 1996 baby boomers are between ages thirty and forty-five.

As stated above, the baby boom was followed by the equally dramatic baby bust, and it is this total demographic shift that creates the projected dependency ratios shown in table 1-2, which is taken from the trustees' 1994 *Annual Report*. This table shows the dramatic shift that will take place in the aged dependency ratio over the next half century. However, it also shows that the total dependency ratio will not be as large over that period as it was in 1960 or 1970. This is because of the implicit counterbalancing force of the youth dependency ratio.

Another important demographic shift that has taken place over the past thirty years is displayed in figure 1-3, which juxtaposes the declining fertility rate of the period 1965–85 with the rapid rise in female labor force participation rates for the same period. The influx of females into the labor force has been both good and bad in terms of the total contributions required for broad social security systems. On the one hand, increased female labor force participation rates exacerbated an already difficult situation, since jobs had to be created not only for the baby boomers (born between 1951 and 1966) as they

Table 1-2. Social Security Area Population and Dependency Ratios, 1950–2040

Calendar year	Population (thousands)			Dependency ratio	
	< 20	20–64	≥ 65	Aged	Total
Historical					
1950	53,895	92,739	12,752	0.138	0.719
1960	72,989	99,842	17,250	0.173	0.904
1970	80,672	113,184	20,920	0.185	0.898
1980	74,549	134,393	26,143	0.195	0.749
1990	74,914	152,525	31,918	0.209	0.700
Intermediate					
2000	81,001	168,547	35,476	0.210	0.691
2010	80,760	185,261	39,945	0.216	0.652
2020	80,657	191,111	53,322	0.279	0.701
2030	81,639	189,628	68,282	0.360	0.791
2040	81,464	194,585	72,456	0.372	0.791

SOURCE: Taken from Board of Trustees (1994, table II.H1, p. 144).

entered the labor force, but also for all the extra females in that cohort who chose to work outside of the home. This put presssure on the education system, the unemployment insurance systems, and in some cases, the public assistance systems. On the other hand, once in the labor force these additional participants became contributors to social security and helped suppress the required pay-as-you-go contribution rates.

Population aging is taking place at different rates in different countries. Table 1-3 shows the projected percentage increase in the population age sixty-five and over between 1985 and 2025 for various countries around the world. As mentioned above, only Canada, the United States, Australia, and New Zealand experienced the baby boom tidal wave. Countries like India and China are experiencing high rates of population aging because of improved life expectancy and also because of fertility controls imposed by the government. In the case of Japan, fertility controls were brought in voluntarily by the population for economic reasons since the 1950s.

It is not just the ultimate size of the aged population that is of importance, but also the rate of change in the proportion of the population age sixty-five and over to those of working age. The systems that require suppport are essentially those that are government sponsored and therefore the requirements for their funding are part of the political process. Hence if required contribution rates must rise rapidly, the ability of the political process to enact such changes must be questioned and analyzed. If countries with low rates of growth in the aged population, like Sweden and the United Kingdom, are able to afford the social security systems that they now have in place, they will face little political

Figure 1-3. Female Labor Force Participation Rates and Total Fertility Rates, United States, 1965–84

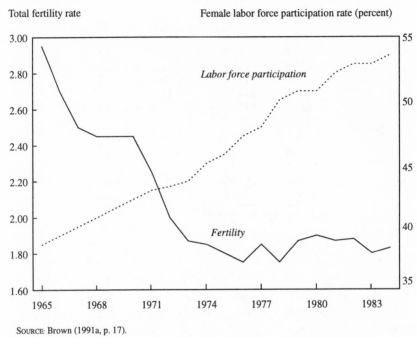

Total fertility rate   Female labor force participation rate (percent)

SOURCE: Brown (1991a, p. 17).

pressure with respect to the funding of these systems over the next half-century. At the other extreme, countries like India and China will experience rapidly aging populations but have not promised their citizens retirement income security systems that will replace a large percentage of their working income and guarantee them a steady standard of living. Thus the aging of their populations will not result in the need to cut back existing programs, but rather in the inability to create such programs.

It is precisely countries like the United States and Canada, with rapidly aging populations and large benefit promises, that will face growing pressure to find ways to cut back existing social security programs providing income transfers from active workers to those over age sixty-five. In fact early indications of this pressure already exist. Such pressures are exacerbated by the current level of debt of the various federal, state, and local governments. In the United States the annual federal deficit is around $300 billion and the total accumulated debt is around $4 trillion. These monies have created an artificially high standard of living for today's population, but will (at least in theory) have to be repaid by some future generation of workers. Thus not only is it expected that the next generation of workers will provide much higher rates of

Table 1-3. **Projected Increase in Population Age Sixty-five and Over, Various Countries, 1985–2025**
Percent

Country	Increase	Country	Increase
India	264	United States	105
China	238	France	67
Hong Kong	219	Italy	51
Canada	135	West Germany	36
Australia	125	United Kingdom	23
Japan	121	Sweden	21
Israel	116		

Source: U.S. Department of Commerce 1987, p 6.

income transfers because of population aging, but they also seem to be expected to pay off the debt from the present excesses at the same time. That represents a very real challenge indeed.

As the baby boom ages, pushes through the various age categories, and is replaced by the baby bust, several economic and social responses can be expected. Despite the ability to predict many of these events accurately, society seems to prefer to anticipate the future by looking at the past. Thus although kindergartens and elementary schools were being built in the late 1950s, it still seemed to come as a surprise to many universities that their student population rose so rapidly in the 1970s. Similarly, while there was a real need for new office space and housing in the late 1970s and throughout the 1980s, it does not seem to have been predicted that these needs would pass, and we are now staring at underutilized housing and office stock. These phenomena have been referred to as "inevitable surprises." What further inevitable surprises are in store for society? More particularly, what knowledge can be gleaned from an understanding of the baby boom–baby bust tidal wave to help determine the appropriateness of the model assumptions underlying the trust fund projections for the OASDI?

Labor Force

In the late 1970s and throughout the 1980s the United States had one of the fastest growing labor forces in the world, as is shown in table 1-4. These rapid growth rates were the result of the baby boom generation entering the labor force, combined with the increasing labor force participation rates of the female population. However, they have now passed. The baby boom generation (now ages thirty to forty-five) has entered the labor force and has secured employment. And it is followed by the baby bust generation, a much smaller

Table 1-4. Annual Average Job Growth Rates, Various Countries, 1975–81
Percent

Country	Rate	Country	Rate
Canada	2.8	West Germany	0.1
United States	2.7	Italy	0.8
Japan	1.0	United Kingdom	−1.0
France	−1.2		

Source: Organization for Economic Cooperation and Development (OECD) data.

cohort. Further, although female labor force participation rates are still inching upward, they appear to be reaching a natural upper bound.

Thus such a demographic analysis would predict a decline in the rate of growth of the labor force and low unemployment rates over the next half-century, and especially after the year 2016, when the baby boom reaches age sixty-five, all else being equal. In this case, the caveat of ceteris paribus is important. Implicit in the prediction of low unemployment rates is the assumption that the next generation of workers will have the skill set necessary for the jobs that are being created. That is far from clear. Even today, with some remaining unemployment (fairly significant from an historical perspective), many jobs go unfilled for lack of skilled entrants. This is an important public policy issue that needs to be addressed more fully than it has been to date. The lack of skilled labor may lead to an unnecessary period of labor shortages combined with continued stubborn unemployment. Nevertheless, the demographics would indicate that some labor force shortages and low unemployment rates lie ahead, although it is debatable how far we are away from effective full employment rates at the present time.

During the past twenty years, the rapidly increasing labor force provided employers with an abundant supply of cheap labor. Thus when it came to a decision whether to buy human labor or to invest in machinery (capital), the economics favored the hiring of labor. Because of this, capital investment has actually lagged behind what it would have been without the baby boom and the increased female labor force participation rates. Given the fact that these two sources of growth in the labor force have now passed, it is likely that there will be more capital investment and a more efficient use of human resources. That is, each worker will be provided with more capital resources and will be able to produce more goods and services per unit of labor than today. Therefore productivity returns should rise—certainly productivity improvement rates should be better than those of the past two decades. This should mean a higher real-wage differential than in recent years, and in turn, that the real-wage differentials assumed in the Trust Fund models are conservative (too low). The demographics would indicate that over the next fifteen to twenty years average real wages in covered employment will rise more rapidly than the models now assume. The economy should be able to achieve this through improved productivity. There is no reason to assume heightened rates of inflation (all else being equal) in the short run.

Indeed, real rates of interest can be expected to be low (relatively speaking) for the next twenty years. This is true because the baby boomers are now leaving their high-debt phase and are entering a period of elevated savings (or so it should be). Hence real interest rates will be depressed, all else being equal. Beyond 2010, however, the story changes dramatically. The reason for this can be discerned in table 1-5, taken from the trustees' 1994 *Annual Report*. From 1995 through 2010, the aged dependency ratio grows at less than 1 percent per year (in fact in the period from 1995 to 2005 it actually declines slightly). However, between 2010 and 2030 it rises from 0.216 to 0.360, a total rise of 67 percent over twenty years, or 2.6 percent per year compound growth.

This means that the U.S. economy must find a way to fund wealth transfers from workers to retired consumers that will grow at 2.6 percent per annum for twenty years. During that period of time, the number of people in the United States age sixty-five and over will rise from 39.9 million to 68.3 million. Under today's assumption as to workplace activity, almost all of these people would be expected to stop being producers and become passive consumers. Further, each one would be expected to turn from a late-working-period saver into a retired liquidator of savings. Their income would come from the liquidation of lifetime savings and pay-as-you-go transfers. This liquidation does not all take place the day a worker retires. Life annuities are also backed by assets. However, from 2010 until the last baby boomer dies, there will be a massive liquidation of assets, and the market will have to pay significantly increased real rates of interest to attract new investors to replace the baby boomers' savings. This downturn in the supply of investable funds underlies the prediction of rising real interest rates after 2010.

One important point needs to be made: full funding or even prefunding of OASDI for the baby boom cohort would not change this prediction. In fact, it makes very little difference whether people provide their retirement income from savings backed by private enterprise assets (such as shares in General Motors or Microsoft) or whether their retirement income comes from pay-as-you-go transfers paid by the active workforce taxpayers of the day. The future predicted inflation will be a source of insecurity for the baby boom generation, retiring between 2010 and 2030. The real issue is how to provide a 67 percent increase in the gross national wealth transfer to retirees over so short a period as twenty years.

Table 1-5. Growth in the Aged Dependency Rates, United States, 1990–2040[a]

Year	Aged dependency ratio	Percentage change in aged dependency ratio[b]
1990	0.209	4.0
1995	0.214	2.4
2000	0.210	−1.9
2005	0.208	−1.0
2010	0.216	3.8
2015	0.242	12.0
2020	0.279	15.3
2025	0.324	16.1
2030	0.360	11.1
2035	0.374	3.8
2040	0.372	−0.5

Source: Taken from the intermediate assumptions presented in Board of Trustees (1994, table II.H1, p. 144).
a. The aged dependency ratio refers to the population age sixty-five or over.
b. Percentage change is calculated by $Z / (Z - 5)$.

In economic terms, if consumption rises more rapidly than production, the result is price inflation. So by accepting two decades of elevated inflation, the real purchasing power of the retirees could be reduced until a new production-consumption equilibrium was established. In theory this would ultimately only erode income from private savings, as OASDI retirement benefits are indexed to inflation. It is extremely difficult to present this as the preferred outcome.

Certainly, increased productivity would help. Returning to table 1-2, which presents the aged and total dependency ratios, and assuming that social transfers to the elderly are three times per capita the social transfers to the young, it can be seen that real productivity gains of only 1.7 percent per year between 2010 and 2030 will cover the increase in wealth transfers required because of the retiring baby boomers. While these are historically very optimistic rates of increase for a twenty-year period, they are not without precedent. This also means, however, that over a twenty-year period, workers would realize a 40 percent increase in their standard of living while the retired elderly would receive no real increase at all. Is this politically acceptable?

Another solution is to apply public policy toward achieving a constant producer-consumer equilibrium. Consider the expenditure dependency ratio. Historic and projected ratios are shown in table 1-6. The expenditure dependency ratio is the same as the total dependency ratio, except that the elderly are given a weight of three and youth dependents a weight of one because that is the ratio of social transfers to these two sectors, respectively.[1] It is an index of the wealth that is transferred from the worker (producer) to the young depen-

1. See Clark, Kreps, and Spengler (1978).

Table 1-6. Expenditure Dependency Ratios; United States 1950–2040
Index, 1950 = 1.000

Year	Expenditure dependency ratio	Year	Expenditure dependency ratio
1950	1.000	2000	1.119
1960	1.257	2010	1.090
1970	1.275	2020	1.267
1980	1.146	2030	1.520
1990	1.126	2040	1.546

Source: Author's calculation, using OASDI intermediate projection.

dents (for consumption as health care and education) and to the elderly (for consumption as health care and social security benefits). Given that it would be logical public policy to keep this wealth transfer index level or constant, then in the period from 1970 to 2010 early retirement from the labor force should be encouraged.

However, in 2010 public policy would have to switch to provide very strong incentives for later retirement. It would probably not be enough just to raise the normal retirement age for OASI from sixty-five to sixty-seven or sixty-eight while still allowing for retirement at age sixty-two with actuarially reduced benefits. Rather, legislation would have to raise the earliest possible retirement age along with the normal retirement age. Alternatively, legislation would have to severely decrease the actuarial value of benefits available for early retirement. Either way, the intent would be to delay retirement to much higher ages. Indeed, as shown below, the normal retirement age within the OAS system would probably ultimately be sixty-nine years, not sixty-seven, as is now legislated.

Even this increase in the age of eligibility for retirements benefits, in and of itself, would still not be enough. Not only will it be necessary to reduce the number of retired nonworkers, but they must be turned into active workplace production units. Thus the private sector must find ways to provide economic incentives to keep capable older workers active beyond the retirement ages that are now becoming widely accepted (bearing in mind that these earlier retirement ages are good public policy today). Employers should be persuaded that this is good practice. It is illogical and unfair to relegate the experience and expertise of capable older workers to empty role structures merely because they attain a certain chronological age. In fact the literature indicates that the ability to stay in the work force would also result in an enhanced health profile.[2]

2. See Brown (1991a, p. 109).

The myth that age results in declining productivity has proven difficult to modify.[3] However, Barry McPherson observes of older workers:

—There is relatively little decline in productivity with age.

—There is some loss of muscular strength and endurance.

—Reaction time slows with age but experience at the task may offset the losses.

—There is little decline in intelligence affecting job performance.

—Older workers are generally more satisfied with their jobs and are less likely to leave an organization for another job (perhaps because they have few alternatives).

—Decremental changes in job-related aptitudes or skills do not occur at the same rate (for example, a hearing loss may not be accompanied by a slow reaction time or by a loss of visual activity), and those that do occur may be compensated for by experience.

—Declining cognitive or physical skills can be overcome by a willingness to resort to coping strategies (such as a reliance on coworkers for assistance, taking work home).

—Older workers are absent less often and have fewer accidents than younger workers.[4]

In reality, one may not have to persuade employers to retain older workers. That will become an economic imperative as the baby boomers reach their normal retirement age (however it is defined) and the labor force turns to the baby bust generation for the production of wealth.

It should also be relatively easy to convince the general public that incentives and a growing pressure for later retirement are, in fact, acceptable. When U.S. Representative Dan Rostenkowski, then chairman of the House Ways and Means Committee, recently proposed an acceleration of the shift in the age of entitlement for OASDI retirement benefits from age sixty-five to age sixty-seven (as is now planned), it received the following editorial reaction: "Speeding up that process saves billions while bowing to the reality that as people live longer—about six years longer than at Social Security's birth—they must work longer too. . . . And it's fair. Current beneficiaries get two to three times more from Social Security than they contributed; future generations can't even get their contributions back."[5]

Other countries around the world are also looking at increasing either the normal retirement age or the length of service required for full retirement

3. See Pifer and Bronte (1986, p. 348).
4. McPherson (1983, p. 376).
5. *USA Today,* April 25, 1994.

Table 1-7. **Scheduled Changes to Conditions for Full Retirement Income Benefits, Various Countries**

| Country | Entitlement age in 1995 | | Scheduled changes |
	Male	Female	
Australia	65	60	No change for men. For women, increasing to 65 over 20 years.
France	60	60	Increase from 37.5 to 40 years of coverage for full pension.
Germany	65	65	Provision allowing people with specified number of years of coverage to retire on full pension before normal age to be abolished by 2001.
Italy	61	56	Increase to 65 for men and 60 for women by 2002. Increase from 15 to 20 years of coverage for pension by 2002.
Japan	60	57	Possible increase to 65 for men. For women, increase to 60 by 2000. Increase from 25 to 40 years of coverage for full pension by 2000.
United Kingdom	65	60	No change for men. For women, increase to 65 by 2020.

Source: Canadian Institute of Actuaries, Report of the Task Force on Social Security Financing, Supplement, February 1995, p. 4.

income benefits from their social security systems. A few examples are shown in table 1-7. How large an increase in the age of eligibility is required to achieve a wealth transfer equilibrium as the baby boomers retire? Using Canadian data I have found that a wealth transfer equilibrium could be retained if the normal retirement age were shifted from age sixty-five in 2006 to age sixty-nine in 2030 (that is, an increase of four years over a period of twenty-four years, or two months per year).[6] Although Canada has had a more severe demographic shift than the United States, projections for the U.S. population would be very similar, leading to the ultimate normal retirement age of sixty-nine for the OAS benefits discussed above.

My analysis assumed that those between ages sixty-five and sixty-nine who faced delayed retirement stayed in the work force with the participation rate now being experienced by those of ages fifty-five to sixty-four. It then contrasted this required rise in the normal retirement age to the impact of improved life expectancy by calculating a series of equivalent ages over the period from 1966 (the end of the baby boom and the beginning of the baby bust) to 2031,

6. See Brown (1994).

Table 1-8. **Equivalent Age at Retirement with Improved Life Expectancy, Canada, 1966–2031**

Year	Age	Year	Age
1966	65.00	2011	69.86
1981	67.30	2021	70.28
1991	68.36	2031	70.72
2001	69.36		

SOURCE: Brown (1994, p. 27).

such that each person would have the same number of years of expected retirement, shown in table 1-8. As can be seen, the required four-year increase in the normal retirement age to maintain a wealth transfer equilibrium is less than the impact of improved retirement life expectancy over the lifetimes of those who would be affected.

If such a production-consumption, or wealth transfer, equilibrium cannot be achieved through a shift in the retired-to-worker ratios, then the final alternative is to encourage all workers in the United States to invest in countries where the workers are willing to work beyond age sixty-five. In that way U.S. retirees will not liquidate U.S. assets upon retirement. Rather, they will call in their dividends from overseas economies where workers are willing to continue working. Thus there could be a worldwide wealth transfer equilibrium that could be maintained in the face of the dramatic aging of all of the northern hemisphere populations shown in table 1-3.

Fertility Rate

In the long term, higher fertility rates have favorable impact on pay-as-you-go funding ratios. As stated by Robert Myers:

If all other demographic elements are constant, higher fertility rates will have a favorable effect on social insurance systems providing old-age retirement benefits. As long as fertility is above the replacement rate (or the actual fertility plus the effect of net immigration achieves this result), there will be a steadily growing covered work force to provide the contributions necessary to support the retired population. This type of chain-letter effect will show relatively low costs for the social insurance program, although eventually the chain must break (because population size cannot increase forever), and the cost of the program will become significantly higher.[7]

7. Myers (1985, p. 3).

So while attempts to increase fertility may prove to be marginally beneficial in the short run, in the long run they will prove a fool's game. Further, in terms of the wealth transfer equilibrium, increased fertility rates mean increased wealth transfer to the youth sector for increased health care and increased education (although only about one-third of the transfer needed for each elderly person).

However, it is not clear that governments can influence fertility rates to any significant extent, if at all. Evidence from countries that have attempted to do so through financial incentives suggests little effect.[8] For example, West Germany offered cash incentives for women to have children and extended mother's holidays and child-care facilities, but the fertility rate continued to slide. In fact, historically, the countries that have had the largest family allowances have also had the lowest birth rates.[9]

What is the long-term future of fertility rates in the United States without government influence? Is the recent upturn a sign of the next wave, or is it only a short-term anomaly? There are two broad schools of thought. Richard Easterlin has postulated that fertility rates rise and fall in a wavelike pattern with a cycle length, from peak to peak or from trough to trough, of two generations.[10] He points out that couples from a small cohort, such as those born in the 1930s, find life relatively easy. Jobs are plentiful, advancement is fast, and wealth is accumulated relatively easily. Such couples will tend to have large families, as was the case in the 1950s. Conversely, couples from a large cohort, such as those born in the period from 1951 to 1966, find life more difficult. Unemployment is high, advancement is slow, and wealth is more difficult to accumulate. These couples tend to have small families. If Easterlin is correct, then the recent upturn in fertility rates in the United States may continue.

On the other hand, the British demographer John Ermisch starts from the same fertility waves of the 1930s through to the 1970s but comes to a different conclusion.[11] Ermisch finds that in a one-earner family, if the worker's real wages rise rapidly and the cost of children remains constant, the parents will have more children. This is what happened in the period from 1951 to 1966. In a two-earner family, however, if real wages rise rapidly but the wife has to leave the work force or interrupt a career path to bear and raise children, then the cost of children rises and fertility rates will not change. Ermisch's data show that the higher a woman's earning power, the longer the gap between

8. See, for example, Hohn (1987, p. 461).
9. See Weitz (1979, p. 21).
10. Easterlin (1978).
11. Ermisch (1983).

marriage and first birth. He also points out that the increased probability of divorce may keep the fertility rate down. In conclusion, Ermisch sees no reason to believe that fertility rates will rise very much, if at all. He anticipates that they will remain level below a replacement rate.

Perhaps the final word should be left to the elder statesman of demographers, Nathan Keyfitz: "Apparently before we see a rise in the birth rate, we will also have to foresee a retreat from women's liberation, the family strengthened and divorce become rare, and women once more subsiding into uncomplaining domesticity. I am not one to make such a forecast."[12] Hence it seems likely that fertility rates will continue to hover at levels below zero population growth rates. In particular, the OASDI trustees' intermediate assumption seems defensible.

Life Expectancy

The trustee's 1994 *Annual Report* indicates that the future cost rates of the OASDI system are surprisingly sensitive with respect to the mortality variable.[13] Without comparing in detail the ranges analyzed between and among the several input variables in the report, it would be plausible to assume that on a seventy-five-year funding horizon the mortality variable would not have been as important as many other variables, including fertility and real wage rates. Indeed, a similar sensitivity analysis in the actuarial report on the Canada Pension Plan (CPP) finds that the mortality assumption is one of the less variable of the modelling parameters.[14] For example, under the CPP valuation a 10 percent geometric decrease in each of the annual mortality reduction factors assumed for 1987 and later years (such that a reduction factor of 0.8 would be decreased to 0.72) has less of an impact on the ultimate pay-as-you-go rate than a 0.1 arithmetic increase in the total ultimate fertility rate (1.95 instead of 1.85), or a 10 percent geometric increase in the net immigration assumption (from 0.4 percent of the population to 0.44 percent), or a 0.25 percent arithmetic increase in the ultimate annual rate of increase in earnings (4.75 percent instead of 4.5 percent), or a 0.25 percent arithmetic decrease in the ultimate annual rate of increase in prices (3.25 percent instead of 3.5 percent). These apparent differences deserve further investigation.

In fact, there is a large literature on trying to project mortality rates. One point of debate is whether or not the human life span is finite, as proposed by

12. Keyfitz (1984, p. 220).
13. See the sensitivity analysis in section G of Board of Trustees (1994).
14. See Canada, Office of the Superintendent of Financial Institutions (1991).

James Fries.[15] The end result of Fries's assumptions would be the rectangularization of the mortality curve. Evidence of its evolution to a "rectangular"
survivorship function can be seen in the rates that have existed since the turn of
the century, as shown in figure 1-4. Fries's hypothesis has been criticized,
however, for example by G. C. Myers and K. G. Manton:

> If one examines the total survival curves from birth onward, they may
> suggest some rectangularization. This, however, combines the effects of
> two very different types of mortalilty reduction, i.e., those due to declines
> in infant and child mortality and those from chronic disease mortality
> reductions at later ages. Not only are these phenomena quite different,
> but they have occurred at different times, i.e., infant and child mortality
> declined rapidly from 1930 to 1960 to presently low levels, whereas
> declines in mortality at later ages are more recent, starting after 1960 and
> associated by many investigators with significant declines in circulatory
> disease mortality after 1968. The figure also clearly shows a stretching
> outwards of the curves over time and a shift on the abscissa toward
> higher ages.[16]

Myers and Manton suggest calculating the standard deviation of the mean
life expectancy at advanced ages in order to provide empirical evidence for this
debate. If the standard deviation decreases as life expectancy increases, then
there truly is evidence of rectangularization. If, on the other hand, the standard
deviation increases along with the increase in life expectancy, then the conclusion must be that there is no finite upper bound, w.

I have performed such calculations using combined male and female U.S.
Medicare data and the following formulae using standard actuarial notation:[17]

$$E[K] = e_x = \text{ISU}(K=0,\bullet,) \, \text{SDO2}_{(K+1)}p\text{SDO2}_{(x)}$$
$$\text{Var}[K] = \text{ISU}(K=0,\bullet,) \, (2K+1)\text{SDO4}(\text{SDO2}_{(K+1)}p\text{SDO2}_{(x)}-e^2\text{SDO2}_{(x)})$$

The results are summarized in table 1-9. The data clearly indicate that increasing life expectancy brings with it increasing variance around the time to death.
Such evidence is not consistent with the assumption that there is a finite life
span.

15. See, for example, Fries (1980).
16. Myers and Manton (1984, p. 347).
17. See Brown (1991b).

Figure 1-4. Female Survivorship Rates for the United States

Percent

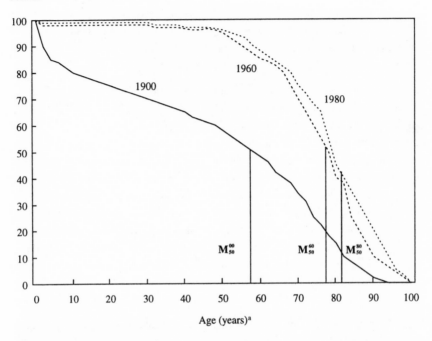

Age (years)[a]

SOURCE: Myers and Manton (1984, p. 347).
a. M_{50}^{00} M_{50}^{60} and M_{50}^{80} represent the ages to which 50 percent of females survive subject to the mortality risks of 1900, 1960, and 1980, respectively.

The work of James Vaupel and A. F. Yashin, taken with the above evidence, gives further cause to pause and reflect about the potential for future mortality improvements.[18] Vaupel and Yashin argue mathematically that current assumptions may seriously underestimate the room for improvement in life expectancy at advanced ages. Their thesis is that the clues provided toward the level of mortality improvement in a heterogeneous population may be misleading. As mortality is reduced at the younger ages, mortality may actually be increased at older ages because more frail individuals survive. Hence the observed rate of progress in reducing the population death rate at the older ages will be less than, but will approach over time, the rate of progress in reducing individual death rates.

For example, a cure for death from juvenile diabetes (such as insulin) will reduce mortality rates at young ages and increase overall life expectancy. However, these diabetics will then die of heart disease brought on by nephritis

18. See, for example, Vaupel and Yashin (1985).

Table 1-9. Life Expectancy and its Variance at Several Ages

	Age					
	80		85		90	
Year	E[K]	Var[K]	E[K]	Var[K]	E[K]	Var[K]
1973	7.00	28.10	5.09	19.15	3.72	13.70
1978	7.70	31.88	5.65	21.93	4.11	15.55
1983	7.96	33.60	5.89	23.21	4.30	16.37
1988	7.96	32.91	5.85	22.48	4.21	15.61

Source: Brown (1991b, p. 94).

in their late forties or fifties, thus raising the mortality rates in these older age groups. Hence the observed rate of progress in improvement for any individual age fifty, as seen through average population statistics, will be less than the true rate of mortality improvement for any particular individual of that age. The true rate of improvement is masked by the heterogeneity of the population. However, if one generation passes without another new cure for a youth disease, then the true underlying rate of improvement in mortality will finally show through in the population statistics—another inevitable surprise!

Vaupel and Yashin maintain that the improvement in mortality rates in the period from 1960 to 1990 (slow in the 1960s and more rapid in the 1970s and 1980s) were completely consistent with their heterogeneity hypothesis. They conclude that mortality rates after age seventy, and especially after eighty, may decline faster in the future than was previously anticipated, with a significant consequence: the elderly population may be substantially larger in the future than currently projected. This would be true even without any medical breakthroughs—solely because the heterogeneity of the population has masked the true underlying rate of mortality improvement.

More recent work by Jacques Carriere on dependent decrement theory indicates the importance of determining the interdependence of various competing risks before determining the possible extention of life as a result of the removal of a specific cause of death.[19] Carriere points out that classical multiple decrement theory is based on the assumption that competing causes of decrement are stochastically independent even though this assumption is usually not true in reality. The level of dependence of various competing risks can lead to a wide variety of projections of future life expectancy.

For example, in his paper "Dependent Decrement Theory" Carriere analyzes the effect of removing heart/cerebrovascular disease from the U.S. population given various levels of dependence between cerebrovascular diseases

19. See, for example, Carriere (1994, 1995).

and other competing risks.[20] Before the removal of the disease, the U.S. median age at death is calculated to be seventy-seven years for a newborn. Under the standard analysis, which assumes that there is no dependence of competing risks, removing heart/cardiovascular diseases would increase the median age at death to eighty-six. However, if there is a 99 percent correlation between heart/cardiovascular diseases and competing risks, then the removal of such diseases will only increase the median age to seventy-eight. If the correlation is 50 percent, the median age rises to eighty-three, and so on.

In a later paper, Carriere presents a similar analysis on the effect of removing cancer as a cause of death.[21] Under the standard assumption of independence of competing risks, this increases the median age at death from seventy-seven to eighty-one. However, if there is a 99 percent correlation between competing risks, the removal of cancer as a cause of death only increases the median to age seventy-eight. And if the dependence is $\rho = + 0.50$, then the median age rises to eighty.

In sum, there does not appear to be any proof that the human life span is finite, and given the work of Vaupel and Yashin, improvements in life expectancy at the advanced age may be more rapid than now anticipated. Nevertheless, the surprising extent to which the trustees' report indicates that OASDI funding is sensitive to the mortality assumption indicates that this area warrants further research.

Immigration

Increased net immigration has an effect on dependency ratios similar to that of increased fertility and possibly even greater, for at least two reasons. First, the impact of immigration on the dependency ratios is immediate, while the impact of increased fertility rates is deferred. Second, if workers come to the United States having completed their education and prepared for the workforce, then the United States is spared the equivalent of the youth dependency ratio—that is, the cost of infant health care and the cost of education associated with the young. Thus it would be natural to expect growing pressures to liberalize the immigration policy of the United States as the impact of the expected rising aged dependency ratio becomes more widely understood.

The Canadian government has already allowed large increases in net immigration to Canada, defended at least partly by the need to decrease the growing domestic aged dependency ratios. However, this recent change in

20. Carriere (1994).
21. Carriere (forthcoming, 1995).

public policy may be ill-timed. The baby boom generation, born between 1951 and 1966, are now thirty to forty-five. Hence any policy that encourages the immigration of workers in this age range will be counterproductive. Only immigrant workers under age thirty will assist in the solution of the growing aged dependency ratios and the growth in the wealth transfer index.

The Economic Council of Canada study *One in Three* confirms this point with a demographic analysis that shows that most of today's immigrants are in the same age group as the baby boom generation.[22] In fact its analysis indicates that increased immigration is not optimally desirable until after the year 2020:

> We noted earlier that the retirement income programs would reach just over 7 percent of GNP by 2031, assuming moderate population growth and maintenance of the present age of eligibility and income-replacement ratio. To reduce this share by only 1 percentage point would necessitate an additional 2.8 million workers in the labour force and no extra retirees by 2031. To accomplish this would require . . . an increase in net immigration in the decade prior to 2031 from 80,000 to 640,000, assuming, as is now the case, that only half of the immigrants would be of workforce age.[23]

Further, as I have pointed out elsewhere, there are two other factors that should be considered.[24] First, although immigrants have historically come to North America from Europe, Europe is now also experiencing declining birth rates and therefore is not likely to be the source of future immigration. Instead, the majority of new immigrants will probably be "visible minorities" and will necessitate special social service programs to enhance assimilation. Second, present U.S. legal immigration criteria set very high standards for potential immigrants. This means that the developing nations may lose many of their best individuals to countries like the United States, thus retarding their own ability to achieve heightened rates of economic development.

In any case, regardless of the public policy arguments for and against increased immigration, the demographics indicate that increased immigration will be a fact of life, especially after the year 2020, and the assumptions underlying the OASDI Trust Fund projections should reflect this.

22. Economic Council of Canada (1979).
23. Economic Council of Canada (1979, p. 81).
24. Brown (1991a, p. 107).

Conclusions

This section has reviewed the demographic and economic assumptions underlying the projections of the OASDI Trust Funds prepared by the Board of Trustees in light of the impact of the shifting demographics. While the effects outlined here are indeed inevitable, they need no longer come as a surprise.

As to the presentation of the projections of the OASDI system by the Board of Trustees, one method of improvement seems worthy of consideration. At the present time the trustees highlight three projections: "low cost," "intermediate," and "high cost." However, each projection is based on a combination of several economic and demographic variables. Thus it is not possible to determine the impact of any one variable on the projected costs of the OASDI system from these projections alone. The report's sensitivity analysis does address these matters, but it is somewhat buried in section G and is not highlighted. In fact, while the high cost, low cost, and intermediate projections are cited in almost every reference to the trustees' report, the sensitivity analysis is rarely presented. It would seem preferable to reverse this emphasis. Indeed, rather than high cost and low cost projections, it might be more productive merely to try, through simulation, to put some confidence intervals on a best estimate projection. This would not be an easy matter, however, because there are correlations between so many of the variables, for example, wage rates and inflation.

On balance, the OASDI trustees' report is an excellent document and, as such, invites academic discussion. The points raised in this section are not criticisms but commentary.

References

Board of Trustees of the Federal Old-Age and Survivors' Insurance and Disability Insurance Trust Funds. *Annual Report.* Washington: 1994.

Brown, Robert L. 1991a. *Economic Security in an Aging Population.* Toronto: Butterworths.

___. 1991b. *Rectangularization of the Survivorship Curve—Facts Versus Appearances.* Actuarial Research Clearing House (ARCH), 89–96.

___. 1994. *Paygo Funding Stability and Intergenerational Equity.* Research Report 94-18. Waterloo, Ontario: Institute of Insurance and Pension Research.

Canada, Office of the Superintendent of Financial Institutions. 1991.*Canada Pension Plan.* Statutory Actuarial Report 14. Ottawa.

Carriere, Jacques F. 1994. "Dependent Decrement Theory." *Transactions, Society of Actuaries,* 46:45–67.

___. "Removing Cancer When It Is Correlated with Other Causes of Death." Forthcoming.

Clark, R., J. Kreps, and J. Spengler. 1978. "Economics of Aging: A Survey." *Journal of Economic Literature* 16 (September): 922.

Easterlin, Richard A. 1978. "What will 1984 be Like? Socioeconomic Implications of Recent Twists in Age Structure." *Demography* 15(4): 397–432.

Economic Council of Canada. 1979. *One in Three—Pensions for Canadians to 2030.* Ottawa: Economic Council of Canada.

Ermisch, John F. 1983.*The Political Economy of Demographic Change.* Policy Studies Institute. London: Heinemann.

Fries, J. F. 1980. "Aging, Natural Death and the Compression of Morbidity." *New England Journal of Medicine* 303: 130–35.

Hohn, Charlotte. 1987. "Population Policies in Advanced Societies: Pronatalist and Migration Strategies." *European Journal of Population* 3: 459–81.

Keyfitz, Nathan. 1984. "Technology, Employment, and the Succession of Generations." *Insurance: Mathematics and Economics* 3 (4): 219–30.

McPherson, Barry. 1983. *Aging as a Social Process: An Introduction to Individual and Population Aging.* Toronto: Butterworths.

Myers, G. C., and K. G. Manton. 1984. "Compression of Mortality: Myth or Reality?" *Gerontologist* 24: 346–53.

Myers, Robert J. 1985. "Implications of Population Change on Social Insurance Systems Providing Old-age Benefits." *Insurance Mathematics and Economics* 4(1): 3–9.

Pifer, Alan, and Lydia Bronte. 1986. *Our Aging Society: Paradox and Promise.* W. W. Norton.

U. S. Department of Commerce, Bureau of the Census. 1987. *An Aging World.* International Population Report P-95:78 (September).

Vaupel, J., and A. Yashin. 1983. *The Deviant Dynamics of Death in Heterogeneous Populations.* Laxenburg, Austria: International Institute for Applied Systems Analysis (IIASA).

Weitz, Harry. 1979. *The Foreign Experience with Income Maintenance for the Elderly.* Ottawa: Economic Council of Canada.

An Economist's Perspective
Diane J. Macunovich

MAKING PROJECTIONS is always a hazardous enterprise—the more so for members of the National Academy of Social Insurance, who are required to forecast at least seventy-five years into the future. A standard method that has been adopted in making such long-range projections is to attempt to identify and work with long-range averages of variables under consideration: in effect, to simplify the forecasting process by ignoring any cyclic variations. This is a laudable methodology, but in this section I raise some questions regarding the methods applied to historic data to identify these long-range averages.

Most economists readily accept that economic variables can be decomposed into a longer-term trend and a series of short-term business cycles. This approach is illustrated nicely for real U.S. GNP in figure 1-5, which is taken from an undergraduate textbook. A considerable portion of macroeconomics is devoted to understanding these short-term business cycles in order to identify the underlying longer-term trend and to forecast future trends and cycles. It is important not to ignore them: as figure 1-6 shows, extrapolating on the basis of the long-term trend and extrapolating simply on the basis of recent experience produces two very different impressions of what the future holds! If an average business cycle were three to five years in length (trough to peak), then at least six to ten years of data would have to be used in calculating a long-term historic average. Anything less would produce a biased estimate.

However, although academics have long accepted the existence of short-term business cycles, there has been little general acceptance of the possibility of other, longer-term cycles. Kuznets traced possible twenty-year cycles in long time series of data, and Kondratieff claimed to identify even longer, fifty-year cycles—but such efforts have been largely empirical, and with little theoretical basis they have been difficult to incorporate into theories for forecasting the economy. These longer-term cycles appear to have occurred at numerous times and places in the past, but there is no way to know whether they will continue in the future—or whether one might be taking place at the present time.

This section focuses on a longer-term cycle of perhaps thirty years' duration which the United States has experienced in the post–World War II period. It is generally referred to as the baby boom and bust, and there is a growing body of evidence supporting a theory that ties this cycle to a whole host of economic and demographic phenomena. To the extent that this theory is correct, it indicates that much of the experience that economists have tended to incorporate into their analyses of long-term trends has, in fact, been the result of these cyclic phenomena. If so, then there is a real danger of misforecasting the future in much the same way as was represented in figure 1-6.

The danger of ignoring the effect of the baby boom and bust can be seen in the simple table reproduced below from the 1991 Report of the Social Security Technical Panel. In an attempt to identify the most likely level of productivity

Figure 1-5. Actual and Potential GNP

Potential real GNP (billions of dollars, 1982 prices)

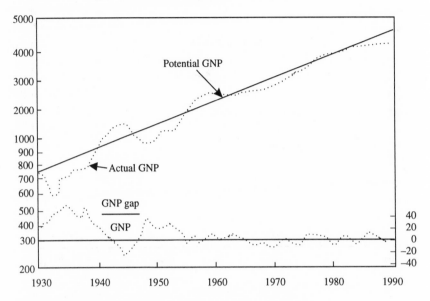

SOURCE: Paul A. Samuelson and William D. Nordhaus, Economics, 14th ed. (New York: McGraw-Hill, 1992).

growth for the period after 1991, the panel analyzed data for the period 1951–89 to produce a series of average growth rates:[25]

Weight applied to each preceding year in deriving average:	1.00	0.98	0.95	0.92	0.90
Average productivity growth:	1.7	1.6	1.4	1.3	1.2

In effect, they were developing averages using different historical periods as a base. When every year is given a weight of 1.00, the historical period used for developing the average is thirty-nine years long (1951–89). Conversely, when each preceding year is given a (multiplicative) weight of 0.90, any experience that occurred more than fifteen years ago is given relatively little weight: the fifteenth year is given a weight of only 0.20 in the average (0.90^{15}), and the twenty-fifth year is given a weight of only 0.07 (0.90^{25}). Using a weight of 0.90

25. U.S. Social Security Administration (1991, p. 22).

Figure 1-6. Forecasting Based on Long- and Short-Term Trends

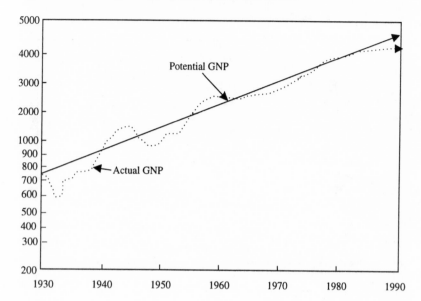

to calculate a long-term average thus effectively assumes that any longer-term cycle that might have been taking place, unnoticed, was no longer than fifteen to twenty years in duration.

However, fifteen to twenty years represents only half of the baby boom and bust cycle. If this had any effect on U.S. productivity, then a much longer-term average (the 1.7 percent in the table above) must be taken in order to factor out its full effect: a fifteen-year average (the 1.2 percent in the table above) factors out only half of the boom-and-bust effect.

Simply comparing averages based on different historic periods is, nevertheless, an extremely crude method of analyzing historic data for forecasting purposes. Ideally, it would be possible to understand underlying causal relationships and apply these when forecasting. But even the more sophisticated ARMA (autoregressive moving average) procedures recommended to Social Security Administration (SSA) staff by the 1991 Technical Panel do not go this far. As a demographic economist, my interest is not in simply observing empirical regularities like the baby boom and bust and their effects on other socioeconomic variables, but rather in attempting to explain them theoretically

Figure 1-7. Log of Relative Cohort Size, United States, 1900–2009[a]

Relative cohort size (logged)

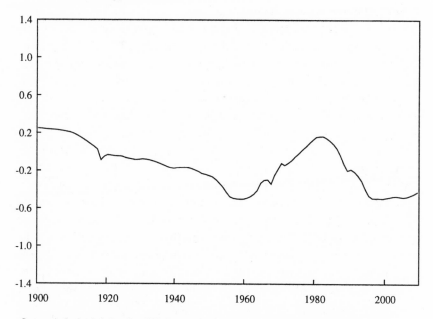

SOURCE: Author's tabulations from U.S. Bureau of the Census, *Current Population Reports*, Series P-25, various years.

a. Relative cohort size is defined as the ratio of the population ages twenty-one to twenty-three to the population ages forty-five to forty-nine.

in order to be able to sort out trends and cycles and begin to develop longer-term forecasts with some reliability. The soundest basis for such theory is the work of Richard Easterlin, which focuses on relative cohort size: the number of persons born in a particular period (a birth cohort) relative to the number of persons in the parental cohort.[26] This variable is closely related to age-specific fertility approximately twenty years earlier. The actual pattern of U.S. relative cohort size (defined here as the number of persons ages twenty-one to twenty-three relative to the number ages forty-five to forty-nine) over the past fifty years is shown in figure 1-7.

My own research has already allowed me to quantify the effect of this variable on the relative wages of young males and from there, on a host of other factors, including fertility, marriage and divorce, and male and female enrollment and labor force participation rates. Work currently in progress indicates

26. See Easterlin (1980).

that there may be equally strong causal relationships between this variable and the industrial structure, the growth rates of GDP, productivity and average wages, inflation, and interest rates (and hence, savings rates). Research in the literature provides even more evidence that all of these factors are closely interrelated in a system driven by relative cohort size. This is supported by recent findings that variables describing the age composition of the population are highly significant in macroeconomic models.

If this is the case, then to base forecasts on recent experience is to treat observations from one portion of a cycle as if they were observations on a linear trend line (as indicated in figure 1-6), and runs the risk of missing a major turnaround in all of these series—a turnaround that evidence indicates has already begun to occur. The argument within SSA is that fluctuations are not important in its seventy-five-year forecasts because they tend to balance each other out over the forecast period. This would be true if economists recognized the cycles and chose the midpoints of those cycles to calculate long-term forecasting averages. But it can be demonstrated that the current cycle may be near its "low" point, so that the use of recent averages seriously biases forecasts toward "high cost" alternatives. The remainder of this paper attempts to place all of the available evidence into a comprehensive framework to show that a fairly plausible argument can be made in support of a relative cohort size explanation for recent economic and demographic phenomena.

First-Order Effects of Relative Cohort Size: Male Relative Earnings, Unemployment, Inflation, Interest, and Savings Rates

The primary effect of relative birth cohort size, as postulated by Easterlin and demonstrated by Finis Welch and Mark Berger, among others, is on the relative earnings of young males—that is, on their earnings relative to those of older males.[27] This effect occurs largely because of the fact that young, less experienced workers are not perfect substitutes in the labor market for older, more experienced workers, and the production function is sensitive to the balance of these two types of workers. If there is an oversupply of one type of worker relative to the other (for example, an oversupply of assembly-line workers relative to management) the wages of the oversupplied group will tend to go down relative to the wages of the undersupplied group (there will be an increased demand for managers to train and supervise the inexperienced workers, relative to their supply, thus pushing up the wages of the managers). In addition, the age group in relatively greater supply will experience increased

---

27. See Easterlin (1968, 1980), Welch (1979), and Berger (1984, 1985). Relative cohort size also has an effect on female wages, but this is more complex and is addressed separately below.

levels of unemployment and part-time employment, which will lead—through the "discouraged worker effect"—to reduced labor force participation rates.

Imperfect substitutability is the main (but not the only) source of declining relative wages. Easterlin postulates a number of other effects, including overcrowding in the family, leading to less parental time with each child; in the schools, leading to higher student-to-teacher ratios and half-day sessions and hence, to lower average performance; and in the supply of college graduates relative to those with less education, leading to a decrease in the premium earned by a college education and hence, reducing the incentive to pursue further education.[28] These other effects would tend to decrease the wages of younger workers relative to those of older workers, all other things being equal.

Although labor economists have been aware of the effect of imperfect substitutability for some time, they examined it in isolation and therefore assumed that once relative cohort size improved for younger males (that is, once the peak of the baby boom had entered the labor market in 1978–80), their relative wages and employment prospects would immediately begin to improve. This did not happen. In fact young males' relative wages continued to decline for the first half of the 1980s, leading the labor economists to believe that they had overestimated relative cohort size effects and to turn to other factors for analysis.

My own work has demonstrated, however, that relative cohort size effects on relative male wages are indeed very strong, but that two other forces have also had a significant influence on them during the postwar period.[29] One is the size of the military (since the military draws predominately from the pool of young men and therefore affects the ratio of younger to older males in the civilian labor force), and the other is the size of the U.S. trade deficit (since imports tend disproportionately to represent the skills of less experienced workers and hence tend to "replace" younger workers more than older workers).[30] The first of these effects dominated in the late 1960s and early 1970s (with the Vietnam war), and the second dominated in the 1980s. By allowing for both these effects, the effect of relative cohort size can be correctly estimated, and the relative earnings of young males can be very closely fitted econometrically, as shown in figure 1-8. Using this model it can be shown that,

28. In regard to overcrowding in the schools, it is interesting to note that the current "echo baby boom," which is just approaching school age, appears to be encountering many of these same effects—even though it is the result simply of increasing numbers of births, rather than increasing birth rates. A recent newspaper article reported overcrowding in New York City kindergartens, due to "unforeseen" increases in enrollments ("The Great Kindergarten Shuffle Succeeds," *New York Times*, October 10, 1994, p. B1).

29. See Macunovich (1994b).

30. This latter is an effect documented by, among others, Murphy and Welch (1992) and Revenga (1992).

Figure 1-8. Average Annual Male Relative Earnings, United States, Projected and Actual, 1955–2007[a]

Male relative earnings[a]

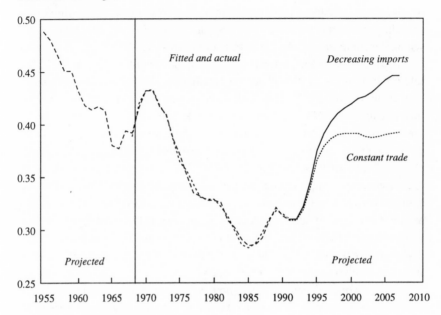

SOURCE: Macunovich (1993a), pp. 1–18.

a. Ratio of income of males with one to five years of experience to income of families with head ages forty-five to fifty-four. Family incomes are for year five.

on the basis of improving relative cohort size, young males' relative earnings are likely to continue the strong improvement that they have experienced since 1985 (a slight attenuation in the upward trend in the early 1990s appears to have resulted from the labor market entry of the Vietnam War mini–baby boom). It is important to note that this discussion has focused on relative male wages. The absolute levels of male wages have only begun to improve in real terms the last three years, also as an effect of relative cohort size, as explained below.

With regard to inflation, interest, and savings rates, evidence in the economic literature is not as strong as that for relative earnings, largely because macroeconomists have until recently tried to ignore effects of changing age structure in the population and deal only with a single aggregate "representative agent." However, some analysts have now begun to discuss the effects of age structure in the context of life cycle consumption and savings models. That is, the most commonly accepted models of consumption and savings tend to recognize that individuals vary in their patterns of savings over their life cycle, in an attempt to smooth overall consumption. Thus in early adulthood, when individuals face major expenditures on housing, cars, children, and furnishings, and their earnings are low relative to later in life, they act as net dissavers (borrowers); and conversely, as they grow older their average earnings rise and their average expenditures fall, and they begin to save for retirement. Gregory Mankiw and David Weil have estimated a strong effect of age structure on housing prices in the United States, identifying the entry of the baby boom into the housing market as the cause of the severe house price inflation of the 1970s and 1980s, and the entry of the baby bust as the cause of recent house price deflation. This effect has been confirmed in the work of Ray Fair and Kathryn Dominguez, who found significant effects of age structure on all forms of consumption, including housing demand, and on money demand. Similarly, Henry McMillan and Jerome Baesel document a strong effect of age structure (the proportion of young to old in the population) on real interest rates and inflation because of differential patterns of savings and consumption with age: a higher proportion of young adults in a population will produce lower aggregate savings levels—and hence higher interest rates. The other side of this phenomenon—the potential meltdown effect of a retiring baby boom on financial markets, asset values, and interest rates—has been described by Sylvester Schieber and John Shoven.[31]

Although some analysts maintain that the potential age structure effect of the baby boomers on personal savings is not large enough to explain the full drop in national savings rates in the United States over the past two decades, studies of this phenomenon to date have focused only on the behavior of the baby boomers themselves. However, it could be that the baby boomers have affected the propensity to save in age groups other than their own. For example, because baby boomers' earnings were depressed and they experienced an inflated housing market (both effects of the large size of their own cohort), many of their parents drew on their own savings in order to help with down payments.

In addition, recent work by Gary Becker and Kevin Murphy that incorporates fertility and human capital accumulation into a macroeconomic model of growth postulates an inverse relationship between the return on human capital (the "education premium") and the return to physical capital (the interest rate), both of which affect and are affected by fertility rates.[32]

Finally, it should be pointed out that Easterlin also presents a mechanism whereby misguided government policy could be seen to exacerbate any effects

31. See Mankiw and Weil (1989), Fair and Dominguez (1991), McMillan and Baesel (1990), and Schieber and Shoven (1994).
32. Becker and Murphy (1990).

of relative cohort size on inflation and unemployment rates.[33] He suggests that the increased levels of unemployment in the 1970s (which he felt were brought about by increasing relative cohort size) led the government to attempt to stimulate job creation by providing tax breaks on investment in physical capital by firms. However, physical capital has been shown in econometric studies of factor substitutability to be a complement to experienced labor (the use of more physical capital creates an increased demand for more experienced workers) and a substitute for less experienced labor (machinery is used to replace unskilled workers). Thus this policy led to an inflationary increase in the wages of older workers, and at the same time exacerbated unemployment among younger workers: the notorious "stagflation" of the late 1970s.

Second-Order Effects of Relative Cohort Size: Fertility, Marriage and Divorce, and Female Labor Force Participation

Easterlin provides a further insight that is important in determining the secondary effects of relative cohort size. Noting that individuals tend to evaluate their earnings relative to some internalized measure of a desired standard of living, he hypothesizes that this internalized standard is most strongly affected by the standard of living experienced in the parental home.[34] (He does not deny that there are other sources of influence, such as an individual's peer group, but simply points out that this is one major influence which can be fairly readily quantified.) That is, an annual salary of $30,000 will be viewed very differently, on average, by someone who grew up in a home in northwest Washington, D.C., than by someone who grew up in northeast Washington, D.C. Because relative earnings are a measure of the earnings of young males relative to those of older males, then on average, this measure can also be used to approximate earnings relative to material aspirations—the desired standard of living as a function of the standard of living experienced in the parental home—in aggregate in the population.

What happens when these relative earnings decline sharply? For example, from the 1960s through the 1980s relative earnings fell from a level close to 0.6 to only 0.28 (that is, the proportion of his parents' *recent* annual income that a young man could reproduce in his *first year* out in the labor market decreased from 60 percent to only 28 percent). Easterlin hypothesizes that in the face of such a decline in ex ante individual earnings, young adults would make several demographic adjustments in order to attempt to keep their ex post per capita

33. See Easterlin (1980).
34. Ibid.

disposable income at a desired level. They might spread individual earnings over fewer dependents: marry later or not at all, have fewer children, and make sure their spouse worked as well, in order to keep per capita disposable income high. They might forego various family benefits in order to maintain material consumption at some desired level, producing lower aggregate fertility and marriage rates and higher aggregate female labor force participation rates (as well as higher aggregate divorce rates, due to the added stress levels and the increased independence of young women brought about by their increased labor force participation). In addition, because delayed or foregone marriage does not imply delayed or foregone sexual activity for males (especially since an increasing relative cohort size creates an abundance of younger females relative to older males), and given imperfect contraception, there would likely be increased levels of out-of-wedlock childbirth and increased proportions of female-headed families.

Easterlin's theories have not been popular with feminists, on the grounds that they tend to focus on relative cohort size effects on young males and to imply a very passive role for young women. However, this is an extremely narrow interpretation of the implications of Easterlin's work. My own research has demonstrated that although their actions were shaped by the norms of the society they lived in, young women have hardly been passive in the face of such dramatic changes in relative earnings.[35] Like their male peers, they too had material aspirations that were largely a function of the standard of living experienced in their parents' homes. In accordance with societal norms, they looked first at the potential earnings of males in order to determine the probability of achieving their own material aspirations, and they saw this as increasingly unlikely. They thus anticipated that they, too, would enter the labor market—whether because they believed that they were less likely to marry, or because they foresaw the need to supplement their husbands' earnings. To prepare themselves, they enrolled in higher education at increasing rates. Then, partly because of the shared desire to maintain per capita disposable income at desired levels, and partly because they were marrying later due to increased college enrollment, they reduced their fertility levels.[36] All three of these effects—declining fertility, increased female college enrollments, and increased female labor force participation—can be explained well with an econometric model based on the female wage and on relative male earnings, which,

35. See, for example, Macunovich (1993a, 1993b, 1994a) and Fair and Macunovich (1993).
36. It is well documented that a later age at first childbirth results in lower completed family size. See, for example, Morgan (1994).

Figure 1-9. Fertility Rates for Women Ages Twenty to Twenty- Four, United States, Projected and Actual, 1954–92[a]

Fertility rate

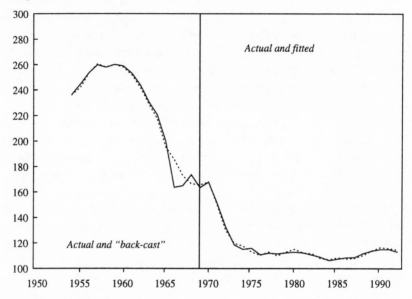

SOURCE: Macunovich (1994b, p. 21).
a. Back-projected for 1954–68.

in turn, are a function of relative cohort size. Predicted and actual levels of these three variables are presented in figures 1-9 through 1-11.

It must be emphasized once again that this analysis is not meant to deny that there could, in addition, be an increasing secular trend toward female college enrollment and labor force participation. Rather, it is intended to show that there was a strong effect of relative cohort size operating at the same time—and that the change in attitudes toward female labor force participation that is often cited as the cause of these increases might well, in fact, have been a result of the groundswell of change arising from increasing relative cohort size.

Third-Order Effects of Relative Cohort Size: Industrial Structure, GDP, Productivity, and Average Wages

In this section the discussion enters a more specultive realm, where research findings are (as yet) hard to come by. This section attempts to indicate the logical ramifications of many of the trends discussed in the two previous sections.

Figure 1-10. Proportion of Women Ages Twenty to Twenty-Four in Labor Force or Enrolled in School, United States, Actual and Projected, 1952-2008[a]

Proportion

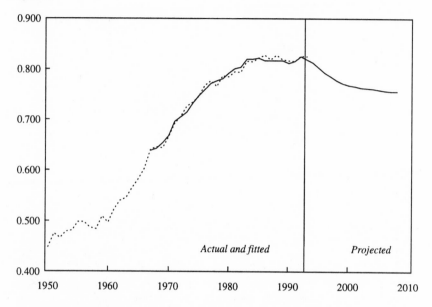

SOURCE: Macunovich (1994, p. 19).
a. Projection assumes that all factors except male relative income are held at 1992 levels.

What happens when increasing proportions of women enter the labor force, and when increasing proportions of families have two wage earners? Although it is well documented that women do indeed face a double burden of market work and work in the home, there is no doubt that having two wage earners—or being the single earner in a one-adult household—increases the tendency to purchase market replacements for the goods and services traditionally produced by women in the home.

It is important, here, to recall the U.S. method of calculating GDP: it is the sum market value of all new final goods and services produced and exchanged in the market. Thus any unpaid work such as housework, and any intermediate goods such as the windshields and tires a firm will purchase to install in new cars, are excluded. In order to calculate productivity, this dollar value of final product is simply divided by the total number of paid hours worked in the market.

But over the past thirty years there has been a "commoditization" of many goods and services. That is, they are now exchanged in the market, and thus included in the measures of GDP and productivity, whereas before they were part of the excluded nonmarket economy. This phenomenon covers a host of

Figure 1-11. School Enrollment Rates for Women Ages Twenty to Twenty-F our, United States, Projected and Actual, 1946–91

Enrollment rate

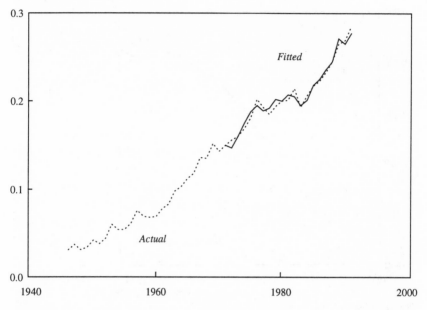

SOURCE: Macunovich (1993b, p. 38).

goods and services, from meal preparation to lawn maintenance to child care to housekeeping. When these services are produced by a non-wage earner, they are not counted in GDP—and yet their end product, in the form of healthy and productive workers, is certainly reflected in the market value of goods that *are* included in GDP. Thus before the entry of large numbers of women into the labor market, the work which they had performed in the home was reflected in the final product included in the measure of GDP, but not in the number of workers thought of as producing that GDP, since only market wage earners were counted. Economic activity was made to look very favorable by measuring the results of all work performed in the economy, but only counting paid workers as having produced that result.

As increasing proportions of women enter the labor force and replace their services in the home with purchased market services, there are three major effects on the measures of economic activity. The first is that many of the goods and services that heretofore had been treated as intermediate products helping to produce healthy and productive workers begin to be counted as final products. To the extent that this has occurred, measures of GDP growth have been falsely inflated: they are now reflecting work that has always been performed in the economy but previously was not acknowledged as such.

The second effect is that measures of industrial structure begin to skew strongly toward the service and retail sectors and away from agriculture and manufacturing. The SSA reports that the proportion of U.S. jobs in manufacturing declined from 29.9 percent in 1950 to 24.3 percent in 1970 to 16.7 percent in 1989, while the proportion of jobs in the retail and service sectors rose from 26.5 percent to 31.4 percent to 41.8 percent over the same periods.[37] This change is not so much due to the fact that more retail and services are being consumed now than when our parents were young: it is simply because more of them are being purchased in the market now, rather than being produced in the home. The much lamented low-wage service jobs are not new: they used to exist in the home, but now they exist in the marketplace.

These goods and services are traditionally considered to be low productivity in the sense that they are not highly mechanized and thus require high levels of labor input per dollar value of output. So measures of economic activity have begun to include large proportions of low productivity work that earlier had not been counted: this alone will place a severe drag on measured rates of growth in productivity. Again, it is not that the balance of work has actually changed, but rather that the ways of counting that work have changed!

Moreover, to the extent that any of these newly commoditized goods and services are counted as intermediate rather than final, they will not be directly counted in measures of economic activity, while the wage earning workers who produce them will. This, too, will lead to drastically reduced measures of labor productivity.

In sum, increasing relative cohort size leads to declining male relative earnings, which leads to increasing female labor force participation, which leads to the increased commoditization of "low productivity" work, which leads to reduced measures of productivity growth simply because the measures of GDP and productivity are so imperfect. While it might be argued that these measures work acceptably when there is little change in market behavior, they fall apart completely in the face of dramatic changes in female labor force participation. But, as can be seen from figure 1-12, the great increase in female labor force participation rates has ended. It was this increase that led to the increased desire to purchase replacements for home services, which, in turn, drove the shift toward growing proportions of low wage, low productivity service jobs in the U.S. economy. With the recent attenuation in female labor force participation rates, the momentum of the shift toward such low produc-

37. Yang and Goss (1992, p. 20).

Figure 1-12. Labor Force Participation Rates for Women Ages Twenty to Twenty-Four, United States, 1952–93

Percent

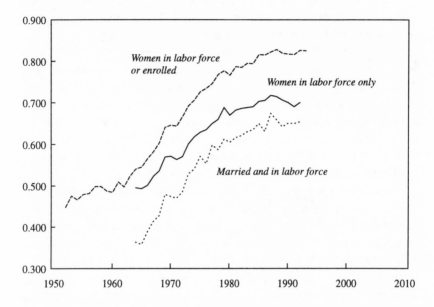

SOURCE: Author's tabulations from Bureau of Labor Statistics, *Current Population Survey*, Public Use Tapes (various years, March).

tivity jobs will also slow down. This assumption is supported by the recent announcement by the Bureau of Labor Statistics (BLS) that new job creation between spring of 1992 and the fall of 1994 occurred primarily in occupations earning above average wages.[38]

The pattern of real average wages for both males and females is closely related to these relative cohort size effects on GDP and productivity. Around the turn of the century, as industrialization began to pick up pace in the United States, males were increasingly drawn into the industrial workforce. Before this time mill workers had largely been young women and children. Through their unions men now negotiated two conditions: that young women would be laid off once they married, and that men would be paid a "family wage."[39] The two are not unrelated. Although the feminist literature presents this as a period of the accession by capitalism to paternalism (men reinforcing other men's

38. "Statistics Reveal Bulk of New Jobs Pay over Average," *New York Times*, October 17, 1994, p. A1.

39. On the commonly acknowledged "marriage bar" see Goldin (1990).

rights to the unpaid services of women in the home), it is more logical to assume that capitalism willingly acceded because the arrangement was financially beneficial. That is, these two measures ensured that the vast majority of male wage earners would be supported in the home by unpaid labor that would effectively make them more productive in the workplace. Industrial employers were simply acknowledging that with each male worker they were, in fact, obtaining the services of two workers—the man and his wife. And from this understanding followed a form of statistical discrimination in which it was assumed that any male worker would have this home support and therefore qualify for a family wage, whereas any female worker would lack such support and therefore would not produce a marginal product worthy of a family wage.

It is a particular shortcoming of the economic literature that by focusing on the male-female wage gap, the productivity effects of women's "double burden" have been discussed solely in terms of the presumed lower productivity of women in the market due to their responsibilities in the home.[40] For some reason the other side of this effect has not been considered seriously: that men with a stay-at-home wife will tend to be more productive than men with a working wife or no wife at all. And yet this was the basis of literature of the 1950s that ultimately led to the concept of economic efficiency through specialization and exchange in the home.[41] At most, economists have discussed and measured an observed wage gap between married and unmarried males, which has been termed the "marriage premium."[42] It has been argued that women might choose more productive men as partners, leaving lower-wage males without spouses. However, my own research shows that the most striking effect on men's wages is caused by the presence of a stay-at-home spouse, not marriage per se.[43]

Other researchers have begun addressing this topic.[44] Recent studies on earnings of male executives report that those with stay-at-home wives earn more than those with working wives, even after controlling for differences in hours worked, education, experience, field of employment, and career interruptions. Men with stay-at-home wives averaged salaries 25 percent above those with working wives in 1993 ($121,630 as compared with $97,490) and their pay increases between 1987 and 1993 averaged 40 percent more. This suggests

40. See, for example, Becker (1981) and Fuchs (1989).
41. See, for example, Parsons (1949, 1955) for the earlier period and Becker (1981) for the later.
42. See, for example, Blackburn and Korenman (1994) and Korenman and Neumark (1991).
43. Author's work in progress.
44. For example Linda Stroh, as reported in "Men Whose Wives Work Earn Less," *New York Times,* October 12, 1994, p. A1.

either that firms discriminate in their executives' compensation (another version of the statistical discrimination model), or that having a stay-at-home wife actually enables a man to be more productive in the hours that he spends at work. The latter does not seem surprising, given the distractions inherent in having to take care of domestic responsibilities, such as running errands and making phone calls during the work day, to name but a few. A newspaper article in 1989 noted that corporations were "pressuring" their male executives to marry.[45] Although it speculated they were motivated by fears of homosexuality and emotional instability, it seems much more reasonable to assume that the corporations were simply demanding that their executives live up to their part of the bargain inherent in a family wage.

It also seems reasonable to assume that over the past thirty years, as increasing numbers of employers have accepted the reality of male workers with working wives, they have become increasingly unwilling to pay a family wage. This would account for the fact that the much-heralded closing of the male-female wage gap has resulted largely from a lowering of male wages, rather than from a rise in real female wages.[46] Thus it appears that the gradual disappearance of the family wage has led to a stagnation of the average real male wage since 1974: any productivity gains from technological change and increasing levels of education have been counterbalanced by the loss of the family wage premium for a stay-at-home spouse resulting from increasing relative cohort size and consequent increasing female labor force participation and lower marriage rates. This is consistent with the findings of McKinley Blackburn and Sanders Korenman, who demonstrate a marked decline in the marriage premium for men throughout the 1970s and 1980s.[47] The real wages of males have been rising, but the rise been masked by the fall in married men's earnings as an increasingly large proportion of them lose the premium associated with a stay-at-home wife. However, since the increase in female labor force participation, and the decline in marriage rates, have attenuated since the peak of the baby boom entered the labor market, the depressive effect of losing the family wage premium should also have attenuated. This assumption is supported by the recent BLS announcement, noted above, that new job creation in the past two-and-a-half years has occurred primarily in occupations earning above average wages.[48]

45. Keith Bradsher, "Young Men Pressed to Wed for Success," *New York Times* (December 13, 1989), p. C1.

46. Goldin (1990).

47. See Blackburn and Korenman (1994).

48. "Statistics Reveal Bulk of New Jobs Pay over Average," *New York Times,* October 17, 1994, p. A1.

Figure 1-13. Female Real Hourly Wage in First Five Years of Work Experience, United States, 1964–91[a]

1991 dollars

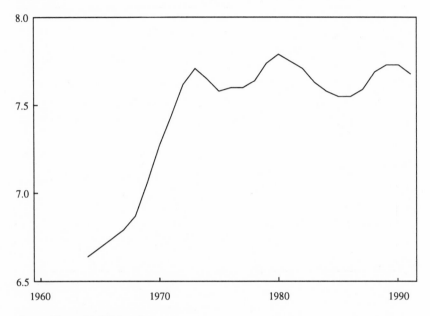

SOURCE: Macunovich (1994b, p. 3).
a. Holding education constant at 1968 levels.

And what has happened to real female wages during this period? Figure 1-13 presents the pattern of the real female wage between 1963 and 1991, holding education constant, for women in their first five years of work experience, a period when average levels of experience change very little. As can be seen, real wages rose dramatically from 1963 to 1972 and have been essentially stable since, with only cyclic variation, corresponding to business cycles. This pattern runs counter to the common perception that the average female wage has risen strongly over the period since 1975, and has thus drawn increasing proportions of women into the labor force. My own work shows that the wage pattern appears to result from a complex set of occupational changes made by women during this period, again in response to relative cohort size effects.

In order to understand those responses it is necessary to distinguish between two categories of jobs: "dead-end" jobs, characterized by relatively flat wage-to-experience profiles, and "career" jobs, with relatively steep wage-to-experience profiles. Before the baby boom generation entered the labor market, when there was an excess demand for labor in the economy, the market was

Figure 1-14. Wage Profiles for Dead-End and Career Jobs

Annual salary (thousands of constant dollars)

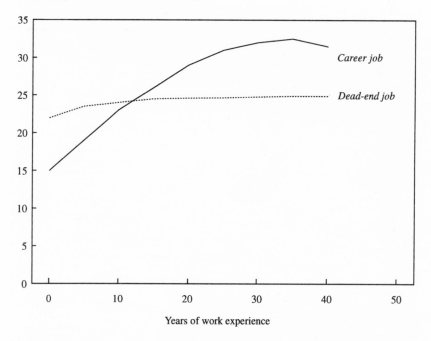

Years of work experience

forced to pay a premium in order to attract workers into dead-end jobs. The result was the relationship illustrated in figure 1-14, with higher starting wages in dead-end jobs than in career jobs. As the baby boom entered the market in the late 1960s and early 1970s, this premium gradually disappeared because the growing labor surplus meant that workers preferred a dead-end job to no job. Then, beginning in the mid 1980s, the premium on dead-end jobs began to return as the baby bust generation entered the labor market.

What type of worker is most likely to respond to a premium on dead-end jobs? Women, who anticipate some discontinuity in lifetime labor force partic-ipation and therefore weight immediate earnings relative to future earnings even more heavily than workers who do not anticipate discontinuity. Hence before the baby boom generation entered the labor market, many women were attracted into dead-end jobs by the wage premium. But as the premium disap-peared, they no longer saw any benefit to these jobs and instead began looking more toward career jobs, switching out of clerical, teaching, and nursing jobs into professional and management jobs. Then in the mid-1980s, as the baby boom was absorbed and the premium on dead-end jobs began to return, women once again started moving back into nursing and teaching, part-time and "mommy track" jobs, which tend to have flatter wage profiles.[49]

The result of women moving from one set of occupations into another was the observed stable wage from 1972 to 1992. This was because as women moved increasingly into career jobs, they tended more and more to replace their time in the home with purchased goods and services. Thus these high-wage jobs for women ultimately induced the creation of additional retail and service jobs—which tended to be filled predominately by women. For each high-wage female worker, a demand was created for some equivalent, low productivity, low-wage female worker; the higher the wage in the first job, the higher the number of low-wage equivalents created. This tended, in the aggregate, to produce a seemingly stable average female wage, controlling for changing average education and experience.

The Net Effect

What has been described here is a coherent picture of an economy driven not only by the size of its population, but by the age composition of that population. The theory embraces nearly the whole set of variables that concern the SSA in making its seventy-five year forecasts. It is attractive in that it appears to explain, in a comprehensive way, most of the truly puzzling aspects of the U.S. economy in recent years. This theory suggests that recent experience has been close to the "bottom" with regard to a number of variables such as fertility, marriage, savings, productivity, and wage growth rates. Forecasting on the basis of that recent experience will underpredict the average levels of all of these variables. The theory of relative cohort size provides strong justification for rethinking some aspects of the SSA low cost projections (such as combining the higher rates of real interest and female labor force participation with the higher rates of fertility and lower rates of marriage), and treating them, rather, as the best estimate projections.

It must be pointed out that not only did all of the available time series move in the appropriate direction to support this theory as the baby boom generation moved into the labor market, but now, as the baby bust generation begins entering, they all show signs of turning around. Thus, for example, beginning in 1985 the male relative wage turned around strongly (see figure 1-8), together

49. It should be noted that studies such as Blau (1984) which find no evidence of premiums on dead-end jobs were carried out using data from the mid- and late 1970s, by which time the labor market effects of the baby boom had eliminated the premium. On the flatter wage profiles of "mommy track" jobs see "Back From the Mommy Track," *New York Times*, October 9, 1994.

Figure 1-15. Proportion Married for Full-Time Workers Ages Twenty to Twenty-Two, United States, 1964–92

Proportion

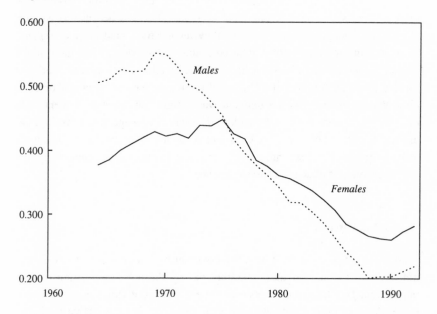

SOURCE: Author's tabulations from Bureau of Labor Statistics, *Current Population Survey*, Public Use Tapes (various years, March).

with the return on college education, and almost immediately thereafter the fertility rate in the twenty- to twenty-four age group began to increase (see figure 1-9), while the female labor force participation rate in the same group began to decline (see figure 1-10). Similarly, marriage rates for this group reversed a twenty-year decline, and divorce rates came down (as shown in figures 1-15 and 1-16). The recent strong turnaround in the real average wage is consistent with the fact that female labor force participation rates have reached their peak and even begun to decline (see figure 1-12)—and hence, so has the creation of new low-wage, low-productivity service and retail jobs. The sharp reduction in inflation in recent years is also consistent with these other phenomena.

While it might be questionable to credit tests of significance on time series data for a period as short as thirty years when the tests involve a single set of time series data, it would seem that the overwhelming evidence of common movements in all series lends support to the hypothesis that relative cohort size is a significant factor driving all of the variables of interest, and therefore that

Figure 1-16. Proportion Divorced for Ever-Married Full-Time Workers Ages Twenty to Twenty-Two, United States, 1965–92

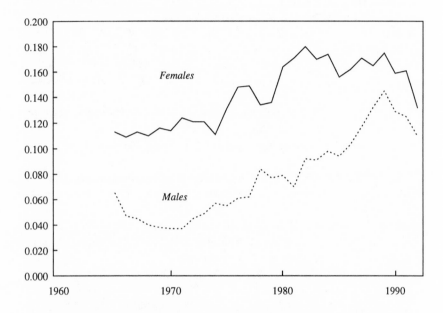

SOURCE: Author's tabulations from Bureau of Labor Statistics, *Current Population Survey*, Public Use Tapes (various years, March).

these variables should be considered in this comprehensive framework.[50] Doing so provides a completely new perspective on the socioeconomic phenomena of the last thirty years and suggests that current forecasts for the future should be reconsidered. It would seem that this theory deserves further examination. It is the only comprehensive theory available, initial evidence is highly supportive, and if true, it provides a key variable for forecasting other variables, at least over the next twenty-five years.

References

Becker, Gary S. 1981. *A Treatise on the Family*. Harvard University Press.

Becker, Gary S., and Kevin M. Murphy. 1990. "Human Capital, Fertility and Economic Growth." *Journal of Political Economy* 98(5, part 2): S12–S37.

50. See, for example, McCloskey and Ziliak (1994) in their discussion of methods of determining *economic* significance as opposed to *statistical* significance.

Berger, Mark C. 1984. "Cohort Size and the Earnings Growth of Young Workers."
    Industrial and Labor Relations Review 37(4): 582–91.
___. 1985. "The Effect of Cohort Size on Earnings Growth: A Reexamination of the
    Evidence." *Journal of Political Economy* 93(3): 561-73.
Blackburn, McKinley, and Sanders Korenman. 1994. "The Declining Marital-Status
    Earnings Differential." *Journal of Population Economics* 7(3): 247–70.
Blau, Francine. 1984. "Discrimination Against Women: Theory and Evidence." In
    Labor Economics: Modern Views, edited by William A. Darity, Jr. Boston: Kluwer-
    Nijhoff.
Easterlin, Richard A. 1968. *Population, Labor Force, and Long Swings in Economic
    Growth. Columbia University Press.*
___. 1980. *Birth and Fortune: The Impact of Numbers on Personal Welfare*. Basic
    Books.
Fair, Ray C., and Kathryn M. Dominguez. 1991. "Effects of Changing U.S. Age
    Distribution on Macroeconomic Equations." *American Economic Review* 81(5):
    1276–94.
Fair, Ray C., and Diane J. Macunovich. 1993. "Estimated Relative Income Effects on
    the Labor Force Participation of Women and Men 20–24." Williams College,
    Williamstown, Mass., Department of Economics.
Fuchs, Victor R. 1989. "Women's Quest for Economic Equality." *Journal of Economic
    Perspectives* 3(1): 25–41.
Goldin, Claudia. 1990. *Understanding the Gender Gap*. Oxford University Press.
Korenman, Sanders, and David Neumark. 1991. "Does Marriage Really Make Men
    More Productive?" *Journal of Human Resources* 26(2): 282–307.
Macunovich, Diane J. 1993a. "Cohort Size Effects on Enrollment Decisions." Williams
    College, Williamstown, Mass., Department of Economics.
___. 1993b. "The Missing Factor: Variations in the Income Effect of the Female Wage
    on Fertility in the U.S." RP-165. Williams College, Williamstown, Mass., Depart-
    ment of Economics.
___. 1994a. "Relative Income and Price of Time: Exploring their Effects on U.S.
    Fertility and Female Labor Force Participation." Paper prepared for the Workshop
    on Expanding Frameworks for Fertility Research in Industrialized Countries. Spon-
    sored by the National Academy of Sciences and the National Institute of Child
    Health and Human Development, September 22–23.
___. 1994b. "Why the Baby Bust Cohorts Haven't Boomed Yet: An Aggregate Analy-
    sis of Cohort Size Effects." Williams College, Williamstown, Mass., Department of
    Economics.
___. 1995a. "The Butz-Ward Fertility Model in the Light of More Recent Data."
    Journal of Human Resources 30(2): 229–54.
___. 1995b. "Marriage and Divorce in the U.S.: Evidence of Cohort Size Effects."
    Journal of Population Economics (forthcoming).
Mankiw, N. Gregory, and David N. Weil. 1989. "The Baby Boom, the Baby Bust and
    the Housing Market." *Regional Science and Urban Economics* 19: 235–58.

McCloskey, Donald N., and Stephen T. Ziliak. 1994. "The Standard Error of Regressions." University of Iowa, Department of Economics (March).

McMillan, Henry M., and Jerome B. Baesel. 1990. "The Macroeconomic Impact of the Baby Boom Generation." *Journal of Macroeconomics* 12(2): 167–95.

Morgan, S. Philip. 1994. "Characteristic Features of Modern American Fertility: A Description of Late-Twentieth-Century U.S. Fertility Trends and Differentials." Paper prepared for the Workshop on Expanding Frameworks for Fertility Research in Industrialized Countries. Sponsored by the National Academy of Sciences and the National Institute of Child Health and Human Development, September 22–23.

Murphy, Kevin M., and Finis Welch. 1992. "The Structure of Wages." *Quarterly Journal of Economics* (February): 285–326.

Parsons, Talcott. 1949. "The Social Structure of the Family." In *The Family: Its Function and Destiny,* edited by Ruth Nanda Ashen. Harper and Brothers.

___. 1955. "The American Family: Its Relations to Personality and to the Social Structure." In *Family, Socialization and Interaction Process,* by Talcott Parsons and Robert Bales. Free Press.

Preston, Samuel H. 1993. "Demographic Change in the United States, 1970–2050." In *Demography and Retirement,* edited by Anna M. Rappaport and Sylvester J. Schieber. Praeger.

Revenga, Ana. 1992. "Exporting Jobs? The Impact of Import Competition on Employment and Wages in U.S. Manufacturing." *Quarterly Journal of Economics* (February): 255–84.

Schieber, Sylvester J., and John B. Shoven. 1994. "The Consequences of Population Aging on Private Pension Fund Saving and Asset Markets." Working Paper 4665. Cambridge, Mass.: National Bureau of Economic Research (March).

U.S. Social Security Administration. 1991. *The Social Security Technical Panel Report to the 1991 Advisory Council on Social Security.*

Welch, Finis. 1979. "Effects of Cohort Size on Earnings: The Baby Boom Babies' Financial Bust." *Journal of Political Economy* 87(5, part 2): S65–S97.

Yang, Eugene, and Stephen Goss. 1992. *Economic Projections for OASDHI Cost and Income Estimates: 1992,* Actuarial Study 108, Social Security Administration pub. no. 11-11551, Washington.

Comment by Stephen C. Goss

In the first of these two very informative and illuminating discussions, Robert Brown provides an excellent review of the way in which the aged dependency ratio, and the aging of the population in general, will affect the future costs of social insurance and private pensions in the United States.

Moreover, he goes on to consider the effects these trends will have on the economy, as does Diane Macunovich. This interaction between demographic and economic factors represents an area that needs to be addressed more in the development of projections of future costs of social insurance and pensions.

Brown believes that mortality is not all that consequential in determining the cost of social insurance programs, and is surprised at how significant mortality is shown to be for Social Security in the sensitivity analysis of the OASDI trustees' *Annual Reports*. These sensitivity analyses indicate the extent to which the long-range (seventy-five-year) cost of Social Security is affected by altering the assumed level of several key demographic and economic factors, one at a time. He observes that the CPP is shown to be less sensitive to a specific change in mortality than to a specific change in some other variables. The problem here is a matter of scaling. When I calculated the sensitivity of the OASDI program to the changes specified for the CPP, I found less sensitivity to the mortality change than to the changes specified for fertility or real earnings growth. The OASDI system, however, was more sensitive to the mortality change than to either the specified change in immigration (likely because about two-thirds of sensitivity variation in U.S. immigration is assumed to be due to illegal immigration) or the specified change in inflation (because the U.S. system is almost fully indexed to inflation).

Brown's suggestion that the sensitivity analysis is so important that it should be highlighted to a greater extent in the OASDI trustees' *Annual Reports* is well made. Indeed, two or three years ago, it was moved up from an appendix to the body of the report to give it further emphasis.

The high cost and low cost alternatives, though, are still very important in policy analysis, as they have been for many years. The technical panels for the Advisory Council are presently talking about ways of describing those alternatives through stochastic methods and treating them as some kind of a confidence interval. That is a tricky undertaking but, if successful, could perhaps enhance the value of these estimates.

Probably the best way to see the importance of demographic factors, including mortality, in determining the future cost of Social Security is to focus on the aged dependency ratio. This ratio is the fundamental demographic indicator of the cost of any mandatory and universal program which, like Social Security, is paid for out of current income on a pay-as-you-go basis.

Under the Social Security program, both the general level of average benefits and the level of tax income are essentially indexed to the growth in the average wage. Thus some of the fundamental economic variables that drive the cost level of the program, productivity and average-wage growth, have similar effects on its tax base, or taxable payroll. Through wage-indexing of the benefit levels, the cost rate (that is, cost as a percentage of taxable payroll) is rendered relatively insensitive to the growth in productivity and the average wage. However, there is no analogous indexing to demographic factors (in particular, mortality) built into the current system. Tax rates are not automatically adjusted to reflect a rise or a fall in birth rates, and the retirement age is not automatically adjusted to reflect increases in life expectancy. Both birth rates and mortality rates contribute directly to the level of the aged dependency ratio that, in turn, essentially determines the cost rate. A change in the birth rate ultimately has a stable effect on the aged dependency ratio because the progressively larger or smaller numbers of births result in progressively larger or smaller numbers of both working-age and aged persons. The effect of a change in the assumed rate of mortality improvement on the aged dependency ratio, however, increases with the passage of time. For example, an increase in the assumed rate of improvement in mortality will result in progressively larger increases in the size of the aged population, with very little effect on the working-age population.

It is necessary to look beyond the year 2040 to fully appreciate the importance of the mortality assumption. Through 2040 the effect of the baby boom generation will be overwhelming. In the period from 1995 through about 2010, the baby boom generation will clearly depress the aged dependency ratio. It will increase the number of people at working age. Between 2010 and 2030 in both Canada and the United States, as Brown indicates, the baby boomers will move into the aged population and create a rather dramatic upswing in the aged dependency ratio. It would be favorable for the financing of Social Security if thereafter, when all the baby boomers have died, the aged dependency ratio were to return to a much lower level. But in fact it will not because of the projected increasing life expectancies based, as Brown suggests, on the continuing improvement of mortality rates into the infinite future. There is no disagreement within the demographic community as to whether mortality rates will continue to improve, but there is considerable debate concerning how rapidly they will do so.

Table 1-10 provides additional insight into the change in the aged dependency ratio, focusing primarily on the effect of the baby boom generation between 2010 and 2030. As Brown points out, over this period in the United States the aged dependency ratio will increase by two-thirds, or 67 percent, at a rate of 2.6 percent per year. This alarming rate of increase of beneficiaries will have to be accommodated by either coming up with the money to pay benefits to them, or reducing their benefits commensurately.

Going beyond this increase in the aged dependency ratio, however, to consider more directly the pertinent ratio of beneficiaries to workers, the news

Table 1-10. Estimated Change in Demographic Measures and OASDI Cost as a Percentage of Taxable Payroll, 2010–30

Percent

Ratio	Change
Aged dependency	67
OASI beneficiaries to workers	51
Workers to population ages 20–64	1
OASI beneficiaries to population age ≥ 65	− 9
DI beneficiaries to workers	4
OASDI beneficiaries to workers	40
OASDI Cost (net of taxes on benefits) to payroll	38

SOURCE: 1994 OASDI Trustees Report, Intermediate Projections.

is not quite as bad. The ratio of old-age and survivors' insurance (OASI) beneficiaries to all covered workers in the United States will only increase by 51 percent over this twenty-year period. The reason why this ratio will grow less is that the number of workers ages twenty to sixty-four will grow very slightly, by 1 percent, while the total number of beneficiaries for the OASI program will actually decline by 9 percent. The increase in the normal retirement age during this period will contribute to the decline in the ratio of OASI beneficiaries to the aged population. In addition, the fact that many Social Security beneficiaries, even for OASI, are under age sixty-five helps to dampen the effect of the changing aged dependency ratio on the cost of the OASI program between 2010 and 2030. Thus while the aged dependency ratio is the most fundamental demographic indicator for a social insurance retirement program that is financed on a pay-as-you-go basis, it is not a precise measure of the cost of the Social Security program.

The Disability Insurance (DI) beneficiaries for this period, of course, will represent very different age cohorts. They will, essentially, be ages fifty to sixty-four or sixty-six, moving through the period, not age sixty-five and over. The ratio of DI beneficiaries to workers rises only 4 percent between 2010 and 2030.

The total number of beneficiaries for the whole OASDI (Social Security) program increases by 40 percent over the period. At the least, this change is not quite as alarming as the 67 percent change in the aged dependency ratio.

The real bottom line for the OASDI program is its cost as a percentage of payroll. If the cost is reduced by the amount of revenue transferred to OASDI based on taxation of benefits, then the result, expressed as a percentage of payroll, represents the effective tax rate that would have to be levied on payroll at that time to provide for the benefits that are scheduled. Over the period 2010 to 2030 this ratio rises by 38 percent, at about a 1.6 percent increase per year. However, this is still a very substantial rate of increase that will need to be accommodated in some way.

There are at least five possible options for making OASDI income equal to outgo by 2030:

1. Reduce benefits by 25 percent by 2030 (12.4/16.5).

2. Increase payroll tax by 4.1 percent (16.5 − 12.4). Implies a 4 percent reduction in gross earnings and a 6 percent reduction in net earnings (at a 33 percent marginal tax rate).

3. Reduce benefits by 12.5 percent and increase payroll tax by 2 percent. Implies a 2 percent reduction in gross earnings and a 3 percent reduction in net earnings.

4. Reduce benefits and gross earnings by 3.5 percent each (12.4 + 100) / (16.5 + 100).

5. Reduce benefits and net earnings by 5.5 percent each (12.4 + 67) / (16.5 + 67).

With option 1, aggregate benefits would be in balance with the income of the program for the year 2030. Further improvement in mortality beyond 2030 would require additional reductions, for a total of about 30 percent below benefits scheduled under present law by 2070.

Option 2 would balance the program on a pay-as-you-go basis solely through increases in the payroll tax, beginning by 2030. The cost rate under present law, less the amount received from taxation of benefits, is projected at about 16.5 percent of payroll in the year 2030. Compared to the 12.4 percent combined tax rate, this is a 4.1 percent differential. Thus the payroll tax rate would have to be raised by 4.1 percent in 2030 in order to provide the benefits that are scheduled under current law. This would result in about a 4 percent reduction in gross earnings for the population on average, and about a 6 percent reduction in net earnings on an after-tax basis (assuming a marginal federal–state–local tax rate of 33 percent).

Options 3, 4, and 5, explore approaches that would combine increased taxes and reduced benefits. Option 3 would eliminate the deficit for 2030 with equal dollar contributions from benefit cuts and increases in taxes. Because taxable payroll is several times larger than benefit payments, this approach would require 2 percent lower gross earnings and 3 percent lower earnings net of tax, but 12.5 percent lower OASDI benefits. Options 4 and 5 would impose similar percentage reductions on benefits and earnings. Option 4 would equalize the reduction in benefits and gross earnings at 3.5 percent. Option 5 would equalize the reduction in benefits and net earnings at 5.5 percent.

Brown also suggests that as the cohorts entering the labor force become smaller, the United States may experience real labor shortages. But he makes a very important caveat: a labor shortage will develop only if U.S. workers have the skills that are in demand for the products desired in the world at that time.

This is an absolutely essential caveat because there is a real possibility that, as the baby boomers start to retire, a very significant shortage of labor will indeed develop in some areas—in services, especially for elder care, and possibly in areas requiring highly specialized skills and advanced technologies. But it is not clear that the labor shortage would result because we are operating in an international economic market, rather than in the United States alone. A reduction in the number of workers in the U.S. work force relative to the U.S. population could be offset in many fields by increases in the work force elsewhere in the world. The rapidity with which still undeveloped countries join the developed world will significantly affect the extent to which a labor shortage is perceived in the United States.

It is generally assumed that the smaller number of workers in the future will result in capital deepening for those workers, and therefore in increased productivity and increased real wage growth. But some caution is due, because capital can easily move across borders. It will go elsewhere if the perceived and real rate of return for capital is better in other countries, particularly if the amount that is being paid for skilled labor is substantially less. Thus the anticipated capital deepening may not be fully realized.

Brown makes another extremely important point when he notes that although aggregate savings in the United States may increase as the baby boomers approach retirement, after they begin retiring, around 2010, they will be liquidating assets at a rapid rate. This surge of asset liquidation (or, at least, drop in savings) is going to cause interest rates to rise and the value of stocks and bonds to fall (or rise more gradually). The cost of housing was clearly affected as first the baby boom generation passed into the stage of household formation, in the early 1970s, and then the baby bust generation, in the early 1990s. Asset values may rise nicely for the next fifteen years, but after 2010 there will be a lot of people wanting to sell assets and relatively few people looking to buy them.

Again however, this is a narrow point of view based on the assumption of a closed U.S. economy. It is important to consider the extent to which financial markets are international, and whether other countries are experiencing a similar net liquidation as their populations age. Likewise, it is not known to what extent other countries will be developing their economies, generating savings, and desiring to purchase financial assets being sold by U.S. retirees.

Finally Brown explores several possible ways of accommodating the aging of the population and its effect on the cost of retirement benefits. Two options seem to have potential: invest abroad, and keep the aged dependency ratio constant.

Investing abroad while the baby boom generation is working makes some theoretical sense, as the foreign holdings could then be divested when the baby boom generation is old, without disrupting the domestic economy. However, the United States is following the opposite course. Moreover, shifting investment abroad would presumably reduce domestic productivity.

The course that the United States is, in fact, pursuing is to influence the aged dependency ratio by imposing lower retirement ages until 2010 and higher retirement ages thereafter. Early out options have effectively permitted a lower retirement age for much of the population in recent years. Increases in the normal retirement age after 2000 for OASDI will probably be met by increases for private pension schemes as well. Further increases in normal retirement age would appear likely. However, it may be more difficult to make workers stay productively on the job longer. Task experience for the older workers may be less and less valuable in an increasingly dynamic employment environment where training and retraining almost never stop.

Macunovich makes two very significant points related to the Easterlin hypothesis concerning the cyclical nature of fertility rates. Both follow from her observation that fertility rates and relative cohort sizes appear to increase and decrease in thirty-year cycles.

First, it is important to look further back than the very near term and very recent history in developing expectations for the long-term future. Selection of assumptions for a seventy-five-year period should be based on analysis of at least thirty-year past periods. Second, when making these future projections, it is necessary to keep in mind the thirty-year demographic trends and their interrelationships with economic variables. In particular, there should be more analysis and modeling of these patterns and their trends. The complexity of such analysis, however, presents problems in a world of limited resources.

On the need to focus primarily on the long-term historical experience in developing long-term ultimate assumptions, she is quite correct. As table 1-11 shows, the track record of the intermediate assumptions for the trustees reports is pretty good. Traditionally, analysis for the long-term assumptions has focused most heavily on the past thirty-year historical average. This fortuitously coincides with Mancunovich's thirty-year average cycle. In fact, for virtually all of the various parameters listed in the table the ultimate assumption, in the far right column, is closer to the thirty-year average than to the fifteen-year average.

About the only exception is the total fertility rate, for which the ultimate assumption is currently 1.9, which is much closer to the fifteen-year average. This is not a result of discounting the longer-term information, but is instead

Table 1-11. Comparison of Intermediate Assumptions of Change in Demographic Variables from 1994 OASDI Trustees Report and Past Experience
Percent (unless otherwise specified)

Variable	Past experience			Ultimate assumption 2003–68
	1978–93	1963–93	1951–93	
Productivity	0.86	1.35	1.69	1.36
Real wage dip	0.44	0.80	1.31	1.00
CPI-W	5.29	5.23	4.11	4.00
Unemployment[a]	6.50	5.70	5.40	6.00
Fertility[b]	1.91	2.07	2.48	1.90
Real interest[c]	4.45	2.62	2.24	2.30

Source: OASDI Trustees Reports.

a. Total unemployment, including military, age- and sex-adjusted to the 1992 labor force.

b. Total fertility rate, that is, the average number of children born to women surviving the entire childbearing period.

c. The average real rate for the first year after the issue of special obligations issuable to the OASDI Trust Funds.

due to the fact that, as Macunovich points out, it is also necessary to pay attention to secular trends and other factors of influence in a society. It is the trustees' judgment that over the past thirty years there has been a shift toward lower fertility rates, particularly as it has become easier for people to plan and to regulate birth, and they anticipate that the lower level will continue in the future. Thus there is general agreement that the long-term average past should be used as the starting point of consideration in developing projections for the future. It is expected that this approach will continue to be used at Social Security, along with greater consideration of the interrelationship of some of these trends and the economic variables, as discussed by Macunovich.

Macunovich notes that the OASDI Trustees Reports have not focused much on longer-term cycles. The primary reason that they have not focused on cycles past the short-range ten-year period is that they have been mainly concerned with relatively short-term business cycles. There has been some analysis of the implications of projecting continuing economic cycles throughout the seventy-five-year period, and it has been found that it makes a difference whether the cycles initially move upward or downward. But including continuing business cycles beyond the first few years does not really have much effect on the long-term estimates.

The thirty-year demographic cycles discussed by Macunovich would, however, be significant. The OASDI analyses do currently reflect some of these kinds of demographic cycles in the overall projection of the size of the population and its distribution by age. Yet some of the effects of these cycles on factors like labor force participation, unemployment rates, and wage-gain and productivity, as suggested by the Easterlin hypothesis, are not currently reflected in the long-term projections. These relationships will definitely be considered in future reports.

In particular, Macunovich points out a strong relationship between the relative wages of young males and relative cohort sizes. She demonstrates that although the Easterlin hypothesis seems to fail at projecting wage levels for the period immediately after 1980, it can be made to produce an extremely good fit with certain adjustments. A case in point is adjusting for the rising trade deficit. Yet while this additional exogeneous variable may have improved the fit for the 1980s, it is clearly also a critical factor to be taken into account when making projections. It seems likely that this increase in the trade deficit could in part be due to the rising expectations of the young people entering the work force in the early 1980s. Rising lifestyle expectations resulted in higher wage expectations and made new workers overpriced for many kinds of work that could be done offshore for a lower price and be imported into the country. Macunovich might consider how this relationship fits with the shifts in cohort size in the early 1980s, and thus with the Easterlin theory.

This example highlights the importance of looking at the economic variables not only with respect to U.S. demographic trends, but also in the international context. Both domestic and international influences have contributed to the increase in the relative size of the service sector of the U.S. economy, the decreasing share for the manufacturing sector, and the increasing trade deficit. If this kind of trend continues, especially in the high-technology sector, then future growth in productivity and the real wage will be adversely affected.

Finally, tables 1-12 and 1-13 present unisex life expectancy at retirement based on period life tables and the ratio of life expectancy to potential working years, respectively. These are used to derive the retirement ages equivalent to sixty-five shown in table 1-14. Taken together, these tables stand in contrast to Brown's table 1-8 showing "equivalent retirement ages," which answers the question: What should the retirement age be in years after 1966 in order to keep the same average number of years after retirement and before death (that is, how to keep the life expectancy at the retirement age constant)? In fact this is rather a conservative approach to the financing of a social insurance program because over time, as that retirement age increases, only the number of years of potential work will be increasing. Since the average number of years of retirement will stay the same, the cost of retirement benefits, as a percentage of payroll, would go down.

The equivalent retirement ages shown in table 1-14 are based on a different criterion; the equivalent retirement age is to change as necessary so that the ratio of the number of years in retirement to the number of years of potential work between age twenty and retirement stays constant. In this way, increasing the normal retirement age would tend to keep the cost of retirement benefits relative to the payroll fairly constant, thus allowing tax rates to remain con-

Table 1-12. Unisex Life Expectancy at Retirement, United States, 1940–2070
Years

Retirement year	Retirement age										
	65	66	67	68	69	70	71	72	73	74	75
1940	12.71	12.12	11.55	10.99	10.45	9.92	9.41	8.92	8.45	7.99	7.56
1960	14.52	13.89	13.28	12.69	12.10	11.53	10.97	10.42	9.90	9.38	8.88
1980	16.33	15.67	15.03	14.40	13.79	13.18	12.60	12.03	11.45	10.92	10.38
1990	17.09	16.42	15.76	15.11	14.47	13.85	13.23	12.62	12.03	11.48	10.90
2000	17.57	16.87	16.19	15.52	14.88	14.22	13.58	12.96	12.36	11.77	11.19
2010	17.92	17.21	16.52	15.83	15.17	14.51	13.87	13.24	12.62	12.02	11.43
2020	18.36	17.64	16.94	16.25	15.57	14.81	14.26	13.62	12.99	12.36	11.79
2030	18.80	18.07	17.36	16.66	15.98	15.31	14.65	14.00	13.37	12.75	12.15
2040	19.22	18.49	17.77	17.07	16.38	15.70	15.03	14.38	13.74	13.11	12.50
2050	19.64	18.90	18.17	17.45	16.77	16.08	15.41	14.75	14.10	13.47	12.85
2060	20.04	19.29	18.56	17.85	17.15	16.46	15.78	15.11	14.45	13.81	13.19
2070	20.44	19.64	18.95	18.23	17.52	16.82	16.14	15.46	14.80	14.15	13.52

SOURCE: Based on 1994 OASDI Trustees Report, Intermediate Projections, from the Social Security Administration, Office of the Actuary.

Table 1-13. Ratio of Unisex Life Expectancy to Potential Working Years, United States, 1940–2070[a]

Retirement year	Retirement age										
	65	66	67	68	69	70	71	72	73	74	75
1940	28.24	26.35	24.57	22.90	21.33	19.84	18.45	17.15	15.94	14.80	13.75
1960	32.27	30.20	28.26	26.44	24.69	23.06	21.51	20.04	18.68	17.37	16.15
1980	36.29	34.07	31.98	30.00	28.14	26.38	24.71	23.13	21.62	20.22	18.87
1990	37.98	35.70	33.53	31.48	29.53	27.70	25.94	24.27	22.70	21.22	19.92
2000	39.04	36.67	34.45	32.33	30.33	28.44	26.63	24.92	23.32	21.80	20.35
2010	39.82	37.41	35.15	32.98	30.96	29.02	27.20	25.48	23.81	22.25	20.78
2020	40.80	38.35	36.04	33.85	31.78	29.82	27.96	26.19	24.51	22.93	21.44
2030	41.78	39.28	36.94	34.71	32.61	30.62	28.73	26.92	25.23	23.51	22.09
2040	42.71	40.20	37.81	35.56	33.43	31.40	29.47	27.65	23.92	24.28	22.73
2050	43.64	41.09	38.66	36.38	34.22	32.16	30.22	28.37	26.50	24.94	23.36
2060	44.53	41.93	39.49	37.19	35.00	32.92	30.94	29.05	27.28	25.57	23.98
2070	45.42	42.78	40.32	37.98	35.76	33.64	31.65	29.73	27.92	26.20	24.58

Source: 1994 OASDI Trustees Report, Intermediate Projections.
a. Potential working years are calculated as those between age twenty and retirement.

Table 1-14. **Equivalent Retirement Age to Sixty-Five for Base Years 1940–2030, United States**[a]
Age in years and months

	Base year							
	1940	*1960*	*1980*	*1990*	*2000*	*2010*	*2020*	*2030*
1940	65							
1960	67	65						
1980	68-11	66-10	65					
1990	69-08	65-07	65-09	65				
2000	70-01	68	66-02	65-05	65			
2010	70-05	68-04	66-06	65-09	65-04	65		
2020	70-10	68-09	66-11	66-02	65-09	65-05	65	
2030	71-03	69-02	67-03	66-07	66-01	65-09	66-05	65
2040	71-08	69-07	67-08	66-11	66-05	66-02	65-09	65-04
2050	72-01	79-11	68	67-04	66-10	66-05	66-01	65-09
2060	72-05	70-04	68-05	67-08	67-02	66-10	66-06	66-01
2070	72-10	70-08	68-09	68	67-07	67-03	66-10	66-05

Source: 1994 OASDI Trustees Report, Intermediate Projections.
a. The equivalent retirement age to sixty-five is calculated such that the ratio of the number of years in retirement to the number of years of potential work between age twenty and retirement (as shown in table 1-13) remains constant.

stant. While Brown's approach to equivalent retirement ages across cohorts assigns all increases in life expectancy to additional years of work, this alternative approach distributes any increase in life expectancy between working and retirement years, in the same proportion as for the selected base year. The result is a slightly slower rate of growth in the normal retirement age.

Tables of equivalent retirement ages on these bases will likely become more familiar in the future as policymakers begin to consider options for eliminating the long-range financing problems that clearly face the Social Security program.

Comment by Sylvester J. Schieber

Robert Brown takes a traditional look at the current challenges in Social Security financing and how possibly to deal with them through a variety of changes in the social and economic fabric: raising immigration, increasing fertility, and similar measures. Diane Macunovich, on the other hand, looks at the effects of cohort size on industrial structure, the growth of gross domestic product over time, productivity and wages, inflation rates, interest rates, and savings. She looks at various aspects of the economy that are central to the growth in cost of the Social Security system.

Brown conveys a sense of angst familiar in discussions about Social Security these days. In contrast, Macunovich holds out a little hope. She does not offer a totally rosy conclusion, but she does give the impression that the outcome may actually turn out better than recent trends would suggest. Despite the fact that these two arguments have been developed around somewhat different frameworks, it is possible to read both and conclude that the normal retirement age should be raised significantly fairly soon. Specifically, the increases should begin sooner than scheduled in the 1983 Amendments to the Social Security Act, and the ultimate level should be raised beyond the age of sixty-seven specified in those amendments.

This conclusion seems to follow from Brown's discussion because he looks at a number of other alternatives and finds that they are not sufficient to resolve the projected long-term imbalance in Social Security. Macunovich's discussion seems to lead to this same conclusion because if the retirement age were raised right now, it would provide insurance against some of the contingencies that may occur, and if the situation does, indeed, turn out better than expected, the retirement age can be lowered again.

Macunovich concludes that the smaller cohorts behind the baby boom generation should, in the end, earn higher wages than the cohorts ahead of them. She suggests that this may ultimately lead to reductions in the female labor force participation rate and increased birth rates, among other effects. All of these outcomes point to some relief of the pressure on Social Security financing.

The story she tells about labor force participation is that the baby boomer cohort of men came into the work force in very large numbers. Because there were so many of them, they were faced with relatively low wages. Aspiring to a standard of living that was similar to that of their parents, they delayed getting married. Yet while reduced wage rates may have delayed baby boomer males' wedding days, it did not delay some of the other interests traditionally linked to the marital state. Thus rates of out-of-wedlock-childbirth increased.

Women, for their part, were not totally passive, Macunovich suggests. They saw that the men were not coming to court and provide for them, so in order to meet their own material needs, they had to go to work. In doing so, they prompted the creation of a whole variety of relatively low productivity jobs in the economy. Specifically, they converted housework and other activities that they had traditionally performed in the home into commercial activities carried out at relatively low wage rates. Wages may now be beginning to grow again, for the baby bust generation. Macunovich suggests that with the rising wages being paid to baby bust men, there will be some slowdown in the labor force participation rate of baby bust women and an increase in their fertility rate.

Figure 1-17 shows the labor force participation rates of men and women in 1950 at various attained ages. For very young women the participation rate was around 40 percent; among those who had just finished school it was higher, at about 45 percent. Then, as women married and began having families in their twenties, female labor force participation rates declined to below 40 percent and stayed below that level throughout most of what are considered to be the normal working years. Labor force participation rates for men, on the other hand, reached 97 or 98 percent by the time they were in their early thirties, when they had completed school and their military service obligations. Male labor force participation rates stayed at this level until men started to retire in their sixties. Moving forward to 1990, as shown in figure 1-18, there is a fairly substantial narrowing of the difference in the labor force participation rates of men and women. This picture is consistent with the story about increasing female labor force participation rates in both of these discussions.

One of the reasons that there appears to be some slowdown in the labor force participation rate of women today might be that they have already attained such high levels that there is little room for continued growth. Parsing out the change in the female labor force participation rates, as in figure 1-19, reveals fairly substantial increases between 1950 and 1970 for women at virtually all attained ages. The increase in female labor force participation rates between 1950 and 1970 certainly were not quite half of the increase during the 1950–90 period but they were significant. The baby boom generation of women, however, largely did not enter the work force until after 1970.

In his discussion of the issue of growing productivity, Brown makes the point that as the smaller baby bust generation enters the work force in the wake of the baby boom generation and realizes increasing productivity, it will also realize increasing wages. He suggests that one of the ways to finance Social Security during the baby boomers' retirement is by taking advantage of this increase in productivity. In fact by capturing productivity increases of 1.7 percent per year for the period 2010 to 2030, it would be possible to finance the added consumption of the baby boomer retirees, assuming that they move into retirement at roughly the same ages as are standard today. The problem with this plan is that the workers who are realizing this 1.7 percent increase in productivity would have to give up all of their productivity increases in order to sustain the consumption of the growing body of retirees. In other words, they would not be able to use any of their productivity increase to improve their own standards of living.

There are, however, at least two other ways to finance the baby boom generation's retirement. The first is through higher Social Security payroll

Figure 1-17. Labor Force Participation Rates by Sex and Age in 1950

Percent

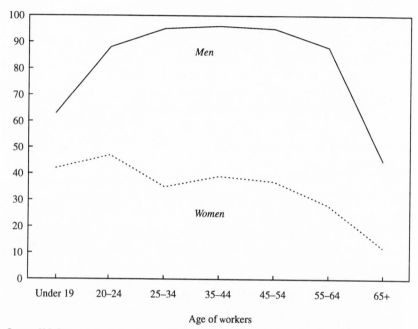

Age of workers

Source: U.S. Department of Labor. Bureau of Labor Statistics, 1989. *Handbook of Labor Statistics*. Bulletin 2340, pp. 13–14, 19–20.

taxes. But the recent political dialogue reflects a rather profound aversion in the United States to paying higher taxes. If this aversion does not fade by 2010, this policy scenario might not be feasible.

The second alternative is to sell off assets. That is, the baby boom generation would sell assets that it is currently accumulating to the baby bust generation. As Brown points out, though, this is not very different than raising the payroll tax because the people who will buy these assets will have to give up consumption in order to do so. In a recent paper, John Shoven of Stanford University and I suggest that there might be some monetary effects on the financial markets when the baby boom generation begins to sell its financial assets.[51] The sell-off of assets by the large baby boom generation to the small baby bust generation might depress the price of these assets. Thus a plan to preserve the baby boomers' retirement needs by selling of their accumulated assets might present very similar problems to those in the tax increase scenario.

51. See Shoven and Schreiber (1994).

Figure 1-18. Labor Force Participation Rates by Sex and Age by Year

Percent

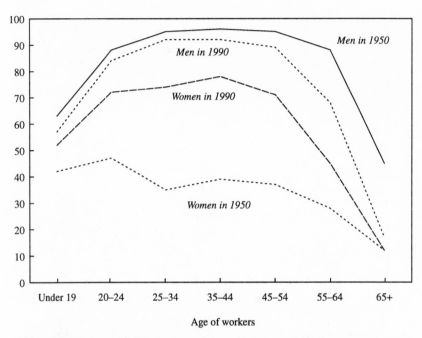

Age of workers

Source: U.S. Department of Labor, Bureau of Labor Statistics, 1989. *Handbook of Labor Statistics.*
Bulletin 2340, pp. 13–14, 19–20.
   U.S. Department of Labor, Bureau of Labor Statistics, 1991. *Employment and Earnings.* p. 164.

Brown's analysis leads us to conclude that raising the retirement age is ultimately the best solution to the problems raised by the baby boom generation's retirement. In this light he discusses the issue of aging and productivity and builds a case that workers can be productive much later in life than current retirement behavior implies. For the most part he is probably correct; but employers' perceptions about older workers and productivity often run counter to what the scientific evidence suggests.

Watson Wyatt Worldwide is currently finishing a survey of major corporate executives in the United States and other countries around the world. The results for the United States were not very different from those of a similar survey that the company conducted three or four years ago, which asked executives and major employers whether there was any relationship between age and productivity. Seventy percent of interviewees answered that productivity increases with age for a while, levels out, and then begins to decline. This

Figure 1-19. Labor Force Participation Rates of Women of Age and Year

Percent

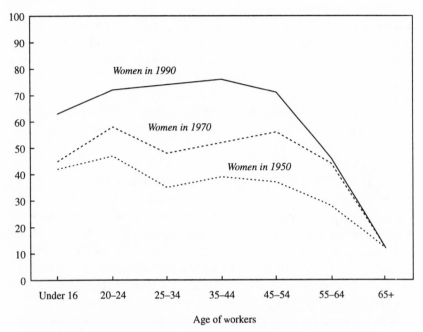

Age of workers

SOURCES: U.S. Department of Labor, Bureau of Labor Statistics, 1989. *Handbook of Labor Statistics.* Bulletin 2340, pp. 13–44, 19–20.
U.S. Department of Labor, Bureau of Labor Statistics, 1991. *Employment and Earnings*, p. 164.

70 percent was then asked at what age it begins to decline. The median answer was age fifty-five.

If employers believe that workers productivity starts to decline in the mid-fifties, the prospect of pushing retirement ages to sixty-five or seventy may be rather limited. There could be some fairly profound demand-side implications in attempting to do so. And if employers do not wish to employ workers for extended periods, a variety of issues could arise as the baby boom generation retires: increased disability, increased unemployment, and increased poverty, all of which make additional claims on alternate programs of the social welfare infrastructure.

Finally, there are the challenges facing private pensions. If Macunovich is right, the problems that Social Security ultimately faces when the baby boomers retire will not be as dire as we currently expect. I think the same is not necessarily true for pensions. Over the past ten or fifteen years, a number of federal regulatory provisions have slowed down the funding of the baby boom generation's retirement benefits through pension programs. Some of these reductions in funding have been fairly profound.

The most important of the regulatory changes was included in the Omnibus Budget Reconciliation Act of 1987 (OBRA87). This legislation changed the funding limits for private-sector employers' plans. Before OBRA87 was implemented, an estimated 7 or 8 percent of larger plans were at the maximum allowable amount of funding. After the new provisions were adopted, this proportion jumped to about 48 percent. Seven or eight years later, more than one-third of large employers still are prevented from putting money into their plan. The majority of them had been putting money in before the adoption of OBRA87.

The problem with the slowdown in pension funding is that every dollar that employers have not been putting into their plans over the last several years will eventually have to be put in, and with interest. Professor Shoven and I estimate that in order to provide expected benefits, private-sector defined benefit contributions would have to rise above current contribution rates by about 60 percent fairly quickly, and stay at that level through the remainder of the baby boom generation's lifetime.[52] Some employers may be willing to make these additional contributions, but not all of them will be able and willing to do so. Some will begin to truncate their plans and simply freeze them in place. So some of the baby boom generation will ultimately receive significantly less from these plans than they have been anticipating. In a truly rational economic model, employees would alter their other savings behavior in response to this possibility. In fact, there are very few people in the United States, especially among rank-and-file workers, who can see through all of the veils of private pensions financing.

Furthermore, John Sabelhaus of the Urban Institute and Barry Bosworth and Gary Burtless of the Brookings Institution have estimated that more than half of the decline in personal savings in the United States during the 1980s was attributable to the slowdown in employer contributions to private-sector employer-sponsored pension plans.[53]

Macunovich is unlikely to find any of the demographic effects in this area that she has found elsewhere. The slowdown in pension saving has been largely the result of legislative change limiting the funding of private pensions. Thus in conclusion, while I hope that Macunovich is right to be optimistic, it would probably be more realistic to follow the conservative line that Brown lays out in planning and expectations.

52. See Shoven and Schreiber (forthcoming).
53. See Sabelhaus, Bosworth, and Burtless (1991).

References

Sabelhaus, John, Barry Bosworth, and Gary Burtless. 1991. "The Decline in Savings: Evidence from Household Surveys." *Brookings Papers on Economic Activity*, 1:1991, 183–256.

Shoven, John, and Sylvester J. Schreiber. Forthcoming. "The Consequences of Population Aging on Private Pension Fund Saving and Asset Markets." In *The Economics of U.S. Retirement Policy: Current Status and Future Directions*. New York: Twentieth Century Fund.

General Discussion

Thomas Jones, as chair of the session, invited participants to direct their questions to the members of the panel.

In answer to the first query, Robert Brown confirmed that the 25 percent reduction in benefits that he proposed as a means to balance the Social Security trust fund was to be applied to the year 2030. If income were to equal outgo in that year, benefit levels would have to be about 25 percent lower than they are scheduled to be under current law. This calculation factored in the current increases in productivity growth, which would increase benefits.

Likewise, Jones sought clarification from Stephen Goss that the difference between his calculation that the payroll tax would have to increase by 4.1 percent (from 12.4 percent combined to 16.5) and Alicia Munnell's earlier comment that long-run actuarial balance could be achieved by a 2 percent increase (1 percent borne by the employee and 1 percent by the employer) was a matter of timing. Munnell was assuming that action would be taken immediately, presumably in 1995, whereas Goss was calculating the balancing effect that would be required if action was delayed until the year 2030. Goss concurred.

Richard Foster said that he was a great believer in econometric analysis, but that the issue of causality often becomes very difficult. He was curious as to what work Diane Macunovich might have done on the wage premium for men with stay-at-home wives. Was it the presence of a stay-at-home wife that enabled these men to work more hours and thus become successful, or did they become more successful and earn higher wages for other reasons, and then become able to afford stay-at-home wives?

Macunovich agreed that this is one of the biggest questions in the literature right now, and one reason why researchers have only looked at the marriage premium, as opposed to the stay-at-home-wife premium. She and a student are currently working on time series of individuals, looking at a man before and after his wife enters the labor force in order to determine the impact of her hours worked and her wages, controlling for education and occupation (among other variables) to eliminate selection bias.

Another participant noted that Macunovich identified imports as an indicator for some changes. Since the import, or trade, deficits that the United States is currently experiencing suggest that there will be trade surpluses in the future, the participant wondered what this would imply in terms of the need for employment to create a surplus from which to pay back these deficits. The current trade deficits imply that the United States is creating capital surpluses that will eventually have to be paid back. Indeed, since the populations of other countries, Japan in particular, are aging more rapidly than the U.S. population, the United States will ultimately develop a trade surplus with them.

Macunovich replied that, although her own forecasts did not assume trade surpluses, this point addressed the sort of work that Sylvester Schieber has done, looking at the longer-term impacts of the baby boom. For her part, Macunovich reiterated that her projections were not entirely rosy, because she foresaw continued problems for the baby boomers due to their cohort size; such an impact on the financial markets would be just one aspect of these problems.

Joshua Wiener asked Macunovich for a little more speculation about the effects of the projected age structure on macroeconomic situations in 2030 or 2040. In answering, Macunovich confessed that since she has been one of the only researchers to try to quantify these effects in recent years, a tremendous number of variables remain to be quantified. She felt that the feedback loops were so complicated that she did not want to be pushed into making too long-range projections before completing the econometric analysis.

On the basis of the work that she had done to date, her general feeling was that current projections have been influenced too much by the negative trends that have been observed most recently; and so she herself would tend to assume somewhat more optimistic forecasts for the various economic variables. In terms of numbers, she was confident of the current Social Security assumptions for productivity levels and wages, although less so for fertility rates. However, because levels have continued to be lower in most recent years, the present tendency is to lower the current assumptions. In contrast, Macunovich emphasized that the current level of assumptions should be maintained.

Bert Seidman referred to Brown's contention that North America faces a greater increase in the elderly population than do the western European countries, and said that it was his impression that the latter were ahead of North America on the demographic curve and therefore were already experiencing such an increase. Furthermore, while western European countries have been raising retirement ages, they have been raising them *to* sixty-five, not from sixty-five. Seidman wondered whether Brown felt that the adjustment policies and changes that these countries have adopted have any relevance to the future of North America.

Brown confirmed that western Europe currently has a much older population than North America, but noted that his own comparison was between the percentage increase in the populations ages sixty-five and over between 1985 and 2025. His point was that, politically, it is not only the ultimate magnitude of the proportion of the population over sixty-five that is significant, but how fast the change in age distribution takes place. Since the population of western Europe is already older, these countries face a much smaller transition from 1985 to 2025 than North America, and so their politicians do not have to sell such dramatic measures to their constituents. The problem is harder in North America, because of the much more rapid rate of change projected.

Lou Glasse of the Older Women's League pointed out that because women tend to live longer than men, they enter retirement needing more income or more resources for their lifetimes. She wondered, first, whether any of the panelists had done any work that might provide guidance on how, or by how much, benefits for women would need to be increased over the long term; and second, whether any of them had researched the opportunity costs for caregiving and their implications.

Brown thought it unlikely that it would be politically feasible to implement benefit differentials based on gender. However, he noted that a lot of work has been done to calculate how much higher the contributions would have to be, and therefore the figures for both Canada and the United States should be easily available.

Goss affirmed that the fact that women tend to live longer than men means that women predominate among Social Security beneficiaries at the very highest ages. Also, poverty rates tend to increase with age. In this context, former representative Jake Pickle had recommended that a 5 percent increase in benefit level be provided at age eighty-five. Poverty may appear to increase with age even though Social Security benefits increase with the cost of living, because the general standard of living in the country increases faster than the cost of living (that is, faster than prices). This gives rise to the perception that, if an individual lives long enough, cost-of-living adjustments alone will not be sufficient to maintain his or her standard of living. Other sources of postretirement income, however, contribute much more to both the perceived and the measured increase in poverty with age. Most other sources of income, including private pensions, have no provision for even keeping up with price inflation.

2

Fund Accumulation:
How Much? How Managed?

Barry P. Bosworth

A<small>N INCREASING NUMBER</small> of Americans have become concerned about the long-term financial viability of the Social Security system, and many younger Americans profess a belief that they will never collect any benefits. This concern is highlighted in a simple summary, shown in figure 2-1, of the financial projections of the Old-Age, Survivors, and Disability Insurance (OASDI) funds provided by the 1994 trustees' report. With constant tax rates, the contributions of the baby boom generation (individuals born between 1945 and 1965) will exceed benefit payments and lead to the build-up of a significant reserve during their working years; but the baby boom generation will begin to retire in the years after 2010, leading to a sharp rise in benefit payments. In the actuaries' intermediate projection, outlays will begin to exceed tax revenues in 2013. Interest income will cover the shortfall for another six years; but starting in 2020, the fund will have to draw upon its assets, which will be exhausted by 2030.

These projections reflect a dramatic change from those of the mid-1980s. In the early 1980s the system was faced with a short-run liquidity crisis as the recession threatened to reduce income below the level of immediate benefit payments by an amount that exceeded the system's reserves. The Social Security amendments of 1983, which were directed primarily toward resolving this short-run problem, also helped to reduce some of the long-term solvency problems by speeding up previously enacted tax increases, raising the retirement age after 2002, and imposing an income tax on beneficiaries, the proceeds of which were to be returned to the OASDI trust funds. Having weathered the short-term crisis and benefited from the legislated changes, the 1984 trustees' report showed the system to be in close actuarial balance over the seventy-five-

Figure 2-1. Income, Outlay, and Assets, of the Social Security Trust Funds, Intermediate Case

Percent of taxable wages

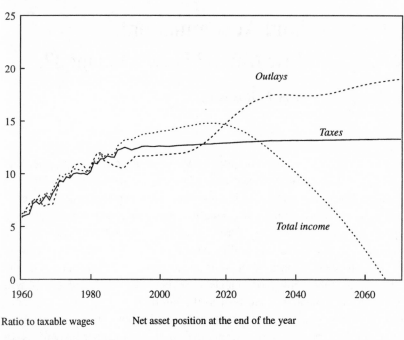

Ratio to taxable wages   Net asset position at the end of the year

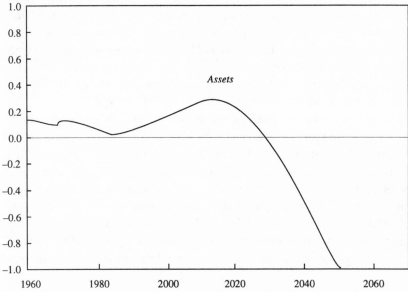

SOURCE: Board of Trustees (1994).

year horizon, and there was a projected build-up of reserves to about $3 trillion in today's prices by 2015.[1]

In contrast, the 1994 report shows a large actuarial deficit, equal to 14 percent of future discounted costs. Furthermore, the reserve is now projected to reach a peak of only a little more than $1 trillion and to be dissipated at a much faster pace. The deterioration of the projected financial position over the past decade, shown in table 2-1, reflects a wide range of changes in the underlying economic and demographic assumptions and methodology used by the Social Security Administration's actuaries, but the result is a steadily more pessimistic assessment of the system's finances. In particular, costs are projected to rise at a much faster pace. For example, the cost rate estimated for 2060 (outlays as a percent of taxable payroll) has been dramatically increased from 15.45 percent in the 1984 report to 18.5 percent in the 1994 report.

The current projections, of course, remain highly uncertain as forecasts of what will actually happen over the next seventy-five years, and the trustees' report includes both high and low cost alternatives to the commonly used intermediate estimates. The projected cost rate is shown in figure 2-2 for all three alternatives. The outcomes range from a situation of continuing surpluses for the indefinite future (low cost) to a liquidity crisis that would emerge as soon as 2015 (high cost).[2]

The sources of the cost increase, as well as the range of uncertainty, can be better understood by separating the cost rate into two components: the dependency rate (DR) and the benefit rate (BR), such that

$$CR = DR \times BR.$$

The dependency rate, the ratio of beneficiaries to covered workers, largely reflects the role of demographic factors and retirement patterns. The benefit rate, the ratio of the average benefit to the average wage, is more indicative of

1. The actuarial balance is computed as the present value of future tax receipts minus the present value of future outlays, plus the difference between the initial trust fund balances and the present value of a target terminal-year reserve equal to one year's outgo. The discount rate is the interest rate earned by the funds on their invested reserves, and the calculations extend over a seventy-five-year horizon. Close actuarial balance is said to exist if the balance is within 5 percent of discounted costs.

2. One major problem with using the alternative projections to evaluate risks to the funds is that there are no associated probabilities for the alternatives. The low and high cost alternatives, for example, do not seem equally likely relative to the intermediate projection. Providing such probabilities ought to be a major goal for future refinements of the actuarial estimates.

Table 2-1. Changes in Estimates of the Seventy-Five-Year OASDI Actuarial Balance by Reason for Change, 1984–94

Percent of taxable earnings

Actuarial balance, 1984	− 0.06
Change in the period of valuation	− 0.45
Economic assumptions	− 0.80
Demographic assumption	0.67
Disability assumptions	− 0.54
Methods	− 1.07
Legislative	0.10
Other	0.01
Actuarial balance, 1994	− 2.13

Source: Board of Trustees of the Federal Old-Age and Survivors' Insurance and Disability Insurance Trust Funds, *Annual Report*, various years, as compiled by John Hambor, U.S. Treasury Department.

changes in economic factors and legislated rules determining benefits.[3] The initial benefit is based on a worker's wage history, indexed to the average economywide wage. Thus the ratio of the average benefit at time of retirement to the average wage can be treated as fixed by legislation. However, in subsequent years the benefit is adjusted only for price inflation. Thus high rates of real wage growth lower the benefit rate.

In the long run, however, changes in the system's costs are driven by the demographic factors—birth rates, immigration, and mortality.[4] For example, in the intermediate projection the dependency rate rises by 80 percent between 1994 and 2070, while the benefit rate declines by 10 percent. Furthermore, at the end of the projection period the dependency rate varies by 100 percent between the optimistic and the pessimistic projections, compared with 17 percent for the benefit rate.[5]

It is all too common to point to the discontinuity in the age distribution of the population induced by the baby boom generation as the primary factor behind the escalating future costs. But the existence of that cohort only distorts the timing. The baby boomers' entry into the labor force since the mid-1960s

3. This is not completely true because the benefit ratio will vary in response to changes in the length of retirement and the proportion of workers who take early retirement with an actuarially reduced benefit. Because benefits are indexed only for price inflation, the benefit rate will decline as the average number of years of retirement rise.

4. The two major economic factors are the rate of real wage growth and the real interest rate. A doubling of real wage growth from the intermediate assumption of 1 percent a year would lower the actuarial imbalance over a seventy-five-year horizon by about 1 percent of taxable wages, half the anticipated shortfall. A 1 percentage point increase in the real interest rate from the assumed 2.3 percent would improve the balance by about 0.6 percent.

5. Not all of the funding imbalance is due to increased costs. The projections also incorporate an implicit tax cut relative to total employee compensation because of continued growth in untaxed employee benefits. The loss of revenues represents about one-sixth of the funding deficit.

Figure 2-2. OASDI Cost Rate, Dependency Rate, and Benefit Rate under Three Alternative Scenarios

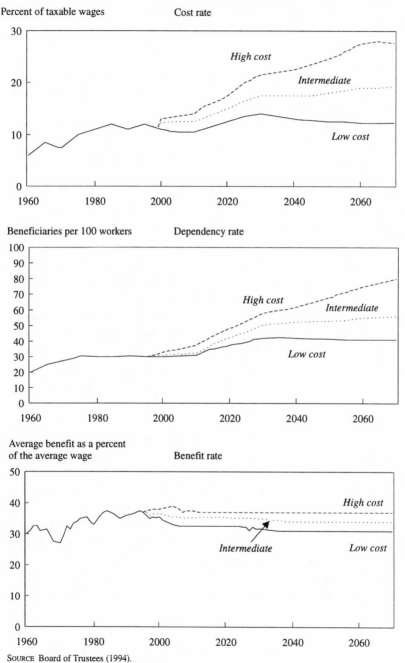

Percent of taxable wages   Cost rate

Beneficiaries per 100 workers   Dependency rate

Average benefit as a percent
of the average wage   Benefit rate

SOURCE Board of Trustees (1994).

has swelled the ranks of the work force and held down the cost rate. This will continue until 2010, when they begin to retire. Cost will then rise at a very rapid rate.

The fundamental force behind the rise in the dependency rate is the slowing of growth in the working-age population. Over the past twenty-five years the dependency rate has increased only marginally, from twenty-seven retirees per one hundred workers in 1970 to thirty-one in 1995, because a rapid expansion of the work force offset nearly all the growth in the number of retirees. In the years to come the growth in the number of retirees will actually slow, falling from an annual rate of 2.2 percent in the 1970–95 period to 1.8 percent over the following thirty-five years, and to only about 0.4 percent in the period 2030–70. This will occur despite the retirement of the baby boom generation. On the other hand, the growth of the population of workers needed to support the system will fall dramatically from an annual rate of 1.6 percent in 1970–95 to 0.45 percent in 1995–2030, and only 0.1 percent in 2030–70. As a result the dependency rate will continue to rise even after the baby boomers are gone.

Despite the uncertainties, it is hard to escape the conclusion that the Social Security system faces serious future funding problems. The magnitude of current tax increases or benefit reductions required to bring the system back to actuarial balance over the seventy-five-year horizon exceeds 2 percent of taxable payroll. That, however, would only be the tip of the iceberg because the simple passage of time would require further increases as the valuation period extends further into the high cost years of the next century. The tax rate would have to rise between 0.5 and 1 percent every ten years just to maintain the standard. A 2 percentage point increase in the tax would cover outlays until 2020.

If the system operates on a pay-as-you-go basis, the intermediate projection suggests that the payroll tax rate would need to increase to about 16.5 percent in 2030, when all of the baby boom generation would be of retirement age, and continue to rise to about 18 percent in 2070.[6] Furthermore, with the inclusion of the hospital insurance portion of Medicare (part A) the increases become much larger. In the intermediate projections the cost rate rises from 15 percent of payroll in 1995, to 25 percent in 2030, and 30 percent in 2070. Overall, the magnitude of transfers from workers to retirees raises some serious concerns about the sustainability of the program. Although the system's short-term financial conditions are strong, today's workers should prefer that decisions to

---

6. Again, the potential variance is very wide. The required tax rate in 2030 could range between 13 percent of payroll in the low cost case and 20 percent in the high cost alternative.

resolve the longer-term problems be made soon, leaving them with a sufficient working period in which to adjust their own saving and retirement plans.

To date, most suggestions for reform of Social Security have focused on methods of reducing future benefits or expanding the tax base.[7] By themselves, however, these actions would not provide a solution, since the size of the future retiree population and their retirement needs would remain the same. The view of a fixed pie of future resources has been generally accepted, and the issue has become how to apportion it between the young and the old—an inherently divisive issue. In this section I will focus on a third option for meeting the higher costs of future retirement—increased saving; that is, expanding the fund of future resources out of which both the needs of the young and the old will be met. This includes the possibility of advance or partial funding for future benefits, as well as some suggestions for changing the approach and responsibility for managing the buildup of a retirement fund.

Proposals for reductions in benefits seem particularly limited because the U.S. program is already quite modest by international standards. For the worker earning half the average wage, the benefit for a married couple is at the poverty threshold, and for a single person, it is below it. Since these retirees will have very few additional assets, an across-the-board cut in benefits would either result in offsetting increases in Supplementary Social Insurance (SSI) payments, or in higher poverty rates. Yet the existing system is so highly redistributional that efforts to concentrate the benefit reductions among high-wage workers risk widespread disaffection and demands to be let out of the system.[8] Alternatively, means-testing of the benefits on the basis of other retirement income, as proposed by some recent public commissions, would go even further toward destroying incentives for retirement saving through private means.[9] Workers would be encouraged to consume during their work lives, since any saving for retirement would be offset by reduced Social Security benefits.

Yet current workers must also recognize than an ever-lengthening period of retirement cannot be supported without some rise in the rate of tax that they pay during their working years. Average life spans have increased continuously, and Americans have taken this additional time, and more, in the form of a longer period of retirement. While the normal age of retirement has remained

7. A wide range of proposals for adjusting taxes and benefits are discussed in Steuerle and Bakiji (1994).

8. Hurd and Shoven (1985).

9. I would differentiate between proposals to means-test Social Security benefits and to treat them as equivalent to private pensions for purposes of income taxation. The latter approach goes more to the principle that two individuals of similar circumstances should pay similar taxes to support government programs.

fixed at sixty-five for men since the Social Security's inception, life expectancy for men at age sixty-five has increased by 25 percent between 1940 and the mid-1990s (from twelve years to fifteen years), and for women by 45 percent (from thirteen years to nineteen years) over the same period. Moreover, life expectancy for both genders is expected to rise by an additional 15 to 25 percent over the next thirty years. If this increase were entirely offset by a later retirement age, the standard of age sixty-five in 1940 would be age seventy-two today and age seventy-four in the year 2030. Yet most Americans are retiring earlier. The average age for men receiving benefits was sixty-nine in 1950 and sixty-four in 1990, and the labor force participation rate of older workers is expected to continue to fall in the future.[10] By the year 2030 the retirement period of an average worker will be nearly half as long as his or her work life. These trends, which increase the population of retirees, could be moderated by raising the retirement age, but this would still leave the slowing of growth in the population of workers and in the contribution base.

Too great a focus on moderating the growth in the cost rate, however, can limit a consideration of other options for resolving the financing of the system. The cost rate is not very useful as a means of measuring the burden that the system places on future generations of workers. It represents the share of wage earnings that must be set aside to finance the retired, but it says nothing about the level of real wages out of which those benefits will be paid. For example, a one-shot increase in the level of labor productivity would raise the real wages on which future benefits are based and add to the future outlays of the Social Security system. Yet the burden of the system on future workers would be less, because the wages out of which the benefits must be paid would have increased far more than the added retirement costs. From this perspective, a focus on the cost rate understates the importance of changes in the growth of productivity and real wages in measuring the future burden. If the current generation could provide a means to sharply raise the incomes of future generations, its retirement would not represent an increased burden, even though the cost rate might rise very sharply. On the other hand, if the growth in real wages continues to deteriorate at the pace of the previous decade, a rebellion by future workers seems increasingly likely.

Pay-as-You-Go versus Funded Programs

To date nearly all industrial countries have financed their social insurance programs by some variant of a pay-as-you-go system, in which each generation

---

10. Decisions to take early retirement have a limited impact on costs because the benefits are actuarially reduced, but they do lower the revenue of the system.

pays for the retirement costs of the currently retired, in return for a commitment for the same treatment from future generations. Such a system has an obvious appeal to the first generation, but at its inception it also appears attractive for subsequent generations.[11] Workers who spend their entire work lives and retirement years within a pay-as-you-go system with constant tax rates will earn a return on their contributions equal to the growth in population plus the growth in the real wage.[12] In effect the formula defines the growth in the pool of resources available to support retirees between the time of contribution as a worker and retirement.

In the decades following World War II, the rate of return within a pay-as-you-go system seemed particularly high. The population of covered workers grew at an annual rate of 2.4 percent between 1950 and 1995; until the early 1970s, average real wages were rising in excess of 2 percent per year. In contrast, the common view of a funded program involved investing contributions in government securities with a real rate of return of about 1 percent. Thus, quite apart from the benefits to the first generation, a pay-as-you-go scheme could be argued to be the right choice for subsequent generations.

The current outlook is much different. The intermediate actuarial projection incorporates an average annual growth of less than 0.3 percent in covered employment over the next seventy-five years. Furthermore, the projected growth in real wages has been cut to only 1 percent annually, and that is still above the average of the last two decades. As a result of the wage increase, the projected return of a pay-as-you-go system is now even well below the interest rate on government bonds. There has also been a significant change in the perspective on the option of a funded program because of the emergence and success of private pension funds, which invest their assets in a combination of bonds and equities and earn a real rate of return in the range of 4 to 5 percent. Thus it would not be surprising were the current cohort of young workers to wish that the founders of Social Security had opted for a funded program. Not only are they stuck with paying the retirement cost of a large baby boom generation, but the economics of the system would not even look good if all age cohorts were of equal size.

11. It has taken the United States a surprisingly long time to complete the transition through the first generation, which receives benefits without having to pay for past retirees. Congress continued to expand the program by enriching the benefit formula and bringing additional portions of the work force into the system. Thus there have been successive waves of cohorts who receive benefits out of proportion to their past contributions. Not even current new retirees can claim to have spent their full work life in a mature pay-as-you-go system. The expansion of the system ended in the early 1970s and the next few years will see a dramatic decline in the return to new retirees.

12. This was first pointed out by Samuelson (1958), and it has been repeated many times since then in articles on Social Security.

A clearer recognition of the benefits of a funded system might not have been enough to change the original decision. A funded program would have required each cohort of workers to receive benefits equal to the present value of its past contributions. Few politicians would have been willing to support a proposal in which the benefits of a new tax would not begin to flow for several decades. It would have delayed for many years the effort to respond to poverty among the elderly. Furthermore, expectations about wage growth and the need for additional capital were much different from today.

The Benefits of Increased Saving

Much of the discussion of full funding versus pay-as-you-go financing has been skewed by an excessive focus on the government bond rate as the relevant measure of the rate of return on a funded system. While that rate is appropriate for evaluating the financial condition of a Social Security fund that limits investments to government securities, it is not at all appropriate for measuring the benefits to the nation or future generations. The Social Security fund earns a 2 percent return because it opts to invest in risk-free government securities; but in buying government securities, it frees up resources that pass through capital markets and can be used by others who are willing to invest in riskier forms of capital earning a higher rate of return. In particular, if the saving of Social Security, the excess of its tax and interest income above outlays, ultimately adds to national saving, it can finance an increase in physical capital. For example, if these funds had been effectively used by corporations to finance their investments over the 1960–93 period, they would have earned an average real return, before tax, of 7.8 percent.

The return in the corporate sector probably overstates the average return on capital in the total economy because corporate capital is more heavily taxed than investments in homes and noncorporate business. There is no reason to assume that all of any increment to national saving would go to the corporate sector. An estimate of the economywide before-tax return to capital can be computed from the prior estimates for the corporate sector, if investments in the different sectors are assumed to yield an equal after-tax return. Existing studies of effective tax rates can be used to calculate equivalent before-tax rates of return for housing and the noncorporate business sector. The result is an estimate of 6.2 percent for the real return on the capital employed in the domestic economy.[13]

13. The marginal effective tax rates are those for 1990, as reported in Fullerton and Karayannis (1993). The overall average return was computed using as weights the net capital stock in 1990 for

How are those benefits distributed? The answer depends on whether the United States is viewed as a closed economy in which all saving must be invested in domestic capital, or if the recent opening of international capital markets and the free flow of resources across national borders is taken into account.

In a closed economy the added physical capital will raise output; and the income derived from that output, under the assumption of fixed full employment, will accrue to the owners of the new capital. After allowing for depreciation, the increase in aggregate income is measured by the previous estimate of the net return to capital. Thus multiplying the net return by the increment to capital yields the increase in net income to the nation. The increase in the capital stock, however, will have secondary implications for the distribution of income between workers and the owners of existing capital. The additional increase in capital per worker will raise the productivity of workers as a whole, and they will benefit through an increase in their real wage. This gain to workers is paid for by a loss of income by holders of old capital. As measured by the rise in the capital-to-output ratio, labor has become more scarce relative to capital so its return rises, while that of capital falls. In effect, entrepreneurs with ideas for new investments and workers gain from the increase in saving, while owners of old capital lose. The direct benefits to the Social Security funds consist of the interest earned on their investments in government bonds and a higher future level of receipts, equal to the tax rate times the rise in the real wage. These benefits are, of course, substantially less than the gain in national income.

In an open economy the process is somewhat different because the increment to national saving can flow abroad. No American is going to invest in a foreign asset that provides a rate of return below that available from domestic investments; and in a completely open capital market it would be most reasonable to assume that the risk-adjusted return of foreign and domestic investment are equal. In fact, rough estimates of the value of U.S. corporate investments overseas suggest that they earn a rate of return equal or above that on domestic capital.[14] If the global market is assumed to be so large that marginal changes in saving within the United States have no effect on the rate of return, the increment to U.S. saving will spill over into the global market where it will

---

the three sectors, as given in Board of Governors of the Federal Reserve (1994). A similar calculation using the rate of return on nonfarm business capital, reported by Oliner and Sichel (1994), resulted in an average yield of 6.3 percent.

14. Data on the current value of foreign direct investments and the income earned are published in the U.S. balance of payments. The average real rate of return over the past ten years has been 8.5 percent, compared with the corporate return of 7.8 percent on domestic investments discussed here.

earn the same return and generate the same increase in U.S. national income as resulted from the rise in the stock of domestic capital. But because there is no increase in the amount of domestic capital per worker, there is no significant effect on wage rates in the United States, and no corresponding loss to old capital. This has some implications for Social Security because, while the funds receive a similar interest return on their investment, they do not benefit from any increase in tax receipts.

As a practical matter, international markets are still in an intermediate stage. While financial capital can flow quite freely between the major industrial economies, the need to balance any net movement of capital with equal changes in current account flows (trade in goods and services) still requires significant changes in relative prices.[15] Thus large outflows of capital would result in a significant currency depreciation in order to achieve a matching change in the trade account. This would be offset by an appreciation in the future, when the income from foreign investments flowed back to the United States. These movements in the exchange rate act as a restraining influence on the capital outflow because the depreciation increases the attraction of investing in the domestic economy.

While the trend is toward a more integrated world economy in the future, the option of investing abroad should be viewed as an escape valve for the policy of increased national saving. It would limit the decline in the rate of return to capital that would otherwise accompany a large surge of saving in a closed economy. Thus the expansion of investment options actually makes a policy of increased national saving more attractive, but it changes the distributional consequences between domestic labor and capital, as explained earlier.

Funding Social Security

Despite the attraction of a higher rate of return, the suggestion that the current pay-as-you-go system might be replaced with a fully reserved system suffers a fundamental flaw. It would require the transitional generation to pay twice—for their own retirement through a fully funded system, and that of the currently and near-retired through the old pay-as-you-go system. The result would be a large drop in the after-tax income of the transitional group of workers. Even if the benefits to future cohorts were significantly positive, it is difficult to perceive how to induce a transitional group to bear the costs.

15. Most empirical studies still place the price elasticity of both U.S. exports and imports at about unity.

However, the fact that the costs of the system, and thus taxes, are projected to rise substantially in the future raises the possibility of an intermediate policy of advance funding of the added future costs. Current workers support a smaller population of retirees for a shorter period of retirement than will be the case when they retire. This situation, combined with a lower growth in the future work force, accounts for the sharp growth in the projected dependency rate. The magnitude of the added burden on future workers could be reduced if the current work force agreed to meet the added cost of their retirement through an increase in their own saving. The result would be a larger future stock of capital, and thus a large pool of income out of which their future benefits would be paid. Although contribution rates would continue to rise in the future, they would be applied to wages that would be higher than in the absence of such a program. In addition, a substantial portion of future benefits would be paid out of the interest earnings of the Social Security funds, rather than relying solely on the contributions of future workers.

With the 1977 and 1983 Social Security amendments, Congress began to move away from a pay-as-you-go system of financing, toward a greater emphasis on the adjustment of taxes and promised benefit levels to maintain an actuarial balance between future costs and future income. Actuarial balance was defined as equality (within 5 percent) of the present-discounted value of future revenues and payments over a seventy-five-year horizon. Those calculations were to be based on current legislation for benefits and tax rates. Because of the future increases in the cost rate, a focus on actuarial balance implied a degree of advance funding and the buildup of a significant reserve. Thus each cohort of workers would pay a portion of their own retirement costs, to the extent that those costs were greater than the costs of the currently retired.

In 1988 Henry Aaron, Gary Burtless, and I examined the economic implications of a system of partial funding in which Congress would consistently adjust taxes to maintain the system in actuarial balance over the seventy-five-year horizon, and the surplus would be set aside to add to national saving.[16] That study was based on the more optimistic assumptions of the 1986 trustees' report. The most important finding was that even the relatively small amount of advance funding implied by a rule of maintaining actuarial balance could, if saved and invested, generate increases in aggregate income sufficient to offset the added costs of OASDI on future workers and more than compensate those

16. Aaron, Bosworth, and Burtless (1989). In view of the current debate about the effect of government policies on the economy, it is interesting to note that we were actually calling for a form of dynamic revenue estimation, allowing for induced changes in future output to be included in the calculation of the benefits of a policy change. However, the assumptions used then, and in this chapter, incorporate very conservative estimates of the benefits of increased capital formation.

generations, through increases in their before-tax income, for the added taxes they would have to pay. The need to move forward the schedule of tax increases in order to maintain actuarial balance would reduce consumption in the short run, but the subsequent faster growth of incomes would allow annual consumption to return to its former level within fifteen years and reach a peak increase of about 3.5 percent at the height of the baby boom retirement, in 2030. In addition, the projections implied that only three adjustments in the tax rate would be required to maintain actuarial balance: increases of about 0.8 percent in the years 1999, 2027, and 2060.

Much has changed since that study was written. Revisions to the trust fund projections since 1986 have resulted in a much faster rate of growth in the cost rate, and the system has already fallen into actuarial imbalance. The fact that Congress has taken no action to restore balance, through adjustments to either benefits or taxes, implies a far smaller reserve buildup and thus a much smaller pool of potential saving. Thus the first assumption of the report—that the current generation would understand the nature of the increased burden that their retirement places on future workers and would be willing to fund a portion of those costs—now seems questionable. Second, the report also required that the current generation recognize the critical importance of setting aside the reserve and letting it contribute to national saving, and thus to the wealth that would be inherited by future generations.

The failure of the first assumption is serious because it reflects the unwillingness of public officials to take actions that impose any costs on current voters. The precedent set by the 1994 response to a looming cash shortfall in the Disability Insurance (DI) program is also discouraging, because Congress simply shifted funds from an OASDI program already out of actuarial balance to meet a more pressing need in the DI program. If public officials will take no action to maintain actuarial balance, the issue of what to do with the surplus will gradually become moot. But, in fact, it is not possible to conclude that inaction was the wrong answer without addressing the second assumption: Can an increase in the OASDI surplus add to national saving?

The Effect on National Saving

The assumption that Social Security surpluses will pass through to an increase in national saving is critical to the notion of using partial funding of the program to offset the increased burden on future workers. National saving is the sum of saving in the private sector (household saving and the retained earnings of corporations) plus the saving of the public sector. In the period between the end of World War II and 1980 the national savings rate averaged about 8 percent of national income: a private saving rate of 8.5 to 9 percent, offset by the public dissaving of 0.5 to 1 percent. More recently the situation has deteriorated significantly. The private saving rate fell during the 1980s to reach an average of 6 percent in the period 1990–93, and public sector dissaving ballooned to 3.8 percent, resulting in a national saving rate of only about 2 percent of national income, as shown in table 2-2.

A funded Social Security system would create a third source of national saving. However, that saving would not add to national saving if its existence, in fact, caused a decline in private saving or an increase in the dissaving of the public sector. There has long been debate about whether the introduction of Social Security, or an increase in the promised benefits of the program, would lead to an offsetting reduction in private saving. Suffice it to say that the issue has not been resolved to everyone's satisfaction. The choice between a funded program or the continuation of a pay-as-you-go program, however, would have no effect on the magnitude of the promised future benefit. It is this promise, the future liability of the system, that should influence private saving, not the magnitude of any annual surplus of the program. Thus, except to the extent that funding would make the future promise more credible, there is little reason to expect that partial funding would lower the private saving rate.[17]

More critical is the response of the government component. To some extent, the issue is entangled in a debate as to whether Social Security is a transfer program or a retirement program. To some, including many of it supporters, Social Security is simply a system of transfers between different groups in society and therefore there is no reason to separate it from other government activities. Its revenues are part of those of the general government, and each Congress must decide how to allocate its scarce resources among competing claims. The assignment of a specific category of government revenues to a specific type of expenditure is viewed as bad budget policy.

The emphasis on keeping Social Security within the general government budget is evident in the fact that, although the status of Social Security was formally changed in 1985 to that of an off-budget agency, nearly all public analyses and discussions of the budget treat the total as inclusive of Social Security. In particular, the current proposal for a balanced budget amendment includes Social Security, and there is every indication that the 104th Congress intends to use the current surplus of the Social Security funds to finance other

---

17. Although, in polls, young workers often say that they do not expect to receive Social Security benefits, their response could be attributed to growing public cynicism toward all aspects of government and any notion of a community of interest. There is no evidence that they have acted on their professed beliefs by increasing their own saving.

Table 2-2. Net National Saving and Investment, United States, 1950–93
Percent of net national product

Category	1950–69	1970–79	1980–89	1990–93
National saving	8.5	7.9	4.3	2.0
Private	8.6	8.9	7.1	5.8
Government	– 0.1	– 1.1	– 2.8	– 3.8
Investment	8.5	8.2	4.2	2.1
Domestic	8.1	7.9	6.1	3.2
Foreign	0.4	0.3	– 1.9	– 1.0
Statistical discrepancy	0.0	0.3	– 0.1	0.1

SOURCE: National Income and Product Accounts.

programs. While cuts in Social Security benefits may be off the table, the same is not true of the surplus.

Yet as long as Social Security is an integral part of the total budget, there is no reason to anticipate that a surplus in the fund would actually lead to a rise in national saving. The decision to fund a portion of the program would be a purely internal matter, offset within the government sector as a whole.

If Social Security is a transfer program, there is a strong argument for abandoning the effort to build up additional reserves, cutting the tax rate, and reverting to pay-as-you-go financing. From a political perspective, the existence of large reserves would simply make the future problem of Social Security worse. If the current generation of workers are undeservedly credited with having contributed to a retirement fund from which they immediately withdrew the proceeds to finance current consumption, they will argue, on their retirement, that the reserve is something meaningful which they are entitled to have returned. Income taxes on future workers would have to rise to repurchase the securities previously issued to the Social Security fund. Yet the current generation will simply have substituted a wage tax for the income taxes that would normally be needed to finance current outlays of the operating budget. If all government revenues are to be commingled, the excess funding of Social Security merely represents a shift to greater reliance on regressive wage taxes to pay for programs formerly financed with personal and corporate taxes. It would be better to revert to a broader-based tax to finance these government activities.

Most Americans, however, view Social Security as a retirement program and seem to agree with the policy of setting aside the surplus as a vehicle for saving. They are normally very surprised to learn that the surplus is being used to finance other programs, and that in most public discussions the budget deficit is defined to include the finances of Social Security. From the perspective of a retirement program, it makes sense to fund a portion of the future costs, as is done with private pension plans, to reduce the burden on future generations of workers.

Thus an effective program to use Social Security as a vehicle for raising national saving must involve a change in the budgetary process to more clearly differentiate Social Security from the operating budget of the government. This will require significant change in the way the fiscal choices are presented and in the economic concepts governing the decisions. In one dimension this has already occurred, in that the primary responsibility for short-run economic stabilization has shifted effectively from the Congress to the Federal Reserve. The shift reflects both the observed inability of the Congress to make timely decisions, and a new perspective on the importance of fiscal policy for economic stabilization in a situation of increasingly integrated global capital markets. In the future, the role of national fiscal policy will be analogous to that of the states' budgetary policies within the national economy. Just as the states have come to recognize the futility of an independent fiscal policy, federal fiscal policy is losing its relevance to the short-run behavior of the United States economy.

A commitment to differentiate between the retirement accounts and the budget would require the federal government to make its decisions within budgetary rules that are similar to those of the states. Most states present their budgets in ways that exclude their retirement programs, and nearly all have sought some degree of funding of those liabilities. As they have built up their pension reserves, they have been able to resist the temptation to increase their own borrowing as an offset. In a few states, such borrowing is prohibited by the constitution, but in most it is not. Some evidence that their retirement account surpluses have added to saving is provided in figure 2-3. While the annual state retirement fund surpluses have grown steadily, to over 1 percent of GDP in the 1990s, the nonretirement budget balance has fluctuated about zero, with no clear tendency to rise or fall over time.[18] In fact, state retirement accounts have grown to the point that they represent an increment to national saving of about 1 percent of national income in the mid-1990s. The ability of most states to make rational decisions about their pension liabilities should suggest that the federal government is at least capable of doing the same.

There are several options for increasing the degree of separation between the Social Security funds and the federal operating budget in ways that might

18. Admittedly this situation may be changing. A few state governors have discovered that they can alter the rules governing the funding status of their public pension funds in ways that allow them to reduce contributions. Other states have attempted to alter the funds' investment decisions to subsidize other activities.

Figure 2-3. Retirement and Nonretirement Budget Balance of State and Local Governments

Percent of GDP

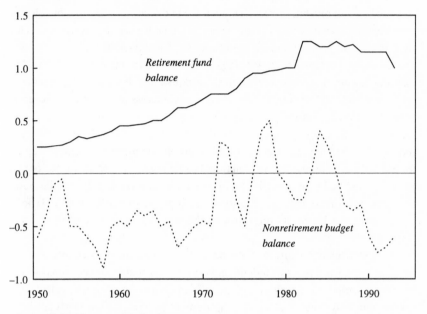

SOURCE: National Income and Product Accounts.

reduce any temptation to use the funds' surplus as a justification for a larger budget deficit. The most direct, but not necessarily the best, approach would be to adjust the proposed balanced budget amendment currently before Congress to exclude the surplus of the Social Security fund. This would save the OASDI surplus, but would do so as part of an amendment that many view as too inflexible a rule for the budget itself.

A more practical approach would be to change the status of the Social Security system to that of an independent agency and remove its revenues and expenditures from the budget documents and the annual proceedings in which Congress makes budgetary decisions. Congress and the administration would exercise oversight responsibilities, and Congress might continue to exercise the power to veto changes in contribution rates and benefit formulas. The Board of Trustees would be assigned broader responsibilities to propose specific actions, as necessary, to maintain the funds' actuarial balance, and would be held accountable for the management of the investments. While movements in the fund balances would affect the economy, the year-to-year variations would be small and of little consequence for fiscal policy. At minimum, the change would prevent the public presentation of the budget deficit from being smaller than it actually is. It would approximate the states' treatment of their retirement accounts.

Furthermore, it would be possible to devise a system in which the funded portion of the Social Security program were moved to the private sector. Workers could be offered the option of shifting a portion of their contribution to a privately managed, defined contribution program. This would raise the complex but not unsolvable problem of how to reduce the OASDI benefit of such individuals in an actuarially correct fashion that does not worsen the financial position of the remaining fund. It is complicated both because of the redistributional elements of the benefit formula and because the inflation protection built in to the public program is not duplicated in private programs. In addition, given the observed political pressures to broaden the conditions under which existing Individual Retirement Accounts (IRAs) can be cashed out for nonretirement purposes, it could be argued that this proposal would not effectively translate into added national saving.

In the typical case, the size of the private account would be small, and it may be too much to expect individuals to be willing to devote the time required to become knowledgeable about investment decisions. It might be preferable, instead, to follow the practice of some private retirement programs and allow workers to choose between a limited number of privately managed funds that would be under strong regulatory supervision by the Social Security system.

Ultimately, there is no means of guaranteeing that partial funding of Social Security would lead to higher national saving. But such a cynical view of the ability of the public and its elected officials to make rational decisions when the issues are clearly put before them raises questions that go far beyond Social Security financing alone. The program itself continues to attract a high level of public support, even among those who question whether they will receive a benefit. Yet continuing to rely solely on pay-as-you-go financing will lead to serious problems as future demographic and economic trends lower the rate of return. Those problems could be easily resolved by a shift to advance funding of a portion of the future liability.[19]

Finally, the fiscal experience of the 1980s should not be used as evidence that a surplus in the OASDI accounts cannot add to national saving. Many factors contributed to the emergence of a large fiscal deficit and the difficulties

19. The experiences of other countries where benefit promises exceeded the financing capabilities of the system are important here. Such situations have given rise to strong incentives for young workers to avoid the system, and the resulting funding crises have led to ill-conceived efforts to redefine benefits in ways that have led to capricious redistributions of income among and within age cohorts.

of taking action to reduce it. Mistakes were made in combining an increase in defense spending with a tax reduction in the early 1980s, and the positive benefits of supply-side economics never materialized. And there is still the difficulty of adjusting to a situation in which the built-in growth in existing programs exceeds the growth of the economy and thus of tax revenues.[20] To a large extent these problems developed before the onset of a Social Security surplus. As the reserve of the OASDI funds has grown, the overall deficit has actually declined.

Management of the OASDI Fund

The creation of an OASDI reserve would also raise significant questions about its investment policies. At present the OASDI reserves are invested in Treasury securities that earn the average rate of interest on government bonds in excess of four years. Rather than engaging in market purchases, with their associated broker fees, the bonds are purchased directly from the Treasury in the equivalent of the private placement market for corporate bonds. Over the past ten years the average rate of real return has been about 5 percent, but it is expected to decline to 2 percent in the intermediate projections, which is more in line with the average historical yield.

It is sometimes suggested that some of the future financing problems could be reduced if the OASDI funds were free to invest in private securities and earn a higher rate of return. As the recent experience of Orange County, California, demonstrates, such a recommendation should not be made lightly, or without a clear understanding of the consequences.

First, from the perspective of society as a whole, this change would yield few benefits. It would make the financing position of the OASDI system appear stronger, but it would not in itself increase national income. Imagine that the OASDI system sold off $1 trillion of its Treasury securities and replaced them in its portfolio with an equal number of private securities paying a higher rate of return. The higher return would presumably reflect the higher degree of risk inherent in the private debt. However, a simple swap of public and private debt between the OASDI trust fund and the private markets would have no appreciable effect on total saving, the stock of physical capital, or output. The return and the gain in national income is given by the before-tax return on capital, as discussed above. The trust fund would report a higher rate of return, while the private sector would hold the lower-yield Treasury securi-

20. In this respect, the current problems of the operating fund are a precursor of the future difficulties of Social Security.

ties previously held by the fund. The resources out of which the consumption of future workers and retirees must be financed, therefore, would remain the same.

Society would not benefit from a policy that simply shifts the distribution of financial assets between the OASDI fund and the private sector unless there are barriers to portfolio diversification in private markets.[21] Modern capital markets are highly integrated, however, and investors can easily alter the composition of their portfolios to achieve the mix of return versus risk with which they feel most comfortable. As a result the interest rate differential between corporate and government bonds increases in recessions and other periods when risks are perceived to have grown. There is no discernible correlation between the yield spread and changes in the share to total credit market debt accounted for by the government. As shown in figure 2-4, the higher proportion of very low-risk governments in the private sector portfolio might induce some increase in the demand, and hence in the price, of risky equity issues, but in any global market the effect would seem small.

Instead, the significance of a policy of investing in private securities lies in the fact that the Social Security system would capture a larger portion of the return on capital for its own purposes. If the original decision to advance-fund a portion of the future liability had not, in fact, translated into increased national saving, the decision to invest in private securities would operate much like a tax, albeit a voluntary one. A larger share of the nation's capital income would accrue to the Social Security funds in return for their agreement to assume more of the investment risk. As a result tax rates would not have to rise so much in the future, because the system would extract resources to meet retiree payment more through interest and less through taxes. Investing in private securities might affect future attitudes about who is truly paying for the consumption of the retired; but the total amount of resources available for consumption would remain the same. Even so, it could still be held that the current investment policy seems excessively conservative for a broad-based retirement fund with very long-term and relatively predictable liabilities, and that a higher return would reduce workers' perception that they pay all of the costs.

If increases in the Social Security fund did add to national saving and the stock of wealth, a more interesting situation would arise. Why should the fund only be credited with a 2 percent return if its actions had actually added something closer to 6 percent in future income to the nation? Such a policy camouflages much of the benefit of advanced funding. Furthermore, if the

21. See Aaron, Bosworth, and Burtless (1989, pp. 101–04).

Figure 2-4. Corporate versus Government Bond Rate Differential

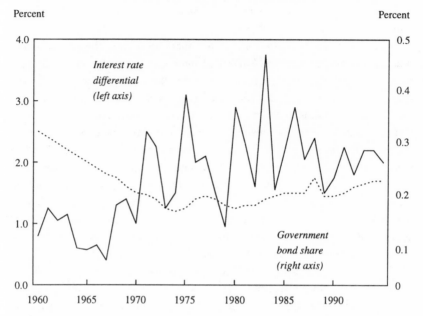

Percent   Percent

SOURCE: Interest rate differential is the corporate BAA rate less the government fixed ten-year maturity. The government share of the market is publicly held debt as a share of total credit market debt.

difference between the total return of approximately 6 percent and the 2 percent received by the funds were allowed to accrue to the private sector, it would presumably be consumed in the proportion in which private income is currently divided between saving and consumption. Alternatively, if the Social Security system were to capture a larger portion, that increment to income would presumably be saved.

If the funding rule by which the system is to be kept in close actuarial balance operated symmetrically, a higher rate of return would push the system toward an actuarial surplus and a reduction in contribution rates relative to the prior assumed path. Workers would probably save about the same portion of that gain in after-tax income as does the private sector as a whole. In that case, a decision to invest in a riskier portfolio of assets would involve no net gain to the national saving rate.

But such an outcome is not required. It would be equally reasonable to allow the reserve to build up beyond the minimal level—as long as it involved no increase in tax rates, since Social Security would still be far short of a fully funded status. The result would be a much larger, but gradual, rise in the national saving rate. In the near term the rise of private income, and thus consumption, would be postponed, and a larger portion of the benefits of increased saving would be retained for the future. This would go a long way toward eliminating any need for taxes on workers to rise in the future.

Finally, if Social Security extracted a larger portion of the return on its saving, there should be no appreciable effect on investment. Business firms are largely indifferent to the source of their funds as long as the interest cost is the same. Private savers would not be disadvantaged either, since they could balance off their greater holding of the debt from the government by combining it with a portion of more risky assets.

Any proposal for public investment in private securities immediately raises concern about who would make the decisions and how the capital might be allocated among competing projects. But in the near term there would be no greater need for concern than with existing large state and private pension funds. Furthermore, management of the fund could be distributed among a substantial number of private fund managers, over whose investment choices Social Security would have no direct control. The agency would evaluate the managers' performance on the basis of relative rates of return and the risks that they involved. In effect, Social Security would be investing in a broad cross-section of the entire capital market. Public scrutiny and review would be beneficial in encouraging Americans to focus on these types of issues.

Quantitative Magnitudes

The magnitudes of change implied by a shift to partial funding of Social Security can be illustrated by using the intermediate projections of the trustees' report as a baseline. First, in order to restore actuarial balance the financial position of the Social Security fund is reestimated to include a tax rate increase of 2 percentage points in 1995. Second, the change in the investment policy is assumed to result in a 1 percentage point increase in the assumed yield on its assets over the next seventy-five years. These changes are shown in figure 2-5. The tax increase alone would allow the fund to continue to build up its reserve until about 2023, but the fund would begin to run deficits again in about 2055, and it would be exhausted near the end of the seventy-five-year horizon.

On the other hand, if the restoration of actuarial balance is combined with a change in investment policies that allows the fund to earn just 1 percent more than the rate on government securities, the reserve stabilizes at a level roughly equal to the taxable wage base. Given that the taxable wage base averages 40 to 45 percent of GDP, this amounts to an increase in the long-run capital stock from the present level of about 3 times GDP to 3.5 times. The increase in national saving represents 3 to 4 percent of national income at its peak, and

Figure 2-5. Assets and Annual Saving of the OASDI Trust Funds with Alternative Investment Policies

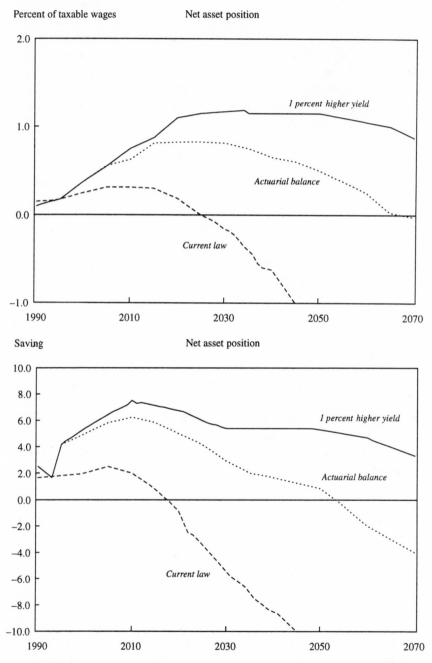

Percent of taxable wages   Net asset position

Saving   Net asset position

SOURCE: Author's calculations as explained in text.

about 1 to 2 percent in the long run. While there is some tendency for the saving of the fund to decline as a share of taxable wages near the end of the forecast horizon, it remains strongly positive throughout. In effect, these two changes would eliminate any problems with the Social Security fund for the foreseeable future.

The qualitative nature of the results of these policy changes can be readily inferred.[22] First, the calculations shown in figure 2-5 make no allowance for the increase in wages, and thus benefit payments, that will occur. However, because the increase in taxable wages precedes the rise in benefits, the financial position of the funds will actually improve as a result of taking account of the effects on the rest of the economy. While the increase in future benefit payments are substantial, the much larger rise in GDP still results in a net gain to the nonretiree population.[23]

Second, because the Social Security system captures a larger portion of the income from its investments and reinvests the proceeds, the decline in its saving that would normally follow from a future rise in the cost rate against a constant tax rate, is largely eliminated. There is no apparent need for further adjustments of tax rates in future years. The differences in saving is shown in the second panel of figure 2-5 as the gap between the two lines labeled "actuarial balance" and "1 percent higher yield." On the other hand, because the saving rate is maintained, consumption rises more slowly and takes longer to return to its earlier level. In effect, the benefits of saving the surplus are pushed further into the future, but ultimately they are much larger.

Conclusions

The deteriorating long-run financial position of the OASDI fund can no longer be dismissed as a minor problem. In responding to this situation, it is important to note that the implicit yield to the average contributing worker in a pay-as-you-go system is also going to fall dramatically in future years. At the same time, the success of private retirement funds has increased public awareness of the benefits of a funded retirement program. The sharply escalating cost rates projected for future years provides the United States with the opportunity to shift over to a partially funded program for the public portion of the retirement system, without the need to impose double taxation on any transitional generation.

22. I have not attempted a full economic simulation of the policy changes within the model developed in Aaron, Bosworth, and Burtless (1989) because of time constraints and the need to recalibrate the model to the current economic assumptions.
23. See Aaron, Bosworth, and Burtless (1989).

Furthermore, the current practice of limiting investments of the OASDI fund to government securities represents an unduly cautious investment strategy, and one that hides from public view the benefits of a partially funded system. A combination of a tax increase to restore actuarial balance and a mildly more aggressive investment policy could essentially eliminate future financing problems.

Many will believe that the solution presented here is overly simplified, and that such small changes in funding could not be sufficient to offset a near doubling of the future dependency rate. But these arguments fail to recognize that OASDI benefits will only increase by 2 percent of GDP between the mid-1990s and 2070, from 4.8 to 6.8 percent; and even in the trustees' high-cost projection, the increase is only 4 percent of GDP. The magnitude of these changes is less than the variations in the share of GDP devoted to defense over the past two decades. While Social Security represents a large proportion of the government budget as currently presented, it is a small element in the total economy. Given the high return from added capital formation and compounding growth rates, challenges of this magnitude can easily be met, as long as society is willing to act sufficiently far ahead of the need.

References

Aaron, Henry J., Barry Bosworth, and Gary Burtless. 1989. *Can America Afford to Grow Old?* Brookings.

Board of Governors of the Federal Reserve. 1994. *Balance Sheets of the U.S. Economy* (C.9 release), data diskettes.

Board of Trustees of the Federal Old-Age and Survivors' Insurance and Disability Insurance Trust Funds. *Annual Report.* Washington: 1994.

Fullerton, Don, and Marios Karayannis. 1993. "United States." In *Tax Reform and the Cost of Capital: An International Comparison,* edited by Dale W. Jorgenson and Ralph Landau, 333–68. Brookings.

Hurd, Michael E., and John B. Shoven. 1985. "The Distributional Impact of Social Security." In *Pensions, Labor, and Individual Choice*, edited by David A. Wise, 193–215. University of Chicago Press.

Oliner, Stephen D., and Daniel Sichel. 1994. "Computers and Output Growth Revisited: How Big is the Puzzle?" *Brookings Papers on Economic Activity, 2:1994,* 274–334.

Samuelson, Paul A. 1958. "An Exact Consumption-Loan Model of Interest With or Without the Social Contrivances of Money." *Journal of Political Economy* 66(6): 467–82.

Steuerle, C. Eugene, and Jon M. Bakiji. 1994. *Retooling Social Security for the 21st Century: Right and Wrong Approaches to Reform.* Washington: Urban Institute Press.

Selected Bibliography

Boskin, Michael J., and others. 1986. "Social Security: A Financial Appraisal Across and Within Generations." NBER Working Paper 1891.

Boskin, Michael J., Lawrence J. Kotlikoff, and John B. Shoven. 1988. "Personal Security Accounts: A Proposal For Fundamental Social Security Reform." In *Social Security and Private Pensions*, 179–206. Lexington, Mass.: Lexington Books.

Bosworth, Barry, Rudiger Dornbusch, and Raul Laban, eds. 1994. *The Chilean Economy: Policy Lessons and Challenges*, 257–320. Brookings.

Burtless, Gary. 1993. "The Uncertainty of Social Security Forecasts in Policy Analysis and Planning." Paper prepared for the Public Trustees of the Social Security and Medicare Boards of Trustees, Washington.

Feldstein, Martin. 1976. "The Social Security Trust Fund and National Capital Accumulation." In *Funding Pensions: Issues and Implications for Financial Markets*, 32–64. Conference Series 16. Federal Reserve Bank of Boston.

Friedman, Benjamin M., and Mark J. Warshawsky. 1993. "The Cost of Annuities: Implications for Saving Behavior and Bequests." *Quarterly Journal of Economics.* 105: 135–54.

Jorgenson, Dale W., and Ralph Landau, eds. 1993. *Tax Reform and the Cost of Capital: An International Comparison*, 333–68. Brookings.

Munnell, Alicia, "Public Pension Surpluses and National Savings: Foreign Experience." *New England Economic Review.* March 1989, 16–38.

Myers, Robert J. 1993. *Summary of the Provisions of the OASDI System, the HI System and the SMI System.* Washington: Mercer Meidinger Hansen Inc.

Weaver, Carolyn L., ed. 1990. *Social Security's Looming Surpluses.* 17–28. American Enterprise Institute Press.

Wise, David, ed. 1985. *Pensions, Labor, and Individual Choice.* 193–215. University of Chicago Press.

Comment by Carolyn L. Weaver

Barry Bosworth's careful analysis of Social Security funding and investment policy tackles three primary economic issues: the long-range financing problem, the comparative effects of pay-as-you-go financing and advance funding on national saving, and the management and investment of trust fund monies.

On the first issue, which involves a discussion of the size and determinants of the long-range financing problem and the sharp deterioration in the financial condition of Social Security over the past decade, I would simply underscore a few of Bosworth's key conclusions. First, despite considerable uncertainties surrounding future economic and demographic developments, "It is hard to escape the conclusion that the Social Security system faces serious future funding problems." Second, traditional solutions, such as increasing the pay-roll tax by about two percentage points to close the reported long-range gap, deal "only with the tip of the iceberg." Increasing life spans, together with continued low fertility, are expected to produce a rising cost rate and growing financial problems even after the retirement of the baby boom. This is gener-ally obscured by the truncated, seventy-five-year projection period used by the actuaries. As Bosworth notes, the payroll tax would have to be increased by between 0.5 and 1 percent every ten years (from its overall base of 15.3 percent in the mid-1990s) just to maintain the ongoing solvency of Social Security in future decades! Third, there is the potentially much larger problem in Medicare to consider, which, together with Social Security, "raises some serious con-cerns about the sustainability of the [Social Security] program." Finally, he stresses the importance of focusing on policies that increase national saving and, thus, the size of the economic pie, rather than only on ways of slicing the existing pie among workers and retirees.

If the picture that Bosworth paints seems gloomy, the situation may well turn out to be worse. His discussion is based on the Social Security Board of Trustees' intermediate cost projections, which have been revised upward quite significantly over the past decade. As Bosworth certainly recognizes, there are reasonable prospects of even larger financial problems setting in even more quickly than currently projected.[24]

On the second topic, the relative merits of pay-as-you-go financing versus advance funding, Bosworth provides a helpful discussion of the economic benefits likely to accompany a shift toward partial or full funding, and how the distribution of these benefits might be expected to vary between workers and taxpayers, for example, or between the trust funds and the economy, depending on the level of funding and the choice of investment strategies. As he notes, a pay-as-you-go system offers young workers the prospect of a rate of return of not more than about 1.5 percent, which is well below the return on government bonds, let alone on real capital investment. Little wonder that public opinion polls show that young workers are discontented with how they are likely to fare under Social Security and are interested in alternatives that involve real saving. Both the economy and individual workers stand to benefit from a system built on real saving and real capital investment.

24. See Carolyn L. Weaver, "Social Security: Solvent Until When?" *Washington Post,* March 7, 1995, p. A17.

And there's the rub: how can we move from the current pay-as-you-go or inadequately funded system to a system that is substantially funded without raising taxes or cutting spending and making somebody worse off; and how can we ensure that saving and real capital investment result? On the latter, about which so much has been said, the government can undermine any apparent saving through the Social Security trust funds by relaxing fiscal restraint in the rest of the budget, putting workers in the position of helping to fund current consumption rather than bolster saving with their extra payroll taxes. Bosworth argues that this can be handled within the context of the present system by distinguishing more carefully between the accounts and assets of the trust funds and the other accounts of the federal government. I am less sanguine that accounting changes can effectively constrain Congress. Moreover, Congress can spend the surpluses just as effectively by expanding Social Security benefits or bailing out Medicare (as it recently did Disability Insurance), and changes in federal budget accounts would be hard pressed to constrain this.

On the problem of transition, Bosworth dismisses full funding, not on economic grounds but on the grounds that it has a "fundamental flaw." Full funding "would require the transition generation to pay twice for retirement," once for their own, through full funding, and once for those who are or soon will be retired, under the old pay-as-you-go system. Even if a funded retirement system would be advantageous in the long run, the drop in after-tax income of the transition group of workers would preclude the adoption of such a plan.

In response I would say that if the question is whether or not people would agree to bear substantially larger taxes in the hopes of faring better down the road—with no changes in investment policy, federal fiscal policy, or the ownership of the proceeds of the additional saving—then it would be entirely illogical to support full funding in any event, double tax or no. Nothing in the current system would ensure that the benefits of full funding would be achieved, or that any of these benefits would be captured by those who made them possible.

But beyond that, the term "double tax" sounds so deterministic. While current workers would, no doubt, have to pay more, it is far from obvious how much more. It would depend on a variety of factors, including the rate of return on their saving (the greater the return, the smaller the added cost of meeting any particular level of retirement income for themselves). It would depend on the way the liability under the old system was met (it would make a big difference to the distribution of the burden among present and future workers and retirees, for example, whether the liability were to be met by increasing the payroll tax or some other tax, possibly a consumption tax, by reducing government spending, or by issuing new debt). And it would depend on how large the liability was seen to be. If the liability was defined as the present value of all benefits scheduled to be paid to people already on the rolls as well as to everyone who has already paid taxes, it would include some payments that cannot now be met and that some people do not expect to receive. The political uncertainty attached to long-range benefit promises, which is now quite substantial, would be completely ignored. If workers and retirees value more secure benefits, they will be willing to pay some price in terms of forgone benefit promises in order to achieve it.

To be sure, the transition to a new, fully funded system would be costly. How costly and for whom can not be known without a clear understanding of the transition plan and the kind of system to be attained. Is the goal a fully funded system with assets managed and controlled by the federal government, as is now the case, or by individual workers through a system of personal savings accounts with individual ownership of the proceeds of these accounts?

As an aside, Bosworth suggests that the double tax problem can somehow be avoided by partial advance funding. This is not convincing. Any plan to convert from a system of unfunded debt to a system involving some real saving will involve added costs. The smaller the increase in saving, the smaller the economic benefits likely to accrue.

Bosworth's final topic, the investment and management of trust fund assets, receives little attention. This is unfortunate, because it could have enriched the debate over full funding and reform proposals designed to enhance the role of the private sector. Who makes the investment decisions and how? Whose money is at risk? In a system holding substantially more assets, we can expect the answers to these questions to have potentially significant effects on the allocation of capital in the economy, on expected rates of return under Social Security, and thus on the economic well-being of present and future generations.

If the goal of reforming investment policy is, as I believe it should be, to short-circuit the direct and indirect spending of surplus receipts by the government, to bolster rates of return, and to achieve the full benefits of capital accumulation, then means must be found to move toward private investment of Social Security monies while keeping the government at bay—that is, in a position to neither "play the market" nor influence others to do so.

One option under discussion, which is modeled after the Thrift Savings Plan for federal civil service employees, would involve subcontracting the investment of trust fund monies to competing professional money managers who would be authorized to invest passively in broad index funds. The hope is that this would depoliticize investment decisions and, by removing surplus Social Security receipts from the federal coffers, improve the chances that the surpluses would contribute to saving.

Unfortunately, this option leaves Congress in a position to influence the allocation of capital in the economy and thus the distribution of wealth and income. Nothing would prevent Congress from imposing restrictions on allowable investments or funds, or manipulating the allocation of investments to different funds or asset classes. This option also leaves Congress in a position to use the surpluses to fund increases in Social Security or Medicare benefits. The Thrift Savings Plan largely escapes these problems because it is a voluntary defined contribution plan—workers own their retirement accounts and can shift their monies among investments as they see fit.

Another, more promising, approach is to give individual workers (not a government board or private money managers) the right to control the investment of some or all of their own Social Security taxes—in effect, moving further in the direction of the Thrift Savings Plan. This might be accomplished through a two-tiered Social Security system, in which the first tier offered a flat or means-tested payment to retirees, financed on a pay-as-you-go basis, and the second was a defined contribution plan, fully funded with workers' contributions. In the second tier, taxes could be channeled directly into individual private savings accounts, possibly along the lines of IRAs. By design, there would be no surplus tax receipts to be managed by the federal government and, thus, no funds available to underwrite an expansion in the rest of the budget. Investment decisions would be highly decentralized and competitively determined.

Reforming Social Security to accommodate a defined contribution component would enable individuals to be directly involved in their retirement-savings decisions and to accumulate legally enforceable claims to future benefits. Workers would take on new financial risks, but they would be spared some considerable political risks. Their ability to make informed decisions about work, retirement, and saving, which are conditional on having reasonable expectations about future Social Security benefits and taxes, would be greatly enhanced.

It is worth noting that this option does not preclude subsidies to lower-paid workers or to any other group deemed socially deserving. These subsidies should be well targeted, above board, and financed from the general revenue, however, unlike those under the present system that are complex, hidden, poorly targeted, and financed by payroll taxes. Separately financing subsidies would promote a more open debate about their value, while ensuring a more appropriate, progressive means of financing what is clearly income redistribution. That said, such subsidies would probably be hard to justify in the second tier, the purpose of which is to provide true earnings-related retirement pensions.

Comment by David W. Mullins Jr.

Barry Bosworth presents an excellent overview of the problem of Social Security. I will explore how advances in modern finance may be brought to bear on the problem by focusing on the issue of investment management.

Currently, investment of the social security trust fund is carried out within the Treasury Department, under the fiscal assistant secretary within the Financial Management Service. As assistant secretary of domestic finance, I found that this group did a very thorough job, especially on the cash flow side, making all sorts of estimates to squeeze out every penny. They are, however, constrained by law as to what investments they can make. These constraints are increasing, not receding. For example, the recent statute to make the Social Security Administration an independent agency also mandated that the Treasury Department issue physical paper certificates for the Treasury bonds in the Social Security fund, a remarkable retreat from the march toward settlement efficiency that long ago brought the move to book entry. At one stage, it looked as though Social Security would have to cut paper checks, rather than make direct payments.

The basic Social Security investment routine is to invest in special securities issued directly by the Treasury Department. The average maturity of the initial investments is about fifteen years. These are fixed-rate Treasuries, yielding the average rate of return on Treasuries of maturities between four years and thirty years.

The first question is whether investing in fixed-rate longer-term Treasury securities is a riskless strategy. Certainly there is no default risk, but there is interest rate risk. Financial economists think of interest rate risk as volatility in market values. Many would not think of Social Security investment in those terms, since these securities are, essentially, going to be held to maturity, so that there is no need to worry about the volatility in market values. But still, there is risk. In nominal terms there is risk with a fifteen-year-maturity Treasury at a fixed coupon because the reinvestment rate of the coupon will depend on whether intermediate rates are higher or lower. That will produce a distribution of ending values, rather than a certain ending value at the end of that investment period.

It is even more relevant to think of the risk in real terms. An example of an almost riskless investment in real terms would be Treasury bills whose rates track the inflation rate, producing through time—at least, to a first approximation—a stable real return and a relatively certain value (in real terms) ten, fifteen, or thirty years later. Thus a riskless real investment strategy might involve rolling over Treasury bills. There has been a lot of talk about inflation index–linked bonds. Essentially the same effect can be achieved by rolling bills (which is one reason why there are no inflation-indexed bonds). The Social Security strategy of locking in a fixed rate for fifteen years produces wide variations in outcome in real terms. If inflation unexpectedly decelerates, high real returns result, and quite low returns result if inflation unexpectedly accelerates.

The interest rate risk of buying and holding allegedly riskless long-term Treasury securities can be illustrated by the following example. Suppose someone invested in thirty-year fixed rate Treasuries in 1964. The rate would have been 4 percent. In 1994 the investment would have just matured, returning the principal investment. But because inflation unexpectedly accelerated over the three decades, real returns on this investment would be quite low. Possibly, they would even be negative; certainly, inferior to the yield on a policy of investing in one-year Treasury bills, because over those three decades Treasury bill rates have averaged greater than 4 percent. Obviously an even better policy would have been to invest in two-year Treasuries, which would have picked up a little yield premium, as well as tracking inflation.

The analysis is made more complex by expanding the investment opportunity set. For example, a linear combination of short-term Treasuries and common stock—with only a small amount put in common stock—can be designed to produce exactly the same spread of ending values, that is, the same risk level, as investing strictly in long-term Treasuries. However, such a policy, while it would bear the same risk as the Social Security strategy, might well produce substantially higher returns with no greater exposure to volatility of outcomes.

The advantages of the policy for the Social Security trust fund can be illustrated by reviewing the historical returns on U.S. securities. During the period from 1926 to 1992, in real terms, the average annual return for common stock (broadly diversified Standard & Poor) was 7.1 percent. Over the same period, long-term Treasury bonds earned a return of 1.7 percent, and Treasury bills, 0.6 percent, so there was a fairly wide divergence between different investment alternatives. Obviously, common stocks were much more volatile.

In nominal terms, the standard deviation of Treasury bonds was only about 40 percent of that of common stock.

A nonparametric measure provides a simple way to think of risk. In this case, for how many years out of the sixty-seven did an investment in a given instrument produce negative returns? For common stock, that happened in twenty years; for long-term Treasuries, seventeen. Thus Treasuries are obviously a little safer, and it would not be advisable to invest solely in common stock. But by limiting its investment strategy Social Security is forgoing a lot of return. In effect it excludes a wide variety of investments with attractive risk-to-return characteristics.

It is a basic tenet of modern finance that it is possible to construct efficient investment portfolios that maximize the expected return of the portfolio for any given risk constraint. Achieving efficiency in maximum risk adjusted returns involves optimal mixes of the full range of available securities. This includes stocks, bonds, short-term securities, and, ideally, international securities and other sorts of investments. The driving force is diversification. Diversification among a wide range of investment alternatives reduces risk while maintaining the expected return, thus producing superior risk-to-return combinations. The key is, for a given level of risk, to combine many different investment alternatives, rather than concentrating investment in one instrument. The Social Security strategy clearly violates this fundamental principle.

Modern finance is arguably the most successful field of applied economics, and modern investment technology has been developed and applied extensively over the past several decades.[25] For many years it has been successfully used by managers of large-scale portfolios in public and private pension funds on a global basis. It has been used to construct efficient investment portfolios which maximize return with any given tolerance for risk. In comparison to this well-developed, mature, successful technology, the Social Security investment strategy seems rigid and arbitrary. Tied to a highly restrictive investment opportunity set (essentially limited to long-term fixed Treasuries), it appears to be costly and inefficient. Even accepting the risk level implicit in the Social Security strategy, a sophisticated approach to investment management would be expected to produce substantially higher returns.

In all fairness, there is more to the Social Security strategy than just investing in long-term Treasuries. Social Security investment managers get a special

25. The genesis of this investment technology was in the academic world and included several Nobel prize–winning contributions. Harry Markowitz, William Sharpe, John Lintner and, more recently, Myron Scholes and Robert Merton have made the major academic contributions, while James Tobin's work touches on this area in part.

deal from the Treasury Department, including some free options to bail out of investments at par value when they are not doing well. If optimally exploited, this would allow them to enhance the returns as compared to a fixed Treasury return.

But ultimately the initial assessment of the Social Security strategy still holds, because these options essentially represent a hidden subsidy by the rest of the government. They are not available to other investors. Treasury is allowing the Social Security trust fund to earn a higher than market return on its securities, and the difference is made up by the taxpayers. In comparison, the alternative strategy outlined here would produce higher returns without such hidden subsidies, by constructing them out of market values.

To modernize the Social Security trust fund and end the waste of its inefficient investment strategy might involve, first, broadening the investment opportunity set to include a full range of securities, characterized by deep and liquid markets. This is the necessary raw material for building efficient investment portfolios. Second, it would be necessary to implement the standard analytical routines to construct efficient portfolios that are characterized by appropriate patterns of cash flows through time and constrained to keep risk within acceptable limits. Moreover, there are a wide range of institutional structures within which such an improved investment management process might be achieved.

At one extreme, it would be possible to design a system that is partially or fully self-directed, allowing individuals to select combinations from a menu of investment alternatives. A more limited approach would be to have a Social Security board that made investment decisions. It would be important to establish the independence of this board, and provide it with a staff and the resources to apply portfolio-building techniques and evaluate and farm out portions of trust funds to outside managers. In this scenario, the big issue would be deciding between passive indexed management and more active management; given the size of the fund, there are quite a few efficiency arguments for the former. The third option is just to perform both optimal portfolio construction and portfolio management in house.

In the investment management universe, there are many institutional models. Chile has been discussed. Carolyn Weaver also mentioned the thrift plan that was set up for federal employees, which employs the Wells Fargo index for common stocks and also for bonds.

There are also a number of other examples within the federal government. The Federal Reserve's pension fund is managed in a pretty sophisticated manner, for instance, and has performed quite well, relative to others in the government. Examples at the state level include Calpers, and there are university examples like TIAA-CREF. It is not trivial to extrapolate from these to Social Security because of its size, yet there are many models.

There are great benefits in modernizing the investment process, but care must be exercised in the design and implementation of the investment management system. Orange County, California, is one example of a system that took on too much risk by leveraging up its portfolio in a very old-fashioned way. On the other hand, there are quite a few successful models that illustrate the significance of having an independent, well-designed, well-monitored system.

Furthermore, expanding the trust fund investment opportunity set would probably affect the relative interest rates on Treasuries and private securities. Investors do not really credit their implicit investment in the trust fund as it now stands; but if a significant portion of the fund were shifted outside of Treasuries, the effect would likely be to increase rates on Treasuries, and increase prices and lower rates on other securities. This would be beneficial and would improve the efficiency of asset allocation in the economy. It would exert additional market discipline on the federal budget through higher rates, once the deep and captive pool of Social Security investment has been drained away.

In sum, the current Social Security investment strategy is rigid and inefficient, compared with the alternative of applying standard, mature, successful investment management techniques. The Social Security strategy involves leaving a very substantial amount of money on the table. This is pure waste. It is inefficient in the sense that much higher returns could be achieved with the same risk level by using a modern approach. This is a fundamental finding, both in theory and in practice.

How large would, or could, the payoff be? An additional real return of 1 percent should be the lower bound and, if managed well, a 2 percent enhancement, or even higher, might be realistic. And these figures would be net of subsidy implicit in the options that the Treasury Department currently gives to the Social Security fund management.

There are many institutional approaches available. Given the challenges facing the system, it is less important exactly which model is accepted. The ease with which substantial benefits can be achieved argues to get on with the process of improving the Social Security investment management process.

3

Reexamining the Three-Legged Stool

David M. Cutler

THE PAST SIXTY YEARS have witnessed dramatic improvements in the living standards of the elderly. In the 1930s the Great Depression destroyed jobs and life savings. Thirty years ago the elderly were not starving, but one-third of them were still in poverty. Today the elderly are perhaps the best-off group in society. This improvement in income has been built on expansions in all three legs of the "three-legged stool" of retirement income support—Social Security, employer-provided pensions, and individual savings.

And yet even though retirement income support is seemingly guaranteed, new questions loom. The first question is about the strength of the different legs—which should be more important and which less? The continuing Social Security trust fund imbalance, for example, has sparked a debate about how important Social Security should be relative to private sources of savings. In addition, the change in employer pensions from plans that guarantee retirement income (defined benefit pensions) to those that guarantee only a rate of contributions (defined contribution pensions) has led many to fear that retirement income is becoming less certain. For both of these issues, evaluating the right mix among the sources of retirement income is essential.

The second question is whether individuals are saving enough for retirement from all three sources combined. A common fear is that many people do not save enough for retirement and that if public policy does not encourage saving now, these people will have to be supported later.

To address these two questions about retirement income support, this chapter compares Social Security, employer pensions, and individual savings in

I am grateful to Bradford De Long, Edward Gramlich, Sylvester Schieber, Margaret Simms, Jon Skinner, Howard Young, and especially Peter Diamond and Dallas Salisbury for helpful comments.

terms of their retirement guarantee and their economic effects. Because these systems affect people throughout their lives, the analysis focuses on the age groups for which different issues are relevant. For those who are retired, the important issue is the degree to which the systems provide annuities and insure against common risks like inflation or changes in real returns. For those who are nearing retirement, the issue is the extent to which the programs insure against the need to retire early, and their cost in terms of encouraging excessive retirement. Finally, for those at younger ages, the issue centers around the differences in the amount of choice the systems allow, and their implications for labor market efficiency.

No system is best in all of these dimensions. Benefit systems like Social Security and defined benefit pensions are better at guaranteeing stable retirement income and reducing retirement age uncertainty than are contributory systems like defined contribution pensions and individual savings. Social Security and defined benefit pensions, however, have adverse labor market effects that the other systems do not, and do not allow younger individuals choice, as they might prefer. A mix of these systems is warranted, potentially with Social Security focused on a base level of retirement support, and private savings as an important means of providing support above that amount. Because defined benefit pensions have adverse employment effects and do not substantially improve on Social Security, the growing importance of defined contribution pensions is found to be of little concern.

Examination of the adequacy of savings in total yields substantial evidence that many people reach retirement without sufficient savings. As a result, it does seem that public policies to increase retirement savings are needed.

Retirement Income Challenges

Table 3-1 presents information on sources of income for the elderly.[1] Retirement income support has traditionally had three pillars. The first is Social Security. Almost all of the elderly receive Social Security,and Social Security benefits account for over one-third of income for the elderly.[2] Individual savings constitute the second pillar, accounting for about one-quarter of income for the elderly. Employer-based pensions are the third component, ac-

1. Hurd (1990) discusses income among the elderly in more detail. The present discussion focuses on the income aspects of retirement, and therefore explicitly excludes noncash sources of income such as Medicare and Medicaid. A more general treatment of retirement issues would include these programs.

2. Some of these without Social Security are not collecting benefits because they are still working.

Table 3-1. Income for the Elderly, by Source, United States, 1958–88
Percent

Source	1958	1967	1976	1988
	Elderly receiving income			
Social Security	—	86	89	92
Asset income	—	50	56	68
Pensions and annuities	—	18	29	43
Public assistance	—	12	11	7
Earnings	—	27	25	22
	Share of total income			
Social Security	22	26	39	38
Asset income	23	25	18	25
Pensions and annuities	14	14	13	17
Public assistance	5	3	2	1
Earnings	37	30	23	17

SOURCE: Susan Grad, *Income of the Population 55 and Over*, Social Security Administration, annual reports.

counting for 17 percent of income among the elderly. Both asset income and pensions have expanded dramatically in the past twenty years.

This tripartite system of income support has been remarkably successful in improving the welfare of the elderly over the past half century. In 1959 over one-third of the elderly were in poverty, a higher percentage than for either the rest of the adult population or children. By 1992 only 13 percent of the elderly were in poverty, a rate well below that of children and slightly above that of other adults. Indeed, Lawrence Katz and I show that, measured on the basis of consumption instead of income, the elderly have the lowest poverty rate of any demographic group.[3]

Despite the great improvement in the income of the elderly, important questions remain. The first is the optimal mix of these three retirement components. Several factors have brought this issue to the front. Perhaps the most fundamental is Social Security. Social Security reform is inevitable. At the current rate of taxation and benefit payouts, the Social Security trust fund is expected to be bankrupt in 2029. Whether reform should take the form of tax increases or benefit reductions, however, is an open question. If Social Security benefits are an essential part of retirement income, then tax increases may be the most appropriate way to solve the trust fund problem. Conversely, if private savings are preferable to public savings, benefit reductions may be more appropriate. Reexamining the tradeoffs in the three-legged stool may therefore indicate which direction Social Security reform should take.

3. Cutler and Katz (1992).

Changes in the nature of employer pensions are a second concern.[4] Traditionally, employer pensions were defined benefit plans—the employer guaranteed a certain replacement rate for preretirement earnings.[5] Over the past twenty-five years, however, participation in defined benefit pensions has been essentially stagnant, as shown in figure 3-1. In contrast, there has been a dramatic growth in defined contribution pensions—plans that guarantee a fixed contribution rate rather than a replacement rate. Between 1975 and 1989 the share of primary plan enrollment in defined contribution plans rose from 13 percent to 35 percent, and the number of employees with supplemental defined contribution plans tripled.

The fastest growing defined contribution plans are 401(k) plans, where employees contribute a percentage of their earnings, tax-free, to a retirement account.[6] Employers can match the employee contributions. Earnings in the account accrue, tax-free, until they are withdrawn. The investment of the account is at least partly controlled by the individual. The link to the individual makes defined contribution pensions much more like individual savings than like defined benefit pensions.[7]

There has also been a growth of plans that combine defined benefit and defined contribution aspects. For example, some employers have "cash balance" plans that are indexed to investment returns and pay out a lump sum, but that index payments by career average earnings.[8]

The shift out of defined benefit pensions is not a result of employers replacing existing defined benefit plans with new defined contribution ones. Table 3-2 shows that between 1975 and 1988 only 17 percent of the employees with defined benefit terminations had a successor defined contribution plan. Rather, the increased use of defined contribution plans reflects two factors. The first is changes in the size of employers. As table 3-3 shows, three-quarters of small firms rely on defined contribution plans for their primary pension coverage, compared to only one-quarter of large firms. As the size of employers has shrunk, the percentage of primary defined contribution plans has increased. The second factor is increased use

4. See Salisbury (1993).

5. A typical formula, for example, provided for pension benefits equal to 1 percent of average salary in the last five years of employment for each year of service.

6. There are other types of defined contribution plan as well. This discussion focuses mostly on 401(k)s because they are the most rapidly growing type.

7. Indeed, some of the "asset income" in table 3-1 is likely the proceeds of defined contribution pensions, paid as a lump sum to the retiree.

8. I am grateful to Dallas Salisbury for bringing these issues to my attention.

Figure 3-1. Number of Workers with Defined Benefit and Defined Contribution Pension Plans

Millions

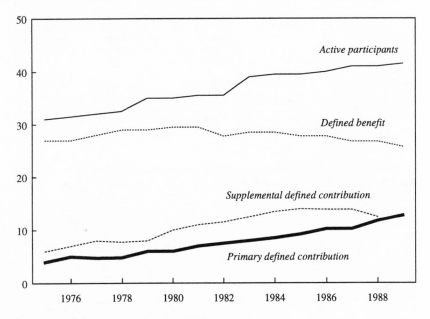

SOURCE: Employee Benefit Research Institute (1994).

of defined contribution plans as supplemental policies in large firms. Table 3-3 shows that almost half of large defined benefit pensions are coupled with a supplemental defined contribution plan.

The economic reasons for these trends have not been fully sorted out. Some have argued that administrative costs created by the Employee Retirement Income Security Act (ERISA) have led firms to prefer defined contribution plans to defined benefit plans. The administrative costs per participant are over twice as high for defined benefit plans as for defined contribution plans. Others argue that the tax-preferred nature of 401(k) contributions make defined contribution plans more attractive. Some have suggested that firms prefer defined contribution plans because they want to avoid the risks associated with market fluctuations or termination costs. Still others argue that nondiscrimination rules in defined benefit plans make it hard for firms to customize these plans to high-wage employees, while there is more flexibility in defined contribution plans. Finally, some argue

Table 3-2. Participants in Terminated Defined Benefit Plans by Intent to Establish Successor Plan, 1975–88

Percent unless otherwise specified

Year	Workers (millions)	Successor Plan		
		Defined benefit	Defined contribution	No new plan or unknown
1975–79	0.3	2	7	91
1980–84	1.8	7	30	64
1985–88	3.3	12	11	77
Total	5.4	10	17	74

SOURCE: Daniel J. Beller and Helen H. Lawrence, "Trends in Private Pension Plan Coverage," in *Trends in Pensions*, 1992, edited by John A. Turner and Daniel J. Beller (Washington, 1992), table 4.17.

Table 3-3. Active Participants Holding Pension Plans, by Type and Size of Plan, United States, 1987

Percent

Type of plan	Number of active participants	
	Up to 100	Over 100
Primary defined benefit plan	25	76
Primary defined contribution plan	75	24
Supplemental defined contribution plan	15	43

SOURCE: Daniel J. Beller and Helen H. Lawrence, "Trends in Private Pension Plan Coverage," in *Trends in Pensions*, edited by John A. Turner and Daniel J. Beller (Washington, 1992), table 4.16.

that increased emphasis on mobility in the work force has led employees to prefer defined contribution plans.[9]

Even if the reasons for the change are not totally clear, some of its implications are. Defined benefit plans are better annuitized than defined contribution plans, since they guarantee a replacement rate on earnings rather than on just the proceeds of investments. Some fear that the shift into defined contribution plans is therefore lowering the annuity value of wealth, and have argued for offsetting the reduction in defined benefit plans with increases in Social Security. Others have suggested reforms that would make defined benefit plans more portable or tax-preferred. It is therefore critical to reexamine the three-legged stool in light of these issues.

The second question that motivates the reexamination of retirement income security is whether individuals are saving sufficiently for retirement through all

9. On the debate in general, see Kruse (1991). Relative administrative costs are discussed in Parsons (1994). In regard to the risk avoidance argument, it should be noted that when a firm switches to a defined contribution plan, its employees wind up bearing much of this risk.

sources combined.[10] The median household nearing retirement holds less than one year's income in financial assets, leading some to argue that saving is not sufficient. Others point to the fact that almost 40 percent of people report using some amount of a lump-sum pension distribution for consumption rather than saving as evidence that people are not sufficiently farsighted. Finally, some cite the fact that the poverty rate of widows is over 20 percent as evidence that families insufficiently prepare for lengthy retirement or death of the husband.[11] If people are not saving sufficiently for retirement, perhaps public policy should encourage or force this saving. This concern is particularly pressing when Social Security benefits are to be cut, or pension coverage is less secure.

Dimensions of Comparison

Because a retirement system has many goals, there are many aspects along which the policies compare. Broadly, there are four types of retirement vehicles: Social Security (including Disability Insurance and Supplemental Security Income), defined benefit pensions, defined contribution pensions, and individual savings. One obvious but important point concerns the ability of the different systems to redistribute income. Several types of redistribution may be desired, whether intergenerational (for example, from future young to current elderly), or intragenerational (for example, from rich to poor, from families with two workers to families with one worker, from men to women). Redistribution is exclusively a province of the public sector. While firms may conduct some internal averaging of costs, redistribution is typically limited by the willingness of employees to work elsewhere. As a result, some public sector involvement is necessary in order to have redistribution in retirement income.[12] Even in Chile, with its privatized retirement system, the government still guarantees a minimum pension to ensure low-income workers a minimum pension.[13] For exactly this reason, ending Social Security is not an option.

Beyond the ability to redistribute, however, the systems differ on other dimensions. It is helpful to group these considerations into three categories, based loosely on the stage in life during which they are relevant. Start at the end

10. Note that this question concerns the microeconomic issue of whether individuals have sufficient assets for retirement consumption, not the macroeconomic issue of whether national savings is appropriate, given demographic trends.
11. See Venti and Wise (1992) on insufficient assets at retirement; Employee Benefits Research Institute (1994a) on consumption of pension distributions; and Quinn and Smeeding (1993) on the poverty rate of widows.
12. See Steuerle and Bakija (1994) for a discussion of redistribution in Social Security.
13. Diamond (1993b).

of life, and consider an individual at retirement age. That individual largely cares about the security of his or her retirement income. If that individual lives a long time, will he or she have sufficient income in old age? If inflation is higher than he or she thought, will that individual have resources to maintain consumption? What if the return to savings is lower than expected? The first question is how the different retirement sources deal with these risks.

Now consider the individual a little earlier in life, when he or she is nearing retirement age. Suppose that the individual plans on retiring at age sixty-five, but that there is some chance that health or other factors will lead to an earlier retirement. This is a risk that the individual would like to insure—by receiving a little more income with early retirement and a little less income if he or she works to an older age. How well the systems deal with this insurance is a second question.

Finally, consider the individual when he or she is young and working. At younger ages, retirement saving is largely an issue of minimizing distortions. Can this individual control his or her own retirement investments, or are they determined by others? Does saving for retirement distort labor supply? Would assets be preserved even in the face of job changes? This set of issues is the third question.

Retirement: Income Security

Consider an individual at retirement age who has only his or her own savings to finance retirement consumption. That individual bears several types of risk. The first is the risk that he or she will live a long time, and thus that personal assets will be insufficient to provide support into very old age. This risk is substantial. In the mid-1970s, for example, about one-third of those turning age sixty-five could expect to die before age seventy-five, another one-third could expect to live to age seventy-five but die before age eighty-five, and the remaining third could expect to live beyond age eighty-five. An individual with a fixed amount of assets would therefore have faced great uncertainty about life span and the ability to consume adequately.

A second type of risk is the variability of inflation rates. In an environment of zero or steady inflation, an individual can plan consumption and savings decisions appropriately. When inflation is variable, however, individuals holding nominal assets bear some risk. If inflation is higher than expected, and income is guaranteed nominally, the real value of retirement support will be low. Conversely, if inflation is lower than expected, the real value of retirement income will be high. Again, the individual would like to insure this risk by having at least some of this retirement consumption guaranteed in real terms.

A third type of risk is the variability of return on assets. This is similar to inflation risk in that it affects the real value of a person's retirement wealth.[14] It may be, for example, that just as a cohort reaches retirement age, the value of that generation's assets falls substantially. This could occur randomly or be systematically related to the size of cohorts. For example, Gregory Mankiw and David Weil show that house prices rose as the baby boom generation started purchasing homes, and argue that prices will fall when the baby boomers sell their homes; Sylvester Schieber and John Shoven argue that the same may be true for stocks, bonds, and other financial assets; and Jerry Green shows that differences in wages resulting from cohort size differentials can explain fluctuations of average consumption over a lifetime on the order of 20 percent.[15] Moreover, the variability of asset income is not limited to financial issues such as changing portfolio values. Any change in plan rules—benefit payments, vesting—act as a change in the pension return. Workers and retirees would like to avoid these risks.

In all of these cases, individuals would like to have retirement income insurance. Or, to view the problem another way, what individuals want in their retirement is a benefit stream, rather than the proceeds of a contribution rate. For several reasons, private markets do not provide this type of benefit insurance.[16]

The first reason, illustrated best with the example of annuities, is adverse selection. When annuities are purchased voluntarily, they are more likely to be bought by those who know that they will probably live a long time. As a result, selling actuarially fair annuities would require insurers to take a financial loss. Instead, they would have to sell annuities at a premium. This, in turn, would limit sales even more strictly to those who expect to live a long time. Equilibrium would occur where only those who expect to live a long time purchase annuities, and annuities sell for a price far above average cost in the population as a whole.

Benjamin Friedman and Mark Warshawsky show that just this pattern obtains in annuity markets. They calculate that adverse selection raises the price of annuities by about 15 percent above what would obtain if purchase were unrelated to expected lifetimes. In addition, they document substantial

14. One can also think of variations in mortality rates as an example of macroeconomic risk.

15. Mankiw and Weil (1989), Schieber and Shoven (1994), and Green (1988).

16. See Diamond (1993a) and Bodie, Marcus, and Merton (1988) for a more detailed discussion of these points.

administrative expense in annuity costs, on the order of 18 to 33 percent. These administrative expenses further reduce the desirability of private annuities. Indeed, it is not surprising that very few people purchase private annuities.[17]

Similarly, private markets do not insure against aggregate risks like inflation or real interest rate fluctuations very well. The reason for this is that aggregate risks are common to every individual in a cohort. When inflation is high, it is high for everyone who is currently retired. When the average asset return is low, it will be low for everyone with the same portfolio. Thus these risks cannot be diversified by members of any one generation pooling the risk amongst themselves. Insurance companies consider these risks to be large (since they affect a whole cohort) and as a result, often choose not to bear them.

Thus the annuities on the market today are nominal, rather than real annuities. Even when individuals purchase variable annuities (which increase the benefits over time) these typically are not adjusted for actual inflation, but increase by a predetermined amount. The annuitant still bears the risk of unexpected inflation. When the risk is borne by the insurer, it is only with a risk premium. Some of the administrative load in the sale of annuities, for example, may in fact be a risk premium for insurers bearing the risk that the average mortality experience will be lower than anticipated.

As a result of this, contribution-based systems like defined contribution pensions or individual savings are relatively poor at insuring retirement risks. In 1989 only 28 percent of defined contribution plans offered an annuity option, and about 30 percent of 401(k) plans offer an annuity option in the mid-1990s. Individual annuity sales are also extremely small. In effect, annuitization is not available from these savings vehicles. Neither one increments wealth if average asset returns turn out to be low.

Social Security and defined benefit pensions insure at least some of these risks. Both provide annuities. They both solve the adverse selection problem by a form of mandatory pooling. In the case of Social Security, the pooling is truly mandatory—individuals must participate in the system. There is no way for sick individuals to opt out, knowing that they would not receive significant benefits. Defined benefit pensions are mandatorily grouped at the firm level. With a large enough pool of employees and a high enough level of participation, the variability of average lifespan to the plan sponsor is likely to be small.

While both Social Security and defined benefit pensions generally overcome the adverse selection problem, they differ in two respects. First, since

17. Friedman and Warshawsky (1988). The administrative costs may be the result of processing costs, the costs of marketing and advertising, or a risk premium for the insurer bearing the mortality risk. There has been no decomposition of the administrative load into these various factors.

pensions are managed at the firm level, the price that the firm faces in providing annuities to its workers is the average mortality experience of those workers. If the firm has employees who are generally healthy, the cost of annuities will be high, and the firm is likely to charge the employees for this in the form of lower benefits, or lower wages while working. With Social Security, in contrast, the whole population is in the same pool and thus pays the same price.

Second, Social Security benefits are indexed, whereas private pensions generally are not.[18] Only one-quarter of private defined benefit plans had any postretirement benefit increases between 1984 and 1989, for example, and only half had any benefit increase in the high-inflation period of 1978 to 1983.

The handling of aggregate risks like inflation is complicated since, by definition, not even the government can pool something that is common to everyone. For example, the fact that Social Security is indexed means that higher inflation leads to additional benefit payments.[19] More generally, when population growth or real wage growth is low (the counterpart to a real return in a pay-as-you-go system), Social Security faces a financing gap. Similarly, when real returns are low, defined benefit pensions face a financing gap.[20]

The two systems deal with these risks in different ways. In the case of Social Security, financing gaps are dealt with through either benefit cuts (making retirees bear the risk) or tax increases (making current and future workers bear the risk). The choice between these two options is, in fact, the current problem facing Social Security. The distribution of the burden between these sources depends on the political process and will not be the same at all times.

With private pensions, determining who bears the risk of aggregate returns is just as difficult. Some assert that the shareholders of the firm offering the pension will bear the risk, since they are the holders of the firm's assets and liabilities. If shareholders and workers implicitly share profits, however, then employers may respond to poor investment returns or poor corporate performance by passing back some of the shortfall to workers or retirees, either by lowering wages or by reducing the generosity of the pension plan. Some evidence suggests this occurs, although the degree to which risk can be passed back to current and future workers is limited by their ability to work for other firms.[21]

---

18. It is possible that the private sector would sell real annuities if the government issued real bonds as a hedge.

19. There is no need to consider the effect on contributions here since the right comparison between Social Security and defined benefit pensions is on benefits only.

20. In the 1980s, by contrast, real interest rates were extremely high, and many defined benefit pensions were overfunded.

21. See Bulow and Scholes (1983).

The effect of adverse shocks on shareholders, workers, and retirees is likely to vary from firm to firm and may change over time. Firms facing different labor market conditions, wage-setting institutions, and financial status may adjust to these shocks in different ways. Even when firms do bear such risks, they may demand some additional compensation for doing so. Thus the total compensation package (benefits plus pensions) may be lower in firms where shareholders have agreed to these stable payments. Unfortunately, there has been no research on the extent to which compensation responds to assumption of macroeconomic risk, nor on the distribution of any gains and losses between current workers and retirees.

The question of who really bears aggregate risk in both Social Security and defined benefit pensions is thus somewhat uncertain, although the retiree is clearly better immunized in either of these systems than in defined contribution pensions and individual savings. Because Social Security is explicitly indexed and there is the possibility of transferring to future generations, it would seem that Social Security has provided a more stable guarantee to the elderly than have defined benefit pensions.

If individuals desire benefit guarantees during retirement, therefore, Social Security is almost certainly the best option. Indeed, many have argued that as defined benefit pensions become less important, it would be advisable to increase Social Security or mandate universal defined benefit plans in order to maintain the level of annuitization. While the desire for some level of annuitization is certainly warranted, two issues are missing from the discussion. First, Social Security already has a long-term financing crisis, and future benefits cannot really be guaranteed until that crisis is dealt with. Second, there have been very few calculations of the optimal amount of annuitization. People who want to leave bequests, for example, do not want to annuitize all of their wealth. The demand for life insurance among the elderly testifies to some desire for less annuitization than people already have.[22] Unfortunately, economists have not had much success in identifying this optimal amount. As a result, there is no reason to believe that dramatic expansions of Social Security to meet the annuitization needs of the elderly are in order.

---

22. Life insurance acts as a reverse annuity. Payments are made while the individual is alive, in exchange for a lump sum payment at death. Presumably, if Social Security is overly annuitizing retirement wealth, individuals can fully offset this with life insurance purchases. Transactions costs and selection factors in this market may make full offset infeasible, however.

Near-Retirement: Retirement Age Risk

The second concern is over the age at which an individual will want to retire. Consider an individual with a defined contribution pension who is planning to retire at age sixty-five. Benefits for that person when he or she turns sixty-five are exactly determined by what he or she contributes when working. In the simplest case, for example, a constant percent of earnings each year are placed in an account for retirement and distributed at age sixty-five.

There is some chance, however, that older people's health will deteriorate during their early sixties, or that they will get fired from a job for which they had specific skills, and that they will want to retire early. If they do so, however, they lose the income that they would have received had they continued working, plus the pension contributions that would have been made on their behalf. This loss may be substantial. In 1992, for example, average earnings among males ages fifty-five to sixty-four were almost $39,000, and average earnings for females were almost $24,000. Employer contributions to pensions are not included in these figures.

Thus it is natural for an individual to want an insurance policy that offers coverage against the risk of needing to retire early. Full insurance would make up for the loss of both pension contributions and wage and salary income. However, full insurance is not optimal because of the problem of moral hazard. If additional payments are made to people who retire early, some of those who would have preferred to retire at a later age will decide to retire early. Unless people can be perfectly screened to determine who would have retired in the absence of a subsidy, some of the money will go to those who were induced to retire by the additional income. In the presence of moral hazard, partial insurance is the right policy. Some payments should be made to those who retire early, since retirement is the right decision for many, but these payments should not make up totally for lost income.

Neither defined contribution pensions nor individual savings provide any retirement age insurance.[23] If an individual retires early, these vehicles do not increase the amount of retirement support. On the other hand, Social Security and defined benefit pensions generally do pay more to early retirees. Social Security does this in a number of ways. First, the Disability Insurance program ensures incomes for many of those in very poor health. Second, the net transfer

23. This is true comparing these vehicles to a defined benefit plan or Social Security with the same present value of income. If defined contribution plans or individual savings provided more retirement income on average than defined benefit plans or Social Security, there would be wealth effects favoring these plans.

in the Old Age Insurance portion of Social Security is greater for those who retire earlier than for those who retire later. Eugene Steuerle and Jon Bakija show that the net gain to a medium-wage male worker from retiring at age sixty-two rather than at age sixty-five is $6,700, and the net cost from retiring at age seventy rather than at age sixty-five is $17,600.[24]

Defined benefit pensions also tend to subsidize early retirement. The extent of the subsidy is difficult to analyze because the provisions vary so greatly, and because determining the profile of contributions requires knowledge of what wages at each age would have been in the absence of the pension plan. The latter task is generally hard, so most analysts look only at pension accrual rates. Laurence Kotlikoff and David Wise show that accrual rates tend to be very high at early and normal retirement ages. They are typically negative after normal retirement age, and often small or negative between early and normal retirement ages. Thus there is some indication that defined benefit pensions also encourage early retirement.[25]

There has been a great deal of economic debate over how much actual retirement behavior is influenced by the early retirement incentives of Social Security and defined benefit pensions.[26] The predominance of retirement at ages sixty-two and sixty-five suggests to many that Social Security and pensions do affect retirement provisions. About 20 percent of those working at age sixty-one retire at age sixty-two, and another 20 percent of those working at age sixty-four retire at age sixty-five. In total, only about 10 percent of people over age sixty-five are in the labor force.

The microeconomic literature on this question is mixed. While most studies support the view that Social Security affects retirement, most of the estimates suggest that Social Security and pension benefits cannot, by themselves, explain all of the increase in retirement. Estimates of the effects of particular pension provisions (especially early retirement "windows"), however, tend to find much larger effects. Further, many analysts have criticized the microeconomic evidence as too limited. By specifying normal and early retirement ages, they allege, Social Security has established norms of retirement behavior that have effects independent of the particular financial incentives they carry. For example, the typical view of retirement is that it should occur as early as possible, but not later than age sixty-five. Thus it seems likely that Social Security and defined benefit pensions have contributed substantially to the moral hazard problem of early retirement.

24. Steuerle and Bakija (1994).
25. See Kotlikoff and Wise (1987).
26. For recent reviews, see Lumsdaine (1994), Steuerle ; nd Bakija (1994), and Hurd (1990).

Balancing the insurance value of transfers to early retirees against the moral hazard of induced retirement is extremely difficult. There are two issues here. The first is a question of aggregate labor supply—is it preferable to encourage more or less labor supply? Given the trends in fertility and Social Security replacement rates over the past several decades, it would now seem advisable to encourage increased labor supply among older workers.

The second question is of the balance at the individual level—have the needs for early retirement increased or decreased and, hence, has the moral hazard problem increased or lessened? As life expectancy has increased and jobs have become physically less demanding, it is plausible that the ability to work at older ages has increased and the incidence of employment-inhibiting disability has fallen. It appears, therefore, that less generous early retirement provisions and increases in the age of normal retirement are now more optimal policies than they were several years ago, and as such, deserve further discussion.

Young Workers: Avoiding Distortions

The final set of issues to consider is the effect of different retirement systems on economic efficiency during the working years. Two aspects are considered here: the amount of choice that each savings vehicle allows individuals, and the labor market impacts of each system.[27]

There are several reasons for individuals to have choice over where their retirement funds are invested. Individuals may have different tolerances for risk bearing. Those with a greater tolerance for risk, for example, may prefer equities to bonds. Younger people may have systematic preferences for some types of assets relative to older people. In addition, competition among investments may result in higher returns. Allowing choice over retirement savings may thus be one goal of a retirement system.

On this metric, Social Security and defined benefit plans fare poorly. Neither allows individuals to direct their contributions at all (nor does Social Security itself invest much of the contributions). This is one consequence of a system focused on benefits rather than contributions. Defined contribution plans and individual savings provide the most choice.

Some economic research has speculated on the right amount of choice. One consequence of a choice-based system is the worry that individuals will not

27. One of the most important aspects of this debate is the macroeconomic effect of funded and unfunded retirement systems on national savings. This is the subject of a different discussion, however. See chapter 2.

invest their assets wisely. In fact, however, individuals tend to be very conservative retirement investors.[28] Individuals with defined contribution plans, on average, invest less in equities and bonds and more in cash and other assets than do managers of defined benefit plans.

A second potential drawback of a choice-based system is that it has higher administrative expenses. Social Security, for example, has generally reported administrative expenses of 1 percent of benefits paid. Administrative and other expenses amount to 11 percent of the benefits of defined benefit plans, and 6 percent of those of defined contribution plans. The fully privatized Chilean pension system, in contrast, has administrative costs of over 20 percent of contributions. Some of the administrative expense that accompanies choice-based systems is valuable. It is the cost of managing individual contributions, adjusting portfolios, and marketing products. A certain amount, however, is likely due to profits resulting from low demand elasticity. As a result, some have argued for a system of group insurance purchase, in which demand may be very elastic, rather than a social insurance model or a pure individual choice model.[29]

The other main consideration is the effect of retirement vehicles on labor supply. There are two particular concerns here. The first is the incentive effects of the Social Security system. In general, income taxation to fund the government distorts the labor supply decisions of individuals, resulting in a deadweight loss from public provision. This need not be true of Social Security. If individuals perceive a link between their Social Security contributions when young and their benefits when old, the "Social Security tax" will be viewed simply as an individual contribution for retirement and will involve no deadweight loss.[30]

Of course, benefits are not related to taxes for everyone in an actuarially fair manner. Social Security redistributes from those with higher incomes to those with lower incomes, making the return to high-income people particularly low. In that sense, it involves some tax. Martin Feldstein and Andrew Samwick report that the net marginal Social Security tax rate for males ranges from 7.5 percent for high earners without a dependent spouse to –33.4 percent for low earners with a dependent spouse.[31]

More important, changes in the actuarial status of Social Security over time have probably contributed to a widespread skepticism that Social Security will

28. See VanDerhei (1992).

29. See Diamond (1993b), which also presents many of the numerical estimates on which the present discussion is based.

30. This is the principle of "benefit taxation" that is at the heart of public finance.

31. Feldstein and Samwick (1992).

not return much of the contributions that current workers are making.[32] A large share of young Americans, for example, expect to get little or nothing out of Social Security, and this share is growing over time. As a result, much of Social Security contributions are probably perceived as a tax rather than saving for retirement.

The evidence of the importance of this distortion is mixed.[33] While many believe that labor supply among prime-age men is relatively inelastic, most economic evidence suggests that labor supply for married women is more elastic. There is likely, therefore, to be some labor market distortion caused by Social Security. Employer-based systems cause much less distortion, since they are less redistributive to begin with, and there is a clearer link between contributions while working and payments received while retired. Along this dimension, private systems are therefore superior to Social Security.

Indeed, the growing importance of the Social Security tax suggests that more public discussion of the structure of the system is in order. Social Security was explicitly designed with two goals: to guarantee a minimum level of income during retirement, and to be a source of savings for retirement. The latter goal is accomplished by linking benefits to contributions—the more an individual saves, the more he or she gets back during retirement. If individuals do not perceive Social Security as a form of savings but, rather, as a tax, the argument for increasing benefits with contributions fails. The remaining goal is therefore income security, which is best achieved by having a flat benefit structure regardless of how much people have contributed. Over time, the optimal Social Security system seems to be moving in the direction of more uniform payouts, regardless of the individual contribution.

Defined benefit pensions, while involving less general taxation than Social Security, have adverse job mobility effects.[34] Individuals change jobs many times over the course of a lifetime, and often these transitions are unpredictable. In a nondistortionary situation, pension wealth would travel with people from job to job. This is true, for example, of Social Security, defined contribution pensions, and individual savings. All of these vehicles provide benefits independent of where the employment took place.[35]

Most defined benefit pensions are not portable, however, and this fact lowers their value substantially. All defined benefit plans have vesting require-

---

32. See Boskin, Kotlikoff, and Shoven (1988).

33. See Hausman (1985) for a review.

34. See Bodie, Marcus, and Merton (1988) for more discussion of the employment effects of pensions in general.

35. Some defined contribution plans provide for increasing contributions with length of service, but this is rare.

ments—usually, five years. Employees who leave a job before that period may have been making implicit contributions to the plan (by receiving a lower wage) but will not receive any benefits. More important, defined benefit plans generally are not indexed between the period when an employee leaves a job and when he or she collects retirement benefits. As a result, benefits earned at a job long before retirement will be worth substantially less than benefits earned at a job just before retirement. Workers who change jobs many times will receive fewer benefits than workers who do not change jobs, even if they are covered by a pension plan for each year.[36]

This loss is often substantial. Hay/Huggins, a consulting firm, has estimated the losses from job turnover for an average worker to be 15 percent of potential pension benefits under defined benefit plans.[37] For some workers, the loss can be as high as 30 or 40 percent.

On the one hand, portability loss exposes workers to the risk of variable job span, which they might otherwise want to insure. On the other hand, it helps employers to retain workers who might otherwise leave the firm. This latter implication is important if high turnover is one reason why firms do not provide more on-the-job training. Determining whether lower turnover is on net beneficial involves weighing these two issues. Few such calculations have been made in the literature, but in the absence of firm conclusions, my sense is that the beneficial aspects of lower turnovers are outweighed by the increased risk borne by workers.

Do Americans Save Enough?

So far, the discussion has considered the tradeoffs between different retirement instruments, assuming that individuals were fully informed about their retirement needs. An equally important question, however, is whether individuals save enough for retirement from all sources of income combined.

The suspicion that, left to themselves, individuals would not save enough for retirement pervades the Social Security debate. It is not difficult to find explanations for why saving would be inadequate. If individuals do not know enough about their retirement needs, or are poor financial planners, or lack self-control, their retirement saving may indeed be insufficient.[38]

36. The hybrid defined benefit-defined contribution plans discussed above solve many of these mobility issues.

37. Reported in Turner (1993). About 25 percent of this estimated loss is due to preretirement consumption of lump-sum pension distributions. This component of the loss should be omitted if the decision not to save the lump sum was rationally made.

38. See Diamond (1977), Blinder (1988), Poterba (1994), and Thaler (1994) for discussion.

As a first step, it is necessary to estimate how much people *should* be saving. As noted above, the fact that so many people consume lump-sum pension distributions is often cited as evidence they do not save enough. This argument is not particularly persuasive, however, since it does not control for liquidity factors that would influence the consumption-or-savings decision. For example, the percent of people consuming some of their lump-sum distribution ranges from 43 percent among those ages twenty-one to thirty, to 26 percent among those ages sixty-one to sixty-four.[39] This is at least consistent with the view that younger people want more consumption power than they are otherwise able to get.

It is more useful to ask whether people who are working accumulate sufficient assets to finance a reasonable level of consumption after they retire. A common economic benchmark is that people should save enough while working to maintain the same level of consumption after they retire.

What does this suggest? Generally, Social Security and pension income replace about 50 to 60 percent of preretirement income. Social Security is a greater source of postretirement income for low-income people, while private pensions are more prevalent among higher-income people. Individuals do not consume all of their income while they are working. If they were consuming 80 percent of income, for example, they would need sufficient assets to replace 20 to 30 percent of their preretirement income for each year of retirement. People who expect to live for fifteen years after retirement (which is roughly the life expectancy at age sixty-five), would require assets of about two to three times income at retirement. More detailed simulations, Bernheim and Scholz, this amount of asset holdings is optimal.[40]

If needs differ between the young and old, individuals will not want to consume the same amount when they are retired as when they are working. But it is not clear, a priori, how needs vary over the life cycle. Since older people are more infirm than younger people, they may want more money to pay for medical expenditures. On the other hand, if the value of leisure-time activities falls with age, people may want less income to spend on these activities in retirement. It is difficult to weight these effects against each other. A benchmark of constant consumption seems useful, however, and thus a wealth level of two to three times annual income is probably about right.

Before considering data on actual asset holdings, it is important to note one point about predicted levels of retirement savings. While Social Security is not means-tested, other forms of retirement income are, including Supplemental

---

39. EBRI (1994a).
40. Bernheim and Scholz (1993).

Security Income and Medicaid. Thus in order to qualify for either of these programs, private income and most assets have to be exhausted first. To the extent people believe they are likely to need these programs, it may be optimal not to save much for retirement.[41] To date, there has not been a great deal of empirical evidence presented on this issue.

Table 3-4 presents evidence on income and wealth among households with a head aged 55 to 64. The median income was $32,000 in 1989. Income was higher for those with a college degree than for those with less education. The median total wealth was $97,200. Thus the median wealth was roughly three times the median income, about the level predicted from the life-cycle model.[42] Indeed, assets were over twice as great as the median income for all education groups. So it might be thought that asset holdings were sufficient.

Three points are worth noting about asset holdings, however. First, even if the median household has sufficient assets for retirement, there are still a substantial number of households with very low retirement assets. As the third column indicates, for 20 percent of all households total wealth was equal to less than one year's income, which is surely a low value. The heads of most of these households do not have a high school degree, or have only a high school degree.

Indeed, recent trends in wealth holdings raise additional concerns along these lines. As table 3-5 shows, pension coverage actually declined between 1979 and 1988 for young men and for men with less education. Other evidence suggests that the financial assets of families with a head aged thirty-five to forty-four were no higher in the early 1990s than they were for the same age group in 1962. If these households do not receive pensions or save individually, they may approach retirement in the same situation as current cohorts.

The second fact about asset holding is that the dominant form of wealth is housing wealth. The median wealth excluding housing was only $28,500 in 1989—less than median income. Indeed, nonhousing assets were only one-quarter of the median income for households whose head lacked a high school degree, and about 80 percent of the median income for those with a head who had a high school degree but not a college degree. Median nonhousing wealth was only significantly greater than median income for those households whose head had a college degree. Over half of the households headed by someone

41. See Hubbard, Skinner, and Zeldes (1995). The rules do vary by program and type of asset.
42. Since housing wealth is included in total wealth, income should include the implicit income that homeowners are paying themselves as rent (equivalently, consumption needs are made greater by the implicit consumption of housing). Without the microeconomic data, I am unable to make an adjustment for this effect. The net effect, however, is to make wealth-to-income levels seem greater than they really are, and thus to minimize the amount of low savings.

Table 3-4. Financial Resources for Households with Head Ages Fifty-Five to Sixty-Four, United States, 1989
Dollars unless otherwise specified

Group	Median income	Total wealth		Nonhousing wealth	
		Median	Percent with wealth < income	Median	Percent with wealth < income
Less than high school education	20,100	46,100	28	5,600	56
High school education	38,800	96,300	18	27,800	36
College degree and above	58,100	210,900	3	126,000	7
All	32,300	97,200	19	28,500	38

Source: Congressional Budget Office (1993).

without a high school degree had less than half a year's income in financial assets.

Thus if housing wealth is not viewed as an asset for retirement consumption, or if it is used to finance only housing consumption, the share of households with inadequate saving is even greater. The question of the fungibility of housing wealth is a long-standing one in the literature. Some analysts argue that individuals do not, in fact, run down housing assets when they are elderly, and thus that housing wealth should not be considered a source of retirement consumption. This can be rationalized with a "mental accounts" view of saving—if individuals think of savings in different "baskets," they may not view housing wealth as substitutable for financial wealth. The lack of a large market in reverse annuity mortgages is commonly cited as evidence of this incomplete substitution.[43]

Others argue that individuals could consume housing wealth if other income were to fall too low.[44] This view suggests that housing wealth ought to be considered as a form of wealth, and that the median family is saving about the right amount. The illiquidity of housing wealth, however, is likely to make it less than perfectly substitutable for consumption, and therefore more weight should probably be placed on the low asset holdings in nonhousing wealth than total wealth including housing.

43. Of course, this could be due to the adverse selection problems in annuity markets noted above. See Venti and Wise (1992), Bernheim and Scholz (1993), and Hubbard, Skinner and Zeldes (1995) for further discussion of the argument presented here, and Sheffrin and Thaler (1988) on the "mental accounts" view, in particular.

44. See, for example, Congressional Budget Office (1993).

Table 3-5. Males with Pension Coverage, United States, 1979 and 1988
Percent

Group	1979	1988	Change
All	70	61	– 9
By age			
25–34	64	50	– 14
35–64	73	68	– 5
By education			
Less than high school	61	44	– 17
High school	71	61	– 10
College degree and above	76	70	– 6

Source: David E. Bloom and Richard B. Freeman, "The Fall in Private Pension Coverage in the U.S." *American Economic Review* (May 1992), 539–45.

The third point to note about asset holdings is that even if the level of saving is optimal given current Social Security rules, it may not be optimal if these rules have to be changed. The point here is related to the old adage "don't put all your eggs in one basket." If some people are relying on Social Security for all of their retirement income, that limits the government's ability to modify the program. Yet it is essential to reform Social Security over the next several decades. One way to ease the pain of this coming transition is to encourage people to rely more on other forms of saving.

It is hard to escape the conclusion that a substantial share of people are not saving enough for retirement. Given the current financing problems in Social Security, public programs almost certainly cannot be used to cover this gap. Therefore it is important to encourage more private saving for retirement. Thinking about how to do so is a major challenge for the public sector. While many have suggested expanded IRAs or premium savings accounts, others argue that extensions of the pension system to lower income workers is more appropriate.[45] The analysis of this issue, however, is beyond the scope of the present discussion.

Conclusions

This discussion has largely summarized the issues involved in comparing retirement income systems and evaluating the overall level of private saving. Four conclusions are warranted.

45. See Venti and Wise (1992), Bernheim and Scholz (1993), and Thaler (1994), respectively.

First, it is important to maintain the Social Security system at a reasonable level, since individuals certainly want some real annuity, and the program offers the most insurance along these lines. It is also the only universal annuity program. The fact that saving is so low, particularly among the poor, suggests that lowering the base amount of Social Security is unwise. As the perceived link between Social Security benefits and taxes declines, however, it will become less essential that Social Security pay out as much to higher-income recipients as it currently does. A flattening of the Social Security benefit profile seems warranted.

Second, the inducement to retirement is becoming an increasingly important problem over time. Reducing the incentives for early retirement in Social Security, in conjunction with an enhanced Disability Insurance program, may be one reasonable reform. Changes in normal retirement ages are a second.

Third, the shift from defined benefit to defined contribution pensions is not particularly worrisome. Defined benefit pensions do not provide any types of benefits that Social Security does not, and they produce labor market distortions that defined contribution plans do not. Indeed, many employees would not have a pension if firms did not have the ability to offer defined contribution plans.

Fourth, it is important that people save more for retirement, particularly those who are less educated. This is particularly true given the likely course of Social Security in the future. In part, increased saving may be achieved by discouraging the use of retirement funds prior to retirement age. Other forms of saving incentives may also be valuable. Designing such incentives is an important public policy challenge.

References

Bernheim, B. Douglas, and John K. Scholz. 1993. "Private Saving and Public Policy." In *Tax Policy and the Economy*, vol. 7, edited by James Poterba. University of Chicago Press.

Blinder, Alan S. 1988. "Why is the Government in the Pension Business?" In *Social Security and Private Pensions*, edited by Susan M. Wachter. Lexington, Mass.: Lexington Books.

Bodie, Zvi, Alan J. Marcus, and Robert C. Merton. 1988. "Defined Benefit versus Defined Contribution Pension Plans: What Are the Real Trade-Offs?" In *Pensions in the U.S. Economy*, edited by Zvi Bodie, John B. Shoven, and David A. Wise. University of Chicago Press.

Boskin, Michael J., Laurence J. Kotlikoff, and John B. Shoven. 1988. "Personal Security Accounts: A Proposal for Fundamental Social Security Reform." In *Social

Security and Private Pensions, edited by Susan M. Wachter. Lexington, Mass.: Lexington Books.

Bulow, Jeremy I., and Myron S. Scholes. 1983. "Who Owns the Assets in a Defined-Benefit Pension Plan?" In *Financial Aspects of the United States Pension System*, edited by Zvi Bodie and John B. Shoven. University of Chicago Press.

Congressional Budget Office. 1993. "Baby Boomers in Retirement: An Early Perspective." Washington (September).

Cutler, David M., and Lawrence F. Katz. 1992. "Rising Inequality? Changes in the Distribution of Income and Consumption in the 1980s." *American Economic Review* 82 (May): 546–51.

Diamond, Peter. 1977. "A Framework for Social Security Analysis." *Journal of Public Economics* 8(3): 275–98.

——. 1993a. "Issues in Social Insurance." Massachusetts Institute of Technology, Department of Economics.

——. 1993b. "Privatization of Social Security: Lessons from Chile." Working Paper 4510. Cambridge, Mass.: National Bureau of Economic Research (October).

Feldstein, Martin, and Andrew Samwick. 1992. "Social Security Rules and Marginal Tax Rates." *National Tax Journal* 45 (March): 1–22.

Friedman, Benjamin M., and Mark Warshawsky. 1988. "Annuity Prices and Savings Behavior in the United States." In *Pensions in the U.S. Economy*, edited by Zvi Bodie, John B. Shoven, and David A. Wise. University of Chicago Press.

Green, Jerry R. 1988. "Demographics, Market Failure, and Social Security." In *Social Security and Private Pensions*, edited by Susan M. Wachter. Lexington, Mass.: Lexington Books.

Hausman, Jerry. 1985. "Taxes and Labor Supply." In *Handbook of Public Economics*, edited by Alan Auerbach and Martin Feldstein, vol. 1, ch. 4. North Holland.

Hubbard, R. Glenn, Jonathan Skinner, and Stephen P. Zeldes. 1995. "Precautionary Saving and Social Insurance." *Journal of Political Economy,* 103 (April): 360–99.

Hurd, Michael D. 1990. "Research on the Elderly: Economic Status, Retirement, and Consumption and Saving." *Journal of Economic Literature* 28 (June): 565–637.

Kotlikoff, Laurence J., and David A. Wise. 1987. "The Incentive Effects of Private Pension Plans." In *Issues in Pension Economics*, edited by Zvi Bodie, John B. Shoven, and David A. Wise. University of Chicago Press.

Kruse, Douglas L. 1991. "Pension Substitution in the 1980s: Why the Shift Toward Defined Contribution Pension Plans?" Working Paper 3882. Cambridge, Mass.: National Bureau of Economic Research (October).

Lumsdaine, Robin L. 1994. "The Effects of Labor Supply Decisions on Retirement Behavior and Income." Princeton University, Department of Economics.

Mankiw, N. Gregory, and David N. Weil. 1989. "The Baby Boom, the Baby Bust, and the Housing Market." *Regional Science and Urban Economics,* 19 (2): 235–58.

Parsons, Donald O. 1994. "Retirement Behavior and Retirement Income: The Role of the Firm." Ohio State University, Department of Economics.

Poterba, James M. 1994. "Personal Saving Behavior and Retirement Income Modelling: A Research Assessment." Massachusetts Institute of Technology, Department of Economics.

Quinn, Joseph F., and Timothy M. Smeeding. 1993. "The Present and Future Economic Well-Being of the Aged." In *Pensions in a Changing Economy*, edited by Dallas Salisbury. Washington: Employee Benefit Research Institute.

Salisbury, Dallas L. 1993. "Policy Implications of Changes in Employer Pension Protection." In *Pensions in a Changing Economy*, edited by Dallas Salisbury. Washington: Employee Benefit Research Institute.

Schieber, Sylvester J., and John B. Shoven. 1994. "The Consequences of Population Aging on Private Pension Fund Savings and Asset Markets." Working Paper 4665. Cambridge, Mass.: National Bureau of Economic Research.

Sheffrin, Hersh M., and Richard H. Thaler. 1988. "The Behavioral Life-Cycle Hypothesis." *Economic Inquiry* 26 (October): 609–43.

Steuerle, Eugene, and Jon M. Bakija. 1994. *Retooling Social Security for the 21st Century*. Washington: Urban Institute.

Thaler, Richard H. 1994. "Psychology and Savings Policies." *American Economic Review* 84 (May, *Papers and Proceedings, 1994*): 186–92.

Turner, John A. 1993. *Pension Policy for a Mobile Labor Force*. Kalamazoo, Mich.: Upjohn Institute.

VanDerhei, Jack. 1992. "New Evidence That Employees Choose Conservative Investments for Their Retirement Funds," EBRI, *Employee Benefit Notes* 13 (February): 1–3.

Venti, Steven F., and David A. Wise. 1993. "Government Policy and Retirement Savings." In *Tax Policy and the Economy*, vol. 6, edited by James Poterba. University of Chicago Press.

Comment by Edward Gramlich

David Cutler focuses on two questions, using his analogy of the three-legged stool: first, whether the legs are in balance; second, whether they are long enough. That is, considering all sources of retirement income, is there enough retirement saving taking place?

On the balance question, Cutler frames the issue well by recognizing that people of different ages usually have different goals. He argues that there are advantages and disadvantages to each of the legs. In particular, depending on an individual's age, both public defined benefit plans and private defined contribution plans can provide advantages. So a sensible system of providing for retirement income would have both, as is now the case. He also shows how there could easily be a generational split on this question: that people of some ages would see the advantages of the public defined benefit plans, and people of other ages would see more advantages in the defined contribution plans.

Two issues that he raises will be very prominent in the public debate about retirement income provision that will almost certainly continue for the rest of our lifetimes. One is whether it would make sense to "flatten" the public benefit system (Social Security) by taking more from high-income people—either in terms of a tax increase or a benefit reduction. The other is whether it would make sense to raise the normal retirement age. Because of my position on the Social Security advisory council, I cannot comment publicly on these issues at this time.

On the question of whether saving is sufficient, there is more to say. The United States is undersaving and has a matured public defined benefit plan. This means the implicit rate of return on the public defined benefit plan will be the growth in the real wage base, which is roughly 1 percent. If national saving is increased, whether through the government or in private pensions, the rate of return will be close to the world real rate of interest, however that is defined. Currently, it is probably on the order of 3 percent. Thus raising national saving produces a big marginal increase in rate of return, as Barry Bosworth argued above.

Cutler approaches the question differently, in a manner that is both interesting and relevant. He determines how much it is necessary for people to save while they are working, so that they will have the same standard of consumption in retirement. While this is a reasonable approach, there are a few problems with the way that he makes this calculation and, implicitly, with the number that he arrives at.

The standard is that individuals plan consumption over their lifetimes. When they retire they must decide what their rate of consumption will be in order to realize their planned standard of living with a reduced rate of production. But is it necessary to achieve exactly the same amount of consumption? This quite interesting question is barely touched upon by Cutler. Once individuals retire they have no work-related consumption needs, so consumption should decline somewhat. On the other hand, older people may have more health-related needs, so their consumption may rise somewhat from that point of view. Or, people may have a better health insurance plan in Medicare than they had while working, which might also affect their consumption of medical services. The relationships are complex. Sylvester Schrieber argued that consumption standards can decline in retirement to maintain true living standard utility.[46] Incorporating this kind of reasoning might make the private savings gap a little smaller than Cutler implicitly calculates.

46. Scheiber (1995).

Cutler implements his model by computing a wealth-to-income ratio in two different ways. He first compares income to total wealth, including housing, and determines that it is necessary to have a wealth-to-income ratio of about three in order to maintain retirement living standards. With Schieber's adjustment it would, perhaps, be slightly less than three. Then he compares nonhousing wealth to income. Yet if he does this, he should also look at income without housing costs. It is inconsistent to use nonhousing wealth alone but include housing costs in income. Income could be adjusted fairly readily, and again, it is likely that the private saving gap that he calculates would decline somewhat as a result.

Cutler does mention very briefly that his estimate of the private saving gap might be rather high because it is based on the assumption in the trustees' report for Social Security that income from both the public and the private plans is about to decline. There is also a question of distribution. If housing is included the wealth stock, one-fifth of people have a wealth-to-income ratio of less than one. If housing is excluded from the wealth stock, two-fifths of people have a wealth-to-income ratio of less than one-half. In this case, however, there is a tail of people who are not saving enough even if the macroeceonomic numbers are acceptable. It is arguable how much policymakers should worry about this tail. It is likely that most of those people are going to be dependent on a public pension plan for retirement income, whatever happens. Yet the aggregate dollar amount involved may not be that large. From Cutler's discussion it is hard to tell whether this is a social problem or not, but the issue deserves further examination.

Thus there is a private saving gap that is generated through what might be called microeconomic reasoning. It nicely complements the saving gap defined by Bosworth's macroeconomic reasoning. There is a strong rationale for raising national saving. Culter stops short of considering how this might be accomplished, but I would like to make a few suggestions here because this will be an important question for the United States in the near future.

The easiest answer is probably to raise national saving by public methods— that is, by reducing budget deficits. This option has been endlessly discussed and need not be elaborated on here.

Slightly more controversial, given that Cutler's microeconomic calculation points to a private saving gap, is that it could make sense to relax the tax treatment of private pension saving. It has been suggested that part of the reason for the decline in private saving through defined benefit plans may have been a series of tax changes in the 1980s that made private pension buildup more difficult.

Thus, accepting Cutler's argument, there are some social benefits to be gained from defined contribution plans. Possibly there should be a comparable relaxation in the provisions for defined contribution saving within the tax system. IRA limits could be increased and 401(k) limits could be increased, for example. This approach leads to difficult tax issues—specifically, whether it is preferable to work with a consumption tax or an income tax; or whether some kind of hybrid, such as exists at present, is actually viable. It is an important question, and ought to be thought about.

But another matter that ought to be considered, and is hardly ever discussed during these types of debate, is how individuals plan for the future. What role do they see Social Security benefits playing? In the past, it has not been very easy to plan in this way. Few people fully understand the Social Security benefit formula, and fewer can accurately predict what their monthly retirement benefits will be. But times are changing. Very soon the Social Security Administration will be going into the information business. Individuals will be able to submit a simple form and receive their earnings record for all thirty-five years of employment, as well as some forecast of what their benefits will be when they retire at a given age. This means that it will be possible for people to know exactly what is in store for them in terms of Social Security benefits. It would be even better if these reports were expanded to show how benefits might vary if savings were increased by a certain amount. Admittedly, the government might be reluctant to go this far, but pension advisory services may. In any case, the first part will provide very useful information.

It is also a question whether it is necessary for public policy or tax policy to make it possible to save more through private pensions. An argument can be made that as long as consumers are properly forewarned about what they might expect from the public part of the system, and they can get further pension advice, there is not much public obligation to support private pension savings further.

The opposite "myopia argument" for the public support of savings for retirement hinges, in large part, on the fact that people just cannot figure out the complexities of the issue. But the new Social Security information service will make it easier, and it might offer a way out of what would otherwise be some difficult policy quandaries. It is also possible, though, that merely giving out the information will not be sufficient. However much information people receive, they often still do not get the point. Clearly it is time to open up the debate about the proper role of information, tax incentives, and related factors in encouraging more pension or retirement saving.

Comment by Margaret Simms

Most of my comments focus on the public policy implications or possibilities of David Cutler's proposals. First, returning to the concept of the three-legged stool, how can the stool be expected to serve different groups within society? Will it act as a chair for some, a stool for others, and an ottoman for yet another group?

Cutler poses the question of whether public policy can encourage savings. So, I would ask what should be done about those who seem to have the least in the way of assets accumulated by retirement. As he points out in table 3-5, households where the head has no high school—or only a high school—education have very low savings or wealth-to-income ratios. In fact, the people who do not have assets are those who have limited disposable income. They may save throughout their lives, but then these savings are depleted—often by an emergency that they cannot pay for out of their current income. It may be medical costs, because they lack sufficient health insurance. It may be burials, because they lack life insurance for their loved ones. Thus it would seem that saving could be promoted among some people through indirect public policies; that is, public policies that address these other problems in their lives that force them to spend down their savings.

On the definition of the asset base, Edward Gramlich correctly points out that if housing is excluded as a form of wealth, then housing costs should be excluded as well. There probably should be a partial adjustment in that regard, since not all housing costs disappear with ownership; even if a house is paid in full, the owner must still pay taxes and maintenance, for example. The right discount will depend on the length of home ownership. Is it really likely that everyone will have paid off their mortgage by retirement?

Both Cutler's analysis and that of Barry Bosworth raised the question of increasing the redistributive aspects of Social Security by various mechanisms, either by raising taxes at the high end, or by lowering benefits at the high end and raising them at the low end. But would increasing the redistributive aspects of Social Security endanger the system for those with whom we might have the most concern. What separates Social Security, in the minds of many people, from other means-tested forms of public assistance, such as welfare or Aid to Families with Dependent Children, is its universality—the assumption that it is an earned benefit. If new policies change that public perception, will they erode support for the system? Given the current political environment, that is not just an idle question.

One further topic regarding Social Security is not discussed by Cutler. It has to do with connection between ownership of assets and eligibility for Supplemental Security Income (SSI). It would be useful to think about what group of people receive SSI. They may very well be people who could be categorized as having moderate assets to begin with, or those with extraordinarily large medical expenses. We should develop an exemption or a level that would enable these people to qualify for SSI and other means-tested programs without forcing them to deplete their assets.

The other issue that should be considered is the level of the normal retirement age. Most of the discussion about this issue has focused on whether retirees should be supported for longer or shorter periods of time. Simply, if they work longer, they will require fewer years of support. The public policy question that nobody has raised is whether to think about this in terms of labor market needs. Should the decision to change the normal retirement age be influenced by a labor shortage or surplus? Cast in this way, the question is not how long to support this group, but whether their presence in the workforce affects job availability for those at the younger end of the spectrum.

Comment by Howard Young

It is certainly true that many private plans—whether defined benefit plans, defined contribution plans, or individual savings plans—have performed very well. But when the private system in its entirety is compared to the Social Security system in its entirety, the track record of Social Security shows nearly fifty years of monthly benefit payments to every eligible individual. The same cannot be said for the private system as a whole. In recent years individual plans have failed, as have funding agencies. Many expectations have been defeated.

It also must be emphasized that Social Security is a portable, universal system and is indexed for inflation. As Cutler points out, Social Security payroll contributions result in uniform costs across the economy for all employers and, therefore, do not give one employer a competitive advantage or disadvantage over another. This is an important point that does not get enough recognition.

On the three-legged stool and the four-legged chair, there is a question of definition. The distinction of government versus employer versus private arrangement submerges the more important distinction between defined benefit and defined contribution plans, which is stronger than Cutler portrayed.

Even with a strong social insurance program, there are still employment-related groups who want some form of a pooled mechanism to meet various specific needs, such as early retirement. This flexibility is offered by private defined benefit pension plans. Defined contribution plans, whether employer-sponsored or otherwise, do not serve that purpose.

It is true that portability is an issue, but the question is how to divide up the pie. One slightly facetious lesson of Cutler's analysis could be that it is optimal to be covered by a defined contribution plan when young, and get hired by an employer with a very good defined benefit plan when older.

In 1989 the General Accounting Office (GAO) published an analysis of results from equal cost defined contribution and defined benefit plans, that is, plans in which the employer would provide the same total contribution. Of course, the result would depend on the design of a particular plan; but the study finds that if a model individual had continuous defined contribution coverage, then no matter how many job changes were made, the accumulated fund could provide an annual pension of $12,100. If that individual were covered successively by five different employers who had identical defined benefit plans costing the same as the defined contribution plan, the individual would retire with an annual pension of $9,800—clearly worse off than the defined contribution scenario. But if that individual stayed with one employer who offered coverage under the defined benefit plan costing the same as the defined contribution plan, he or she would receive an annual pension of $19,100. Thus alternative programs reflect different goals and different expectations.

Similarly, on the question of whether current policies are inducing too much early retirement or too much retirement in general, the other side of the coin is that the absence of defined benefit plans would defeat the goals of people who want additional retirement opportunities. Among auto industry workers, in particular, retirement is a very high priority. It is not evident that the nature of work is changing in a direction that will reduce retirement expectations because, in many respects, white-collar and office work is becoming more like traditional factory work, rather than the other way around. For example, technological developments often mean that jobs are less matched to specific employees, so the individual becomes less significant.

Returning to defined contribution plans, there are problems that might be overlooked by conducting separate analyses of the older, middle, and younger stages of life. Cutler mentions the concern about annuity rates in connection with people who are at or near retirement, but that issue seems to get lost when he discusses the advantages of defined contribution plans for those at younger ages. Under a defined contribution arrangement, the participants take on not only the investment risk but also the risk of unexpected improvements in longevity. When they do reach retirement age, and if they do annuitize their income, they will pay the then-prevailing annuity rates. That is, the annuity rates shown to young participants usually are not guaranteed to apply at retirement. Furthermore, there often are gender-based rates under defined contribution plans which are not employer sponsored.

Investment decisions also are very important in defined contribution plans. Maybe I am a paternalist, but I am not convinced by all of the discussions about the value or efficiency of informed choice. There are arrangements where participants can choose from many investment vehicles and can change their choices every quarter. They have an automated 800-number telephone line that, in at least one place, is referred to as the "lock-in-your-losses line." When participants see their portfolio go down, they call up and revise their investments, but often the new choices will fall even further.

Finally, there is the overwhelming importance of making the contributions at younger ages. If there is going to be a true investment gain, even if that is as little as 1.5 percent a year, consider the role of contributions from ages thirty-five to sixty-five. In the first year (one-thirtieth of the total time period) the contribution provides 4.1 percent of the final accumulation. Similarly, the contributions for the first five years (one-sixth of the total period) provide 20 percent of the accumulated income. Yet these are exactly the years when people have the greatest difficulty in making the contributions. They have the most alternative costs on which they have good reasons for spending the money, and if they change jobs, they have an opportunity to withdraw the money already contributed.

Regarding the investment rate, since the benefit should be considered in relation to final pay, it is not the real investment rate (net of inflation) that must be looked at, but the investment rate net of pay increases. This does not mean average pay increases in the general economy; instead, the reference is to pay increases for individuals, as they go through their career. Accordingly, allowances must be made for merit or longevity increases as well as productivity increases. Thus the gap between the nominal investment rate and what is required to keep up with increased earnings is narrower than might otherwise be thought. In particular, the gap is likely to be less than the real interest rate.

That said, there certainly is a role for defined contribution plans and private savings. Individuals have different goals, so some way should be sought to use Social Security and other defined benefit plans to facilitate phased or partial retirement, in order to provide a gradual transition from full-time employment to full-time retirement.

4

Social Security Income and Taxation: Four Views on the Role of Means Testing

IN THIS CHAPTER four scholars address the issue of means-testing. How and to what extent should the net benefit of federal income security programs vary with income adequacy? Their differing perspectives shed light on the ways in which Social Security benefits are currently related to income, and on proposals for change.

The Shift to Criteria Involving Economic Status in Old-Age Policies: How Far Can the Trend Go?
Robert H. Binstock

THIS SECTION TREATS four topics related to means-testing: the changed political context of policies on aging; the spread of means-testing and other criteria involving economic status; speculation about how far this trend can go and its longer-term implications; and some alternative perspectives to the intergenerational equity paradigm.

The Changed Political Context of Policies on Aging

From the New Deal through the mid-1970s, popular stereotypes of older Americans were largely compassionate and the role of government in responding to their needs grew continually. The media tended to portray older people as poor, frail, dependent and, above all, deserving. The American polity implemented this compassionate construct through the New Deal's Social Security Act, the Great Society's Medicare and Older Americans Act, special tax exemptions and credits for those age 65 or older, and many additional measures enacted under President Nixon's New Federalism, including the Employee Retirement Income Security Act of 1974.

Since the late 1970s, however, the long-standing compassionate stereotypes of older persons have been undergoing a substantial reversal. Throughout the 1980s and into the 1990s new stereotypes have emerged in the media depicting older persons as prosperous, hedonistic, selfish, and politically powerful "greedy geezers." As a cover story in *Fortune* magazine expressed it: "The *tyranny* of America's old . . . is one of the most crucial issues facing U.S. society."[1]

Perhaps the most important factor contributing to this reversal of stereotypes was what Robert Hudson originally dubbed the "graying" of the federal budget.[2] In the late 1970s academicians and journalists began to recognize that benefits to older Americans (mostly Social Security and Medicare) had grown to be more than one-quarter of the federal budget, comparable in size to expenditures on national defense. Today, expenditures on aging are more than one-third of that budget, and defense has fallen to about 18 percent.[3]

As the proportion of the budget devoted to benefits for older people—and projected future expenditures—have become increasingly recognized, curtailing the costs of Social Security, Medicare, and a large proportion of Medicaid spent on long-term care is viewed by many as essential for reducing the national government's deficit and maintaining the health of the U.S. economy.

In addition, various public figures, academicians, and policy analysts have focused on programs for elderly Americans as an important trade-off in any attempt to address domestic social problems. Such trade-offs have been thematically unified and publicized as issues of so-called intergenerational equity, by organizations such as Americans for Generational Equity (active in the 1980s) and the Concord Coalition, founded by former U.S. Senators Paul Tsongas and Warren Rudman in 1992. Their central aim is to reduce Social Security, Medicare, and other expenditures on aging as part of a general effort to reduce the deficit, not to preserve the solvency or the general principles of the social insurance programs.

Proponents of the generational equity paradigm have not only managed to frame policy issues in terms of justice between young and old—as opposed to justice between rich and poor, or between racial and ethnic groups. Their leaders, particularly Paul Tsongas, have been highly inflammatory in speeches and discussions on college campuses and elsewhere, in which they vigorously engage in "elder bashing." Moreover, many so-called analytical observations

1. L. Smith, "The Tyranny of America's Old," *Fortune,* vol. 125, no. 1 (1992), pp. 68–72.

2. R. B. Hudson, "The 'Graying' of the Federal Budget and Its Consequences for Old-Age Policy," *Gerontologist*, vol. 18 (1978), pp. 428–40.

3. Congressional Budget Office. *The Economic and Budget Outlook: Fiscal Years 1996–2000* (Government Printing Office, 1995).

of generational equity proponents regarding expenditures on older persons are misleading. For example, projected long-term declines in the number of workers relative to the retired "dependent" population are used to suggest that, through some sort of demographic ex machina, benefits to aged Americans will be unsustainable in the 21st century—thereby generating anxiety about the future of Social Security. Yet, as several scholars have demonstrated, declines in child dependency expenditures will offset increases in elder dependency expenditures. The total dependency burden will never be as high as it was in the 1960s, even if there is a second baby boom comparable to the first.[4]

Moreover, the productivity of an economy and, hence, its capacity to support dependents within it, is a function of a variety of factors including capital investment, natural resources, balance of trade, and technological innovation, as well as number of workers. If we can free ourselves from the assumption that Social Security must be *exclusively* financed through a worker-by-worker payroll tax—which is *not* the case in many advanced industrial nations—then this concern about increasing dependency ratios, per se, would be revealed as much overemphasized in any event. Under such circumstances the social insurance principle would not necessarily erode. Witness that Medicare Part B, which is 80 percent financed by general revenues, is no more under attack than Part A, which is financed exclusively through the Federal Insurance Contributions Act (FICA). The basic issues for the longer-term are simply whether the economy generates sufficient resources to be transferred, and whether the political will to transfer them to older persons will exist.

Similar misleading discussions have been generated in the arena of health care policy, where it is *erroneously* argued and asserted, for example, that we are wasting a great deal of Medicare expenditures on futile, high-tech, high-cost care for "feeble old geezers." These assertions are not factually correct.[5]

The Emergence of Criteria Involving Economic Status

In this political climate some of the long-standing features for structuring old-age programs have already been undergoing significant change. Since the early 1980s a trend has been established through which Congress has reformed

4. See, for example, R. A. Easterlin, "Economic and Social Implications of Demographic Patterns," in R. H. Binstock & L. K. George, eds., *Handbook of Aging and the Social Sciences,* 4th ed. (San Diego: Academic Press. 1996), pp. 73–93; and W. H. Crown, "Projecting the Costs of Aging Populations," *Generations,* vol. 17, no. 4 (1993), pp. 32–36.

5. R. H. Binstock, "Old-Age Based Rationing: From Rhetoric to Risk?" *Generations,* vol. 18, no. 4 (1994), pp 37–41.

policies on aging to reflect the diverse economic situations of older persons, most often through various forms of means-testing.

The Social Security Reform Act of 1983 began this trend by rendering some Social Security benefits subject to taxation for the first time. The Tax Reform Act of 1986, even as it eliminated the extra personal exemption that had been available to all persons aged 65 and older when filing their federal income tax returns, provided new tax credits on a sliding scale to older persons with very low income. The Older Americans Act programs of supportive and social services, for which all persons aged 60 and older are eligible, have been gradually targeted by Congress to low-income older persons, though not through means testing. The Medicare Catastrophic Coverage Act (MCCA) of 1988 followed this pattern of sensitivity to economic status through the Qualified Medicare Beneficiary program, which requires that Medicaid pay Part B premiums, deductibles, and copayments for Medicare enrollees who have incomes below specific poverty guidelines regarding income and assets.

Legislation in the 1990s has continued to apply the means-testing principle to social insurance programs. The payroll income ceiling on the Medicare portion of FICA has been eliminated. And, in the Omnibus Budget Reconciliation Act of 1993, new levels of income testing for taxation of OASI benefits were established, and 85 percent of benefits above these levels were made subject to taxation. In sum, a substantial trend of politically feasible incremental changes has firmly established the practice of combining age and economic status as policy criteria in old-age benefit programs.

The political impact of the old-age lobby in responding to this trend of means-tested reforms in old-age programs has not been impressive. The aging-based interests have shown no capacity to mobilize older persons as a cohesive, powerful force, in elections or otherwise. A recent letter from AARP's president to the organization's members essentially acknowledges this fact.[6]

How Far Can This Trend Go?

Within the past two years, proposals for more such changes have been made, including several measures in President Clinton's Health Security Act.[7] A September 1994 CBO report, "Reducing Entitlement Spending," presented and analyzed the implications of a number of additional means-tested policy

6. E. I. Lehrmann, "Health-Care Reform at the Crossroads," *Modern Maturity,* January–February 1995, p. 12.

7. White House Domestic Policy Council, *The President's Health Security Plan* (Random House, 1993).

options.[8] Proposals in the 104th Congress for reforming Medicare include means-testing to determine the size of the Part B Supplemental Medical Insurance premiums that Medicare enrollees would have to pay.

How far can this trend go, and what are its long-term implications? The experiences of the enactment of the Medicare Catastrophic Coverage Act and its partial repeal the next year suggest that some such measures may not be politically feasible. Two-thirds of the principal portion of the Act, a substantial expansion of benefits, was to be financed through a progressive, sharply escalating surtax on 40 percent of Medicare participants in middle- and higher-income brackets. Despite AARP's support for the act, there were distinct and highly visible protests from middle-income elders in virtually every Congressional district. Though they comprised only a minority of elderly persons, no popular constituency emerged to provide countervailing support for this program, and Congress gave in to the protesters. This chain of events might not have taken place if the progressive tax had been more finely tuned, and Medicare beneficiaries had been more effectively educated as to what the new benefits would have provided.

Most contemporary proposals, however, involve *reductions* in and taxation of benefits, driven by fiscal concerns rather than major expansion of benefits. The political difficulties in carrying forward the means-testing approach may not be substantial in the years immediately ahead. Yet, in the long run, this trend may not remain viable. Reductions in the benefits that middle- and upper-income people receive from old-age programs pose substantial risks. Such measures could weaken political support for Social Security, Medicare, and other old-age policies among middle-income elderly persons (as well as persons nearing old age or those in younger age cohorts), leaving these programs without a middle-class constituency, as is and has been the case with what are generally thought of as welfare programs. Such programs do not fare well in American politics and are currently under vigorous political attack.

Alternative Perspectives

If the social insurance principle erodes over time and policymaking is dominated by a welfare approach to old-age benefits, the issue of income adequacy will become far more important than the issues of equity. Questions may be raised about the magnitude and largess of old-age "welfare." The political will to use policy to address income adequacy—now and in the future—may not be present. Some old-age groups such as the National Council

8. Congressional Budget Office, *Reducing Entitlement Spending* (GPO, 1994).

of Senior Citizens, and a few others, have addressed the issue of income inadequacy over the years. But most, including AARP, have not addressed it seriously, and, given their constituencies, are not likely to.[9]

Ultimately, the dominant policy framework for addressing old-age policy issues may need to be one that moves away from the generational equity paradigm to a more direct examination of the consequences of poverty and near-poverty in old age. If the social insurance principle erodes severely, the ensuing focus and pressure on old-age "welfare" may force us to confront head-on such issues as a growing number of homeless and frail elderly persons, and whether we really want to reestablish almshouses for poor elderly persons and institutionalize them as a matter of social policy.

A more optimistic scenario would be the replacement of the generational equity paradigm by a *generational investment* paradigm which Vernon Greene outlined in a report issued by the National Academy on Aging.[10] In this investment model, old-age programs and other social programs (such as public education) are perceived as integral parts in a system of *reciprocal* contributions that generations in any society make to one another.

In brief, Greene argues as follows:

—Societal wealth arises primarily from our stock of human capital—the knowledge, skills, aptitudes, and other capacities of our work force.

—The primary source of this human capital is the investments made by the parents and grandparents of those in the work force, through nurturing and rearing, paying taxes and/or tuition to support education, and other direct expenditures of income on their children—all representing considerable sacrifice and deferral of personal consumption and opportunities for accumulating wealth.

—These investments give rise to the claim of a fair return through Social Security and Medicare, which are viewed as public mechanisms for administering the returns on investment to older generations, based on social contribution.

—The value of stocks, bonds, treasury notes, and other sources of retirement income depends critically on the productivity of the work force. Therefore, it is in the self-interest of older people to make sure that younger people prosper.

9. R. H. Binstock, and C. L. Day, "Aging and Politics," in Binstock and George, *Handbook of Aging*, pp. 362–87.

10. National Academy on Aging, *Old Age in the 21st Century* (Washington: Maxwell School, Syracuse University, 1994).

—Adult children and grandchildren benefit from the old-age programs, which often help them avoid substantial financial and in-kind sacrifices that arise from helping their elders.

This paradigm makes the "generational accounts" seem more in balance than the Concord Coalition and others would have us believe. Moreover, if elderly Americans are asked to give up more of their benefits for the common good, such a development is likely to be more palatable to older people if it is framed in terms of their willingness to invest further to help their children and grandchildren, rather than as a demand that they give up excessive "welfare" benefits to which they are not properly entitled.

Whether this particular paradigm or any other is persuasive or not is beside the point. Much more important than the specific paradigms that we apply to analyze the policy decisions that lie ahead will be the fundamental social values to which we adhere. As former Surgeon General C. Everett Koop has put it: "No matter what financial constraints, we must not let our economics guide our ethics, but must let our ethics guide our economics."[11]

Martha Phillips

WARREN RUDMAN AND PAUL TSONGAS formed the Concord Coalition in September 1992 because of their concern about the federal budget deficits. Despite an upturn in the economy, these deficits are still chronic. When President Clinton was sworn into office the public debt stood at $4 trillion; at the end of 1995 it will reach $5 trillion. The federal government will have borrowed about $1 trillion in the first three years of the Clinton Administration. During this time the country has not been at war, has not been in recession, and has not been investing in the next generation or in economic growth.

Thus the Concord Coalition's concern about the budget deficit focuses on the need to reduce the government's dissaving of the diminishing amount of national savings. Increasing the pool of national savings available for investment in human, physical, and technological capital is the key to increasing economic growth and future wealth. Through economic growth, the country will be able to afford the retirement of the baby boomers and continue to have an increasing standard of living.

11. C. E. Koop, "Foreword," in R. H. Binstock & S. G. Post, eds., *Too Old for Health Care? Controversies in Medicine, Law, Economics, and Ethics* (Johns Hopkins University Press, 1991), p. ix.

After the organization was formed and members began rallying to the cause, its leaders were challenged to spell out how they would reduce the deficit. The resulting proposal was boldly called "The Zero Deficit Plan for the Year 2000." It visited each of the four major budget categories: defense and domestic discretionary spending, revenues, and entitlements. In the year 2000, about $40 billion would have been cut out of total discretionary spending, through about fifty specific cuts or terminations. In the revenue category, about $70 billion of tax revenue would have been added in that year, including a 50 cent-a-gallon gasoline tax increase, and higher taxes on alcohol and tobacco. The report also suggested limiting income tax mortgage interest deductions to $20,000 a year.

All of those spending and tax policies still left a deficit of $120 billion in 2000. The only remaining budget category was entitlements. Specific changes were recommended in various programs, including stricter policies on farm price supports and federal employee health and retirement benefits. Suggested changes to Medicare included increasing and indexing the deductible, requiring copayments for laboratory and home health care services, and pegging the Supplemental Medical Insurance premium to 30 percent. After those steps, there was still a deficit of about $70 billion. The report recommended closing the remaining gap through a comprehensive entitlement means test. That one recommendation has brought the Concord Coalition the most notoriety.

Briefly, this means test was set up as follows. It took into account all entitlement payments, not only Social Security and Medicare. (Medicare was calculated at insurance value.) Family income was measured, rather than individual income, and the threshold for benefit reduction was $40,000. The means test formula would first count nonentitlement income (private pensions, earnings, and investment income) and then add entitlement transfers. To the extent that entitlements caused family income to exceed $40,000, there would be a graduated reduction in payments.

For families with incomes over $120,000, 15 percent of benefits would still be payable. For simplicity's sake, it was decided that there would be a 10 percent reduction for every $10,000 of entitlements that took income above $40,000. To avoid little cliffs or steps, the scale could be changed to 1 percent per $1,000. There are a number of ways to set up a graduated reduction.

The means test was not to be implemented cold turkey; it was to be phased in over six years. However, it could as well have been phased in over a longer time, or applied only to people below a certain age.

The Concord Coalition's entitlement means test proposal was developed in the context of balancing the federal budget, rather than from the perspective of improving the long-term actuarial viability of the Social Security trust funds.

One of its guiding principles was that those who can most afford to help reduce the deficit ought to be asked to carry a proportionately larger share of the burden. It did not include any reductions in safety net programs at all.

Although the Concord Coalition did stress the issue of generational equity, it is not fair to charge the organization with elder bashing. In fact, a large part of the membership consists of older people who are shocked that the government is paying them so much money. They think that their working children need it more than they do and that their grandchildren do not have a chance of living the kind of life that they have enjoyed. So they send the money to the Concord Coalition.

The founding of the Connecticut chapter was a case in point. Almost as soon as the idea was proposed, Social Security checks endorsed to the Concord Coalition began arriving in the mail from Connecticut activists and supporters. This does not sound like elder bashing. Admittedly, the organization's older members are not representative of the national population. They are comfortably well off and very willing to make some sacrifice if they are convinced that it is part of a comprehensive, total plan that really would reduce the deficit and lead to greater economic growth for the next generation.

Lastly, the Concord Coalition wanted to begin to shift public thinking about many of these entitlement programs away from the concept of annuity payments and more toward insurance policies. They are there if needed, but hopefully they will not be needed. Benefits should not be seen as a God-given right that is automatically received at a certain age for having worked and paid into the system. That will be a major shift in thinking. The proposal for a means test is a starting point for the dicsussion.

One of the charges against the means test is that it would discourage savings—that people would divest themselves of income-generating assets in order to qualify for full Social Security and Medicare benefits. At the margin that probably would be the case, if it only required a little divestiture. Saving is done by people who are generally younger than retirement age, who have an idea of what they want their retirement income to be, and who know what their target savings amount needs to be. If they understand that Social Security benefits will not be a significant proportion of income at the income level to which they are aspiring (an upper-middle-class income level over $40,000), they would be encouraged to save more rather than less.

A second argument against means-testing is that some people would give away or sell their assets to qualify for full Social Security benefits. Again, that may happen at the margins, but many people would have to divest literally hundreds of thousands of dollars of income-generating capital to reduce their annual incomes to a level at which they could receive some

$12,000 or $15,000 in benefits. People far up on the income scale are not likely to do this.

A third charge against means-testing is that it would cause people to shift their assets into non-income-generating investments. This could be a problem.

It has also been argued that elderly persons today should not be required to participate in such an abrupt change of policy because they have already planned their retirement on the basis of the existing benefit rules, and it is too late for them to change their earning and saving patterns. The counterargument is that comfortably well-off people in this generation should not be given a free ride while financially struggling younger families shoulder more and more of the burden of the deficit. The idea of the means test is to ask those who are most able to trim back to do so. It also requires asking elderly Americans today to share some of the burden of solving the deficit problem, rather than leaving it all to younger generations.

The bill introduced by Representative Dan Rostenkowski in 1994, for example, proposed a series of incremental steps to deal with the long-term imbalance in the Social Security fund. These recommendations amounted to 2.35 percent of payroll. A small amount—perhaps 0.03 percent—of that would be borne by the people who are retired today. The burden of the rest of his proposal would fall on the people who are still working. Obviously, it is possible to change the system in increments. But at what point will people begin to protest that they have done enough and refuse to do any more?

The Concord Coalition is definitely not trying to foment generational war. People of all generations are in this together. The United States faces real difficulty in borrowing $1 trillion every three years to finance current consumption. It is an unsustainable course that must be addressed. Whether establishing a means test for people at $40,000 to $80,000 of income would erode public support for the system is rightly a widespread concern. This is why a shift in perception is important. If the program were perceived more as an insurance policy than an annuity, it might be more politically sustainable.

Moreover, because income distribution falls along something like a bell curve, means-testing would affect a relatively small number of people. Some say public support for Social Security would erode without the approval of that group of people. But it is truly galling for many struggling families to see others with plenty of disposable cash and free time collecting Social Security benefits. Someone at a Concord Coalition meeting in California said, "Well, what we do every month when the check comes in is to go over to Las Vegas and gamble for the weekend, because we don't need it to live." This kind of attitude also erodes support for the Social Security system.

An income level of $40,000 as the starting point for means testing is not immutable. It could be $50,000; some have suggested lower. However, a Roper Starch Worldwide poll that asked people how much money they would need to live comfortably and how much money they would need to fulfill all of their dreams found that elderly people thought that they could fulfill all their dreams for $79,000 a year, but could get along comfortably at something closer to $30,000 a year. Thus setting a comprehensive means test at $40,000 would seem fairly realistic.

Retirement benefits and Medicare form the largest part of entitlements, but the Concord Coalition's proposal would have extended to all programs. It has some fairness, some equity, and some justice to it. Too many people have a retirement stool with fewer than three legs, and they ought to be urged to work and save, and invest more of their own savings toward their retirement. A means test might help to achieve that result.

C. Eugene Steuerle

BECAUSE THE SOCIAL SECURITY system is out of balance for the long run, numerous proposals have been made either to increase taxes or to reduce benefits to middle- and upper-income elderly persons. These proposals, unfortunately, are often considered in isolation—with little or no reference to each other, to current law and recent changes to it, or to the principles and goals of the tax and Social Security systems. As a consequence, the tax treatment of elderly persons proceeds in fits and starts, reduces equity both among elderly persons and between elderly and nonelderly individuals, and unduly distorts work and saving behavior.

Considered separately, many current provisions may appear to make sense. Of great importance, however, is how they combine to take away a share of any increase in income received by a Social Security recipient. If income goes up by one dollar and a person pays 40 cents more in income tax, the effective income tax rate on the additional dollar is clearly 40 percent. If some benefit is independently reduced by 25 cents for every dollar of income, then there is an additional effective "income tax" rate of 25 percent. In this latter case, the money will never appear in income tax accounts, but the combined rate on additional income still equals 65 percent. In fact, budget accounting will usually identify the 25 cents in benefit reduction as a "negative benefit." These types of benefit reductions might as well be called "expenditure taxes," because they operate like taxes hidden within the expenditure structure. Yet whether placed in the direct tax structure or put into a benefit scheme, the tax effects are often the same for the individual.

In the modern welfare state, transfers have come to dominate the use of tax dollars. From a budget perspective, a tax might be viewed as a negative transfer, or a transfer as a negative tax. If a household pays $100 in taxes and receives $60 in benefits, for instance, it pays a net tax of $40. If the government decides to raise the net tax to $50, it can either increase the tax or reduce the benefit by $10. From an economic perspective, it makes no difference which approach is taken if the formula for collecting the money is the same. That is, an individual is likely to react the same way to an additional income tax of 10 cents for every dollar earned and a benefit reduction of 10 cents for every dollar earned.

Today a Social Security recipient faces a variety of direct and implicit tax systems—so many that few experts or members of Congress understand each one or their interactions. The major federal items follow.

THE INCOME TAX. The income tax affects retired Americans mainly by imposing a tax rate on their pension income and on their earnings from saving. For those who do not retire, it is also assessed on all earnings and self-employment income. The income tax also includes some special exemptions and credits for elderly persons.

THE PHASE-IN OF TAXATION OF SOCIAL SECURITY BENEFITS. Under current law, most elderly persons are not liable for income taxation on their Social Security benefits. For those with income (including certain Social Security benefits) above a threshold, however, a portion of Social Security benefits is subject to taxation. For couples with income of more than $32,000, up to 50 percent of benefits may be taxable. For those with incomes above $44,000, the rate is raised to 85 percent. During this phase-in period, an additional $1 of earnings can result in $1.50 or $1.85 of additional income being made subject to taxation, although this higher 85 percent rate may be eliminated under legislation being considered for 1995.

THE SOCIAL SECURITY TAX. A Social Security tax of 15.3 percent (employer and employee tax combined) is imposed against the earnings of an elderly person, whether on Social Security or not. Typically, the tax adds nothing to Social Security or Medicare benefits in later years of retirement. That is, for each $100 earned, the net additional Social Security tax, less additional transfer, is close to $15.30.

THE EARNINGS TEST. For those ages sixty-five to sixty-nine who are receiving Social Security benefits as well as wage earnings or self-employment income, benefits are reduced by one-third of any earnings above a given threshold. Those between ages sixty-two and sixty-five are subject to a separate earnings test that applies at a higher rate and a lower threshold. These benefit reductions are offset, in part, by an increase in Social Security benefits in later years. For those between the ages of sixty-two and sixty-five, the reduction is almost balanced by later benefit increases. For those between sixty-five and sixty-nine, later benefits do not provide a complete offset, but for future retirees the offset will increase over time and soon come close to balancing the earlier reduction. The major exception is the Social Security tax, for which offsets are not provided and little benefit adjustment is likely.

The different types of offsets, such as "delayed retirement credits," however, are quite complicated and understood by few individuals, beneficiaries, or policymakers. Most individuals consider the earnings test to be nothing more than a very high tax rate on their earnings. In many ways, the earnings test is the worst type of tax: over time it raises little net revenue, but it still creates all the distortions associated with the higher tax rates that individuals perceive themselves to be paying.

THE HEALTH EARNINGS TEST. If an elderly person works for an employer who provides health insurance to nonelderly employees, the employer must also provide health insurance to the elderly employee. Medicare then becomes the secondary payer, which means that often it will pay nothing at all. Assume that an individual earns $15,000 in cash and $5,000 in health insurance and that Medicare is also worth $5,000 (the average Medicare expenditure for two elderly individuals currently is close to $10,000). The $5,000 in lost Medicare can be equated to a tax rate of 25 percent; most economists would argue that, in effect, the individual pays that tax in the form of lower cash wages.

THE SOCIAL SECURITY BENEFIT FORMULA. Social Security provides benefits based on lifetime earnings (or more technically, an average monthly indexed wage). As these earnings increase, the rate of return provided by Social Security declines. In fact, for most past generations, the benefit formula provided net benefits in excess of taxes to almost all retirees, even the richest. In the future, however, richer retirees will pay net taxes, and the amount of those net taxes will grow over time. Moreover, because the system is out of balance for the long run, either taxes will go up or benefits will go down, implying that the lifetime net tax burden (taxes less benefits) will increase beyond what is scheduled in current law. This form of taxation is distinguished from those described above by the fact that the tax implicit in the benefit formula is based on lifetime earnings, not annual earnings or income.

Because the Social Security trust funds are out of balance for the long run, a number of changes are required in either Social Security taxes or benefits. This is a factual, not a political, statement. Changes could take a variety of forms: an increase in the extent to which Social Security benefits are made subject to taxation; a slowdown in the rate of growth of annual benefits from one generation of retirees to the next; a change in the price index used to adjust annual benefits; an increase in the retirement age; or an increase in the Social Security tax. Most of these suggestions would adapt or modify existing tax or benefit structures. Considering the tax and benefit structure within Social Security as a whole, the effect of all these proposals would be to decrease the net benefits (benefits less taxes) or increase the net taxes (taxes less benefits) of many future Social Security participants relative to what is promised in current law.

There is no agreement on exactly how this should be done. One of the proposals that has been put forward in recent years is to add yet another form of benefit reduction or taxation, known as means-testing. Means-testing operates very much like an additional income tax: for each dollar of income above certain thresholds, Social Security benefits would be reduced. If benefits are reduced by 20 cents for each dollar of income above $50,000, for instance, then at an income of $80,000, Social Security benefits would be reduced by $6,000. For some taxpayers, Social Security benefits would be reduced to zero.

The proponents of means tests are trying to bring the nation's long-term budget under control, and they should be applauded for this. Many of them are courageously trying to address the major problems of Social Security and Medicare now, rather than waiting until the difficulties of fixing these systems have become more severe. Nonetheless, there are several problems with this new type of tax or means test—problems that might be avoided by adjusting the current implicit and explicit tax system.

One issue is just how this new tax would be integrated into the already complicated tax structure facing elderly persons. In many ways, a means test would operate very much like the current earnings test, which is simply a means test based on earnings and self-employment income rather than total income. While Congress has been shying away from the earnings test over the years, however, a means test would extend it to include income other than earnings, in particular, pensions and returns to capital income.

This effect seems to contradict an objective sought by many proponents of the means test: to increase saving in society. Suppose that a person saves for retirement. In retirement, there are earnings on some savings, while other savings are paid out in the form of pension benefits. These forms of income are already subject to combined tax rates that can easily rise to over 50 percent, especially given the phase-in of taxation of Social Security benefits. In a means-tested system, such earnings would also force a reduction in Social

Security benefits. Together, the various benefit reductions and taxes could add up to a significant reduction in the net earnings obtained from saving.

It is not clear where the earnings test would fit in. Perhaps these multiple means tests would operate in combination. More likely, the old earnings test would be replaced by the new, broader means test. But then delayed retirement credits and other offsets to the earnings test would no longer be available, thus adding to the disincentive to work as well. If the offsets were retained, on the other hand, then the means test would not have much effect on benefits over the long run. Equity concerns might arise if the offsets were retained only for earnings after retirement age, but not applied to earnings put aside earlier and later recognized as pensions.

Another major issue is why a new means test, based on annual income, is required at all. The Social Security benefit formula could easily be adjusted so that fewer lifetime benefits were paid to those with larger lifetime earnings. This type of test primarily acts on lifetime circumstances and opportunity and would require fewer penalties on savings. Although it would raise the net taxes (taxes less benefits) on earnings, it would not place particular emphasis on earnings in later years of life. Means tests that operate only after ages sixty-two or sixty-five create some unusual inequities in the law: they force older workers to face much higher tax rates than are faced by younger workers with the same levels of income.

A means test in Social Security also would encourage some of the behavior now playing havoc with nursing home care provided under Medicaid—in particular, the transfer of assets to children. Suppose taxpayers A, B, and C have equal lifetime incomes, but only A and B save for retirement, and B gives his saving to his children. Taxpayer A is rewarded for her prudent behavior by being forced to transfer money to both B and C. This is patently unfair. By saving more, taxpayer A decreases the transfer that she will receive at retirement; by working more, she pays more taxes to support others rather than provide for her own retirement.

Finally, there is the fundamental philosophical issue of what individuals might reasonably expect when mandated to participate in a partial insurance system. In a system that is unfunded, such as Social Security, expectations must be modest. After all, there are no underlying assets to back up promises to individuals and future liabilities to the government. Because the government has not paid for what it is promising for the future, these promises cannot be held inviolable. In some cases, the government can promise more than it can deliver. Despite these limitations, a case could be made for providing some return in any mandated insurance system. In a mandated pension system, people are forced to save for their own retirement so they do not fully rely on other taxpayers for support. Analogous arguments for mandates are made in favor of requiring every car driver to buy automobile insurance. If it is mandated that individuals put money aside for retirement, then it is questionable whether some of them should simultaneously be told that they are going to get nothing back out of that money later.

Wealthier members of society will still pay some of the cost of supporting those elderly persons who are poorer. As long as there are transfers, somebody has to pay for them. The level of such transfer payments, however, can be determined through adjustments to the normal income tax, the Social Security tax, and the Social Security benefit formula. An additional means test is not really required, and, as a patch onto an already elaborate system, may add more distortions and inequities than its backers really intend.

The Folly of Means-Testing Social Security
Gary Burtless

MEANS TESTING is not very popular. People who receive benefits under government programs do not like their current incomes to be subject to periodic examination by public officials. Voters show greater affection for non-means-tested transfer programs, such as Social Security and Medicare, than they do for means-tested programs, such as Aid to Families with Dependent Children (AFDC) and food stamps. Voter preferences might seem puzzling, since the means-tested programs are far cheaper than redistribution programs which provide benefits that do not depend on participants' current incomes. If voter behavior is driven mainly by the desire to avoid high taxes, as some politicians now believe, it is odd that wage earners should prefer Social Security and Medicare over AFDC and food stamps. The two social insurance programs cost approximately twelve times as much as the two means-tested programs. Most of the cost of social insurance is borne by wage earners rather than taxpayers more generally. Moreover, social insurance is financed with a highly visible, dedicated tax that, for many workers, is larger than the income tax withheld from their weekly paychecks.

The popularity of Social Security and Medicare is not really very mysterious. Most voters know people who rely on Social Security and Medicare. Benefits are considered a rightful repayment for past payroll contributions. Older workers anticipate collecting benefits under the programs when they

The views expressed are the author's alone and should not be ascribed to the staff or trustees of the Brookings Institution.

reach retirement age. Fewer voters have firsthand knowledge of people who collect AFDC or food stamps. Most people probably think it unlikely that they will ever collect means-tested benefits themselves. Unlike Social Security and Medicare, which are regarded as earned rights, AFDC and food stamps are stigmatized by their association with dependency and chronic poverty.

In sum, Americans do not like to collect means-tested benefits. Nor do they like to pay for them. Nonetheless, many policymakers are convinced that Social Security would be improved if benefits in the program were subject to a means test based on applicants' current incomes. Mickey Kaus, the Concord Coalition, and prominent members of the Bipartisan Commission on Entitlement and Tax Reform have all embraced the idea. The main reason for proposing a means test in Social Security is to reduce public spending. Mickey Kaus is explicit on this point: "It would be nice to live in a country with enough money to finance a universal social pension. The problem is that we don't live in such a country. The case for means-testing . . . is simply that we can't afford the current system."

The argument that the United States cannot afford a universal pension will come as a surprise to residents of other rich industrialized countries. The United States is wealthier than almost any other country and it offers old-age pensions that are less generous (relative to average wages) than those available in other rich countries. Possibly the United States cannot afford a universal pension because it has more pressing claims on public resources than these other countries. However, statistics on public spending and taxes suggest that the United States devotes fewer resources to public purposes than other rich industrialized countries.[12] This implies that if the United States cannot afford a universal pension, it is because it cannot afford the tax rate that is needed to sustain such a pension. Americans are unwilling to contribute enough to Social Security to provide pensions to everyone who reaches retirement age.

Value of Social Security to the Affluent

This argument for means-testing reflects a misunderstanding of the affordability of Social Security from the point of view of individual taxpayers. OASDI offers unique insurance protection that is difficult, if not impossible, to duplicate in private markets. When Social Security was enacted in the Great Depression, private old-age pensions were rare. Many industrial and trade

---

12. Japan and the United States spend about the same fraction of national income on government programs; Switzerland spends somewhat less. All other rich countries spend more of their national income on public programs than the United States. In most cases, the gap is substantial.

union plans had collapsed as a result of the stock market crash, leaving retirees and older workers without a dependable source of income in old age. In view of these circumstances, it is not surprising that most voters favored a pension plan backed by public financing.

Even though many people have confidence that private financial markets are more secure today than they were in the 1920s and 1930s, Social Security pensions retain unique advantages that distinguish them from the pensions available in private markets. Based on actual experience over the past half-century, Social Security seems more dependable than privately financed pension alternatives. The program is not affected by financial market fluctuations because benefits are mainly financed out of wage contributions, rather than out of income from capital. Benefits under the program have never been in serious jeopardy because of competitive losses suffered by individual companies, industries, or regions. Nor have benefits been significantly eroded by inflation. Even before they were indexed to the consumer price index by law in 1972, they were informally linked to prices by frequent amendments to the Social Security Act. This kind of protection against inflation is credible in Social Security (although not in private retirement plans) because the benefit promises are backed by the taxing authority of the state.

For people who are (or who expect to be) very well off, the unique advantages of Social Security might seem unimportant. For the great majority of old and disabled Americans, however, the role of Social Security in income security is crucial. Statistics published by the Committee on Ways and Means show that poor family units with a person over age sixty-four derive more than two-thirds of their income from Social Security. Even among nonpoor elderly family units, nearly one-third of income is derived from Social Security.[13] A large percentage of nonpoor family units would be poor were it not for Social Security pensions. In the mid-1980s analysts estimated that almost half of Social Security and Medicare benefits were received by families and individuals whose pretransfer incomes were below the poverty line.

Not only does Social Security play an essential role in maintaining the retirement incomes of most aged American families, it offers a form of income protection that is not otherwise available, even to affluent retirees. In contrast to private pensions and private savings, Social Security benefits are periodically raised in line with inflation. Many retired workers, or their survivors, will live for twenty or even thirty years after pensions begin, so it would seem essential that at least part of their retirement income be protected against sudden and unexpected price increases.

13. U.S. House of Representatives, Committee on Ways and Means (1994, p. 863).

Social Security offers a more subtle protection against uncertainty, too, even for people who are (or who expect to be) very well off. The private savings of many households can be quickly eroded by a series of financial reverses. Fluctuations in financial market continue to make most private retirement incomes uncertain. As a result, the argument for a continued role for social insurance is strong, even for workers who earn high wages throughout their careers.

Because Social Security protection is impossible to duplicate in private markets, it can have real value to affluent as well as middle-income and low-wage workers. Affluent workers should be willing to contribute some of their earnings to sustain a system that offers such valuable benefits. Even though the combined contribution rate for OASDI is 12.4 percent, this does not represent a pure tax on earnings if workers expect to receive substantial benefits in exchange for their contributions. A substantial part of workers' contributions will be repaid to them or their surviving dependents, even if future benefits are scaled back.

The Consequences of Means-Testing

If Social Security benefits were subject to a means test, the payroll contributions of some taxpayers would be converted into a pure tax on labor income. High-income workers would no longer expect to receive any benefits from their contributions, so payroll taxes would become indistinguishable from income taxes, causing all of the distortions in labor supply behavior that occur as a result of an income tax rate increase.[14] Economists do not know whether such a tax increase would cause these taxpayers to work more or less than they currently do. They know only that the distortion of labor market behavior would be increased.

Political Effects

From a political scientist's perspective, means-testing would be expected to cause high-income workers to resent their Social Security contributions much more than they currently do. Social Security contributors who expected to be affected by the means test would find Social Security to be less affordable than

14. For high-income workers whose wages are above the taxable maximum amount, the tax increase is equivalent to a lump-sum change in taxes and will create no marginal distortions. The marginal tax rates facing these taxpayers will be unaffected by means-testing Social Security benefits. For affected workers whose wages are below the taxable maximum amount, means-testing Social Security greatly increases the distortion of the Social Security payroll tax.

the present universal system. These taxpayers would be asked to contribute 12.4 percent of their taxable wages to pay for retirement benefits that would be showered exclusively on other workers and retirees. Thrifty and high-income workers would be left with the formidable task of paying for their own retirements out of the remaining part of their compensation, while workers with low lifetime earnings and those too improvident to save for their own retirement could expect to receive unreduced Social Security pensions.

Under these circumstances many high-income workers would try to persuade their employers to provide them with less taxable money wages and more untaxed fringe benefits, reducing the size of the income tax base. The loss in income tax revenues will offset part of the Social Security savings achieved through means-testing.

More significant, many high-income workers would try to persuade their political representatives to scale back the size of the Social Security program. Although high-income workers and retirees represent only a minority of voters, recent experience suggests that their political voice carries disproportionate weight in public policymaking. For example, most disinterested analyses of the 1988 extension of catastrophic insurance protection in Medicare showed that a great majority of aged Medicare beneficiaries gained under the plan. Affluent retirees and certain middle-income retirees who were already covered by employer-provided insurance plans were made worse off. Yet after these affluent older voters had persuaded middle-income and poorer Medicare beneficiaries to join in vehemently protesting the plan, the administration and Congress were cowed into repealing a program that actually improved the circumstances of most middle-income and poorer beneficiaries.

It seems likely that means-testing Social Security would eventually reduce support for the program among voters who have been important to its sustained political success: affluent older workers and retirees. In addition, it would arouse fierce opposition among voters who up to now have been moderately supportive of the program: affluent active workers.

Reducing the Antipoverty Effects of Social Security

Scaling back Social Security would represent a serious threat to the interests of low-income workers and retirees. In the United States, income redistribution is primarily accomplished through the big social insurance programs, Social Security and Medicare. These programs are largely financed by payroll taxes paid by the currently employed and their employers. Benefits are provided to groups with low current earnings: the retired, the temporarily or permanently disabled, and dependents of deceased workers. As a whole, beneficiaries are less affluent than wage-earner contributors, at least if affluence is calculated from current money income. Within a one-year accounting period, social insurance programs undeniably redistribute income from the better-off to the less well-off.

Viewed over an individual's lifetime, social insurance redistributes income from periods of gainful employment, when a worker has high income, to periods of unemployment, disability, or retirement, when wage income is low. Benefits received in adversity are in part a repayment of contributions made during flush times. This lifetime redistribution takes place for insured workers whether they are poor, middle-income, or wealthy. Even though social insurance formulas are heavily tilted in favor of workers with below-average wages, the amount of lifetime redistribution between rich and poor is clearly much smaller than it appears when redistribution is viewed from an annual perspective.

Although neither Social Security nor Medicare was specifically designed to eliminate poverty, both programs accomplish that goal and are far more important than means-tested transfers in lifting American families out of poverty. Daniel Weinberg estimates that 48 percent of Social Security and Medicare benefits were received by families and individuals whose 1986 pretransfer incomes were below the poverty line. More than one-fifth of Social Security and Medicare benefits went toward reducing the poverty gap, and nearly one-half of the pretransfer poverty gap was eliminated by Social Security and Medicare benefits.[15] Among family units with members over age sixty-four, Social Security alone reduced pretransfer poverty by 72 percent in the mid-1980s, thereby reducing the poverty rate from 56 to 14 percent. Social Security eliminated 85 percent of the pretransfer poverty gap for elderly families.[16]

The effects of Social Security on income poverty are also visible in the time series poverty statistics. In 1959 the income poverty rate of elderly persons was 35 percent, while the rate for the remainder of the population was 22 percent. By 1990 the income poverty rate for elderly persons had fallen to 12 percent, while for the nonelderly, it remained at around 13.5 percent. Taking account of in-kind income, including Medicare, the poverty rate for elderly persons was less than 10 percent in 1990.[17] A large share of the decline in poverty among elderly persons has been due to the rise in Social Security and Medicare benefits since 1960.

15. Weinberg (1991).
16. Committee on Ways and Means, U.S. House of Representatives, (1991, pp. 1171–72).
17. U.S. Department of Commerce, Bureau of the Census (1991, p. 14).

People who favor means-testing in Social Security question the logic of using social insurance as a method of redistribution. Why should poor wage earners be heavily taxed in order to pay for benefits that are mostly received by the middle class and affluent elderly? This criticism rests on the assumption that social insurance is not redistributive enough: it ought to give far less to the affluent or impose lighter burdens on the working poor. In fact, however, social insurance represents a better financial deal to most low-income workers than it does to workers who earn high wages. The pretransfer poor receive a sizable fraction of social insurance benefits. A large share of the remainder is paid out to families not far above the poverty line.

The political popularity of social insurance rests to an important degree on the perceived link between contributions and benefits. Payments are regarded as a right earned by virtue of earlier payroll contributions, irrespective of income level. The link between benefits and contributions makes the program more palatable to taxpayers and makes benefit payments acceptable as a form of government aid to recipients. Those who condemn the system because it dissipates so much of its resources on the nonpoor seem to think that the aim of all social welfare spending is to aid the needy. By and large, the public does not agree. The far more popular goal of social insurance is to protect ordinary workers and their dependents against earnings losses throughout their careers and against high medical bills in old age. It is doubtful whether the immense amount of redistribution carried out through social insurance would continue for long if the link between contributions and benefits were severed.

Economic Effects on Work among Aged Americans and on Private Saving

Means-testing can create a major disincentive for middle-income and affluent workers to save for their own retirement, as well as a large disincentive for older workers to continue working after attaining the retirement age.

For workers with moderate expected incomes in retirement, a means test would substantially raise the penalty for working. For example, Social Security recipients with income levels near the threshold imposed by the means test would face a sharply higher tax on earned income than they do under present law. The higher tax would lead to larger distortions and, in this case, lower levels of work effort among people collecting Social Security. And it would not be popular. The earnings test in Social Security, which is effectively slated to disappear within the next decade, is one of the most hated features of the present system.

The most serious economic problem that would be created by a means test, however, is the substantial disincentive it would create to private pensions and other forms of retirement saving. If one dollar of private pension income led to a 40-cent reduction in Social Security benefits, some workers would conclude that it was better to consume when they were young rather than accumulate savings to finance consumption when they were old. Workers who did not expect to be affluent when they became old would not be affected by this distortion, and workers who anticipated very high incomes in retirement would also be unaffected on the margin. (In fact, some of these high-income workers might boost their saving to offset the anticipated loss of Social Security benefits.) But a large number of American workers would be uncertain whether their retirement incomes would be high enough to be affected by a Social Security means test. Since these workers have comparatively high levels of earnings, they account for an economically significant amount of the nation's saving. Means-testing Social Security benefits would send these comparatively affluent workers a clear message: If you increase your private saving for retirement, the state will sharply reduce your Social Security pension. The U.S. private saving rate is already dangerously low. It makes no sense to offer workers an additional inducement to reduce their saving.

Conclusion

Means-testing Social Security benefits on the basis of retired workers' current incomes is a bad idea. It undermines the economic incentive to save for old age by imposing a foolish tax on private pensions and other retirement income. It discourages work after retirement by penalizing the earned incomes of Social Security recipients. People who believe that Social Security should offer more generous benefits to the poor or less generous benefits to the well-heeled could achieve that goal in a far less harmful way than by means-testing benefits. The income tax schedule could be made somewhat more progressive. Or the Social Security benefit formula—which already imposes a means test based on average *lifetime* earnings—could be made more favorable to low-wage workers. Either alternative would be preferable on economic grounds.

A stronger argument against means-testing is that it threatens the political consensus that has kept Social Security popular for so long. One important reason why Social Security receives such high marks from voters is that it is not viewed as a program for the needy. Instead, it is seen as a program that helps all the nation's citizens, including the needy, the middle-income, and the affluent. By basing Social Security pensions on retirees' current incomes, means-testing can target benefits more narrowly on people in need, but at tremendous political cost. The program will be less popular among the affluent and more vulnerable to political attack from ideological opponents of government redistribution. Public support for the program will almost certainly decline. The ironical result of imposing a means test may be to reduce the amount of income support provided to low-income elderly and disabled Americans.

References

Kaus, Mickey. 1994. "The Case for Means-Testing Social Security." In *Social Welfare Policy at the Crossroads*, edited by Robert B. Freidland and others. Washington: National Academy of Social Insurance.

Weinberg, Daniel. 1991. "Poverty Dynamics and the Poverty Gap, 1984–86." *Journal of Human Resources* 26(3): 535–44.

U.S. Department of Commerce, Bureau of the Census. 1991. *Measuring the Effect of Benefits and Taxes on Income and Poverty: 1990.* Series P-60, no. 176-RD.

U.S. House of Representatives. Committee on Ways and Means. 1991. *1991 Green Book—Overview of Entitlement Programs: Background Material and Data on Programs within the Jurisdiction of the Committee on Ways and Means.*

—. 1994. *1994 Green Book—Overview of Entitlement Programs: Background Material and Data on Programs within the Jurisdiction of the Committee on Ways and Means.*

5

Social Security around the World

Estelle James

THE WORLD BANK study *Averting the Old Age Crisis: Policies to Protect the Old and Promote Growth*, on which this section is based, is an empirically based work, drawing on evidence from over one hundred countries.[1] Although its messages are primarily directed toward developing countries (whose populations are aging most rapidly) and transitional socialist economies (where old-age systems are a major current fiscal problem), it also has implications for industrialized countries. Figures 5-1 and 5-2 show, for various countries, the percentage of the population over sixty years old in 1990 and 2030 and the number of years required to double that segment of the population from 9 percent to 18 percent, respectively.

The World Bank team that worked on this study used two overarching criteria for evaluating old-age programs. First, such programs should protect the old. Second, they should promote, or at least not hinder, economic growth, which is good for both elderly and young people. It was found that current systems in many countries fail both tests. They do not always protect elderly people and they have not promoted economic growth; in fact, they have introduced inefficiencies that impede growth. This means that future generations will get lower wages and pensions than they would have otherwise.

This section outlines the most common problems uncovered by the World Bank study, presents its recommended solutions, addresses some of the major questions that have been raised about the study, and comments on its relevance to the United States and other OECD countries.

---

1. World Bank (1994).

Figure 5-1. Percentage of Population Age over Sixty, by Region, 1990 and 2030

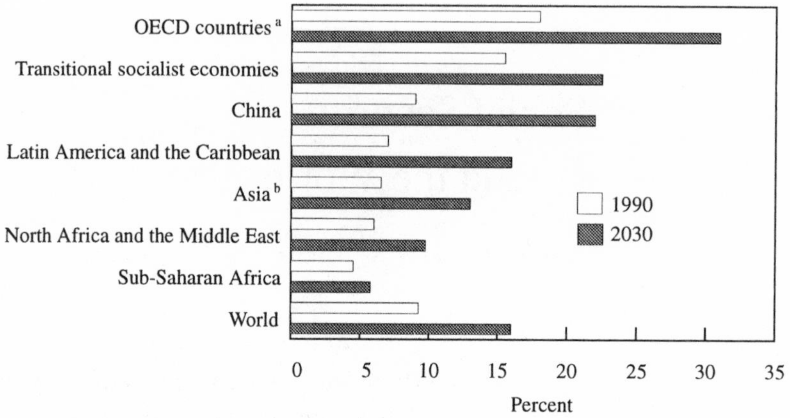

SOURCE: Adapted from the World Bank population database.
a. Including Japan.
b. Excluding China.

The Problems

Most formal systems of old-age security are mandatory publicly managed schemes financed by payroll taxes, largely on a pay-as-you-go basis, meaning that today's workers pay the pensions of those who have already retired. They combine in one program the three functions of old-age systems: saving, redistribution, and insurance. Almost all existing programs are in serious trouble, yet countries that are starting new systems are on the verge of making the same mistakes. A list of common problems follows.

HIGH TAX RATES. When populations are young and old-age systems are immature, small contributions from the large number of workers make possible substantial benefits to the few pensioners. As a result, politicians often set up overly generous benefits. However, as populations age and systems mature, these same benefits require high taxes to pay pensions to the growing number of retirees. Payroll taxes for pensions already exceed 25 percent in Egypt, Hungary, Russia, Kyrgyzstan, Brazil, and Italy. They will exceed 30 percent in many countries over the next thirty years, if pay-as-you-go financing and current benefit schedules are retained. High payroll taxes are regressive and inefficient; they mean lower take-home pay if passed on to workers, and less employment if borne by employers.

EVASION. High taxes that are not closely linked to benefits promote evasion. This is a major problem in developing countries, where tax collection capaci-

Figure 5-2. Number of Years Required to Double the Proportion of the Population Older than Age Sixty from 9 to 18 Percent, Various Countries

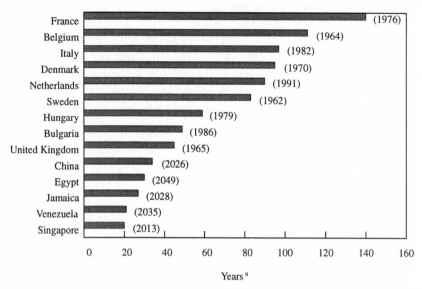

Years[a]

SOURCE: B. R. Mitchell, *International Historical Statistics: Europe 1750–1988*, 3d ed. (New York: Stockton Press, 1990) and World Bank population data base projections.

a. Year in which proportion of people over age sixty reached or will reach 18 percent is shown in parentheses.

ties are limited. In many Latin American countries over 40 percent of the labor force works in the informal sector, in part to avoid payroll taxes for pensions. In Argentina before recent reforms, more than 50 percent of covered workers covered by the system evaded their contributions. Workers who evade payroll taxes are either unprotected, thereby defeating the purpose of the old-age system, or they manage to qualify for benefits despite their failure to pay contributions, which undermines the system's financial viability. Evasion hurts the economy, because people who work off the books are often less productive.

EARLY RETIREMENT. There are many reasons for early retirement, including the availability of public pensions at rates that are not actuarially reduced and, conversely, the imposition of penalties by these plans on those who continue working. In Hungary, more than one-quarter of the population are pensioners, the average retirement age is fifty-four, and the payroll tax is 31 percent; in Turkey, many workers retire with a generous pension before age fifty, or even forty. Over the last two decades the labor force participation rate of men in their fifties and sixties has fallen substantially in almost every OECD country. Early retirees have a twofold impact on Social Security systems: they stop making contributions and they begin drawing benefits. They also deprive the economy of their experience and work effort.

INCREASED BURDEN ON THE PUBLIC TREASURY AND MISALLOCATION OF PUBLIC RESOURCES. In 1990 Austria, Italy, and Uruguay spent more than one-third of their public budgets on pensions. Given the economic and political limits on taxation, high pension spending can squeeze out government spending on growth-promoting public investments such as infrastructure, education, and health services, or can lead to deficit spending that fuels inflation.

LOST OPPORTUNITY TO INCREASE SAVINGS. Many countries believe their growth is hampered by inadequate national saving and yet fail to use their old-age systems as a way to induce people to save more. Indeed, some economists believe that existing systems have induced people to save less.

FAILURE TO REDISTRIBUTE TO LOWER-INCOME GROUPS. Studies of public pension plans in the Netherlands, Sweden, the United Kingdom, and the United States have not found much redistribution from the lifetime rich to the lifetime poor, even though these plans are based on seemingly progressive benefit formulas. This is partly because benefit formulas typically pay higher pensions to higher wage workers, and partly because the rich enter the labor force later and live longer, thereby contributing for fewer years and collecting benefits for more years.

POSITIVE LIFETIME TRANSFERS TO EARLY COHORTS AND LOSSES TO THEIR CHILDREN. In general, covered workers who retire in the first twenty to thirty years of a scheme get back more than they contributed, because they pay low payroll tax rates and for only part of their working lives, yet they get full benefits upon retirement. In contrast, their children and grandchildren pay high payroll tax rates and will get back less than they contribute and at lower rates of return than they could have earned elsewhere, as old-age schemes adjust to the demographic transition. In addition, the total GNP may be lower for these future generations than it would have been under another old-age system, because of the effects on long-term savings and labor supply and its allocation, as described previously.

CURRENT SYSTEMS ARE NOT SUSTAINABLE. In most countries with high coverage, such as OECD and transitional economies, the implicit public pension debt (that is, the present value of pension promises made to old people and workers) far exceeds the conventional debt and comprises more than 100

Figure 5-3. Implicit Public Pension Debt and Conventional Debt as a Percentage of GDP, Various Countries, 1990 ª

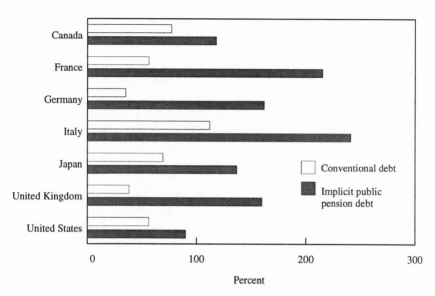

Percent

SOURCE: Paul Van der Noord and Richard Herd, "Pension Liabilities in Seven Major Economies," Working Paper (Paris: OECD Economics Department, 1993).
   a. Implicit public pension debt is defined as the present value of pension promises made to old people and workers.

percent of GDP. This is illustrated in figure 5-3. Current contribution rates are not nearly high enough to fulfill these benefit promises. Either pensions or other government spending will have to be cut, or tax rates will have to be raised. Many developing countries have already reneged on their promises by allowing inflation to take place without indexing benefits. In Venezuela, as shown in figure 5-4, the real value of public pensions fell by 60 percent during the 1980s, due to inflation.

In these and other ways, current government-run Social Security systems have hurt the economy and have failed to protect elderly people, or those who will grow old in the future. Not all of these problems are present in every country, but many of them exist in many countries, suggesting that these common problems result from something inherent in the political economy of the systems. A new system is needed that is more immune to these dangers.

The Solution

A good starting point in designing a framework for reform is the three ways in which people can be supported in their old age: saving, redistribution, and

Figure 5-4. Real Pension levels, Venezuela, 1974–92

Index, 1974 = 100

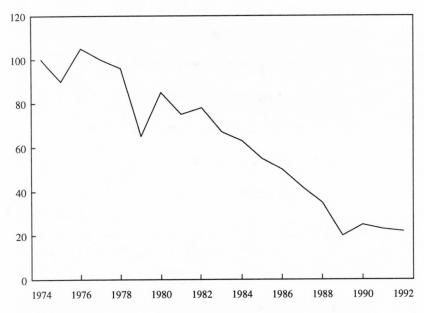

SOURCE: Gustavo Marquez, "El Seguro Social en Venezuela, " Banco Interamericano de Desarollo, Washington 1992.

insurance. The current system in most countries provides all three functions in one dominant, publicly managed, pay-as-you-go, defined benefit system. A reformed system, as shown in table 5-1, would establish separate administrative and financing mechanisms, or pillars, for redistribution and saving, and would use a mix of public and private management, full funding and pay-as-you-go tax financing, and defined benefit and defined contribution schemes.

Many Social Security analysts advocate a multipillar system for old-age income security, but unfortunately each analyst means something different by that term. In the system devised by the World Bank study, one mandatory pillar would be fully funded and privately managed. This pillar is ideally suited for handling peoples' saving. But since a privately managed pillar cannot be relied upon to provide a social safety net, a mandatory, publicly managed, tax-financed, redistributive pillar is also needed. And a third, voluntary, pillar would be used by people who wanted additional old-age security.

The pillar for saving is the most controversial. It is envisaged that this pillar would, in part, perform the function of existing public systems; but in such a way as to link benefits closely to contributions (usually through a

Table 5-1. The Three-Pillar Reformed Old-Age Income Security System

Characteristic	Mandatory publicly managed pillar	Mandatory privately managed pillar	Voluntary pillar
Objectives	Redistributive plus coinsurance	Savings plus coinsurance	Savings plus coinsurance
Form	Flat, or means-tested, or minimum pension guarantee	Personal savings plan or occupational plan	Personal savings plan or occupational plan
Financing	Tax-financed	Regulated, fully funded	Fully funded

Source: World Bank (1994, p. 15).

defined contribution plan) and therefore discourage the evasion and labor market distortions observed in many countries. It would be mandatory for the same reason that current systems are mandatory: because a significant number of people may be shortsighted, may not save enough for their old age on a voluntary basis, and may become a burden on society at large when they grow old.

But the most important characteristics of this saving pillar are that it would be fully funded and privately managed. It should be fully funded, first, because the costs would be clear from the outset and countries would not be tempted to start out by making unrealistic promises that they could not ultimately fulfill. Such promises are difficult to keep, and they are difficult not to keep. By shifting some costs to the early years of a plan, full funding gives a reality check and helps to avoid this dilemma. Second, full funding would prevent dramatically rising contribution rates and large intergenerational transfers, particularly in developing countries with populations that are aging very rapidly. If these countries put in place pay-as-you-go systems or expand their coverage today, they would face a huge increase in the cost of those programs thirty years from now, and a huge intergenerational transfer. Intergenerational transfers can be justifiable, so long as they are openly discussed and chosen by an informed citizenry. The danger with an unfunded system is that these transfers occur automatically, as a result of the aging and maturation process, and sometimes in unexpected ways; for example, the largest transfers can go to rich people in the earlier generations. Moreover, the decision to transfer in such a system would have been made by the generation that gained, while younger generations, who would be the losers, would not have participated in this political choice (many of them would not even have been born when the system was set up and expanded). Thus there are serious questions about the procedural fairness of an unfunded system. The third reason in favor of full funding is that it may help build long-term national savings.

In addition, this saving pillar should be privately and competitively managed in order to maximize the likelihood that economic, rather than political, objectives will determine the investment strategy, and thereby to produce the best allocation of capital and the best return on savings. As can be seen from figure 5-5, throughout the 1980s publicly managed pension reserves earned less than privately managed reserves (based on national averages for countries where data are available) and in many cases lost money. This is not because their managers were incompetent, but because they were required to invest primarily or exclusively in government securities or loans to failing state enterprises, at low nominal interest rates that became negative real rates during inflationary periods. Publicly managed funds may also encourage deficit finance and wasteful spending by the government because they constitute a hidden and exclusive source of funds. Competitively managed, funded pension plans, in contrast, are more likely to enjoy the benefits of investment diversification, including international diversification, that protects them against inflation and other risks, and to spur financial market development, thereby enhancing economic growth. The private managers could be chosen by workers, in the case of personal saving plans, or by employers, in the case of employer-sponsored group plans.

But there are two caveats: countries must have at least rudimentary capital markets before they can establish this funded pillar; and considerable government regulation and regulatory capacity are needed to prevent fraud and excessive risk. Consequently, some countries are not yet ready to handle a funded pillar for mandatory retirement saving.

Even for countries with the necessary capacities and institutions, it is not enough to rely completely on a privately managed pillar to handle saving; a redistributive pillar is needed to keep old people out of poverty, and this must be publicly managed and financed. Some people who are low-wage earners for most of their working lives will not be able to save enough to keep themselves out of poverty in old age as well. Others may run into a spell of bad returns, despite government regulation of the investment companies. The future is always uncertain, and this applies to capital markets as to all others.

The redistributive pillar that would take care of these problems would resemble existing public pension systems in that it would be publicly managed and tax-financed. However, unlike most current systems, the reformed public pillar would be targeted toward low-income groups, thus providing a social safety net for the old. To accomplish this, benefits could be flat, means-tested, or provide a minimum pension guarantee. Because of its limited scope, this pillar could be supported by taxes significantly below current levels.

Figure 5-5. Gross Average Annual Investment Returns for Selected Pension Funds, 1980s[a]

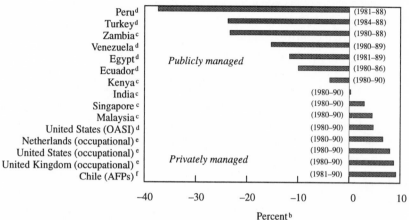

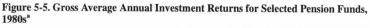

SOURCE: R. Acuña and A. Iglesias, *Chile: Experienca con un Regimen de Capitalization 1981–1991* (Santiago: Economic Conference for Latin America and the Caribbean–United Nations Development Program, 1992); Mukul G. Asher, "Income Security for Old Age: The Case of Malaysia," National University of Singapore, Department of Economics and Statistics, 1992; E. P. Davis, "The Structure,Regulation, and Performance of Pension Funds in Nine Industrial Countries," Working Paper 1229 (Washington: World Bank Policy Research Department, December 1993); India Employees' Provident fund, *Annual Report 37, 1989–90* (New Delhi: Employees' Provident fund Organization, 1991); Carmelo Mesa-Lago, "Portfolio Performance of Selected Social Security Institutes in Latin America," Discussion Paper 139 (Washington: World Bank, 1991); Robert Palacios, "Averting The Old Age Crisis: Technical Annex," World Bank Policy Research Department, Washington, 1994; and U.S. Social Security Administration, Social Security Bulletin (various issues).

a. Simple averages for countries with at least five years of data, as noted in parenthesis.

b. Rate of return after inflation.

c. Malaysia, Singapore, Kenya, India, and Zambia are publicly managed provident funds. Rates reported are returns credited to worker accounts.

d. Peru, Turkey, Venezuela, Egypt, Ecuador, and the United States are publicly managed reserves of partially funded pension plans. Amounts reported are gross returns to the funds. In many cases data on administrative costs are not available.

e. The Netherlands, the United States, and the United Kingdom are privately managed occupational plans; estimated average net returns have been reported by subtracting 1 percentage point from simulated average gross returns. Actual returns and expenses varied by fund.

f. Actual average net returns, after all administrative expenses, are reported for the Chilean Administradora de Fondos de Pensiones (AFP). Average gross returns were 12.3 percent; actual returns and expenses varied by fund.

The third pillar, comprising voluntary saving and annuities, would offer supplemental retirement income for people with the means and inclination to save more, just as voluntary saving does today. This raises an important public policy issue: Should governments offer tax incentives for voluntary saving and annuities? The answer depends on whether such incentives are compatible with the country's overall policy toward taxing consumption versus saving. A piecemeal approach runs the risk of being regressive (since voluntary plans are used mainly by upper-income groups) and of shifting retirement saving from taxed to tax-exempt forms, rather than increasing it overall.

All three pillars would coinsure against individual and economywide risk, providing better protection to the old than could any single mechanism alone. Risk diversification is especially important given the long time periods and great uncertainty involved. Typically, upper-income people realize this fact and have very diversified sources of retirement income, including privately managed investment income, while lower income groups are much more heavily reliant on publicly managed pay-as-you-go programs. The World Bank proposal is founded on the belief that these lower income groups should also get the benefits of risk diversification and access to income from capital, and that this should be built into a national mandatory plan.

This is not an ivory tower proposal. The key features of this framework— separate mechanisms for redistribution and saving, shared responsibility between the public and private sectors, and a mixture of funded and tax-financed plans—have already been adopted by several countries, including Chile and Argentina, where the funded pillar is based on personal saving plans; Australia and Switzerland, where it is based on mandatory employer-sponsored plans; and Denmark and the Netherlands, where employer-sponsored plans are mandated by widespread collective bargaining, rather than legislation.

Some Controversial Issues

In answer to those who have questioned the reformed system described in the World Bank study, it should first be emphasized that the public sector is not intended to play a minimal role. Both the public and the private pillars have very important roles to play. The public sector is asked to do what it can do best—regulate and provide a social safety net—while leaving the management of peoples' saving and the allocation of capital to the private sector, which is more efficient at these tasks.

Another question that has been raised is whether it is good to have a public pillar with such a transparent redistributive function. Maybe this will hurt the poor. Maybe high-income people will not be willing to redistribute and provide an adequate minimum pension in a very transparent public pillar. The implication is that for some reason high-income people would be more willing to redistribute through a nontransparent mechanism.

The willingness of societies to redistribute to low-income groups is indeed questionable, and this could cause social problems in the future. But there is no reason why that willingness would be greater in a messy nontransparent system. As described above, in countries with messy systems, it is difficult to find empirical evidence of real redistribution from rich to poor. The simple fact is that if upper-income people do not want to redistribute, they will probably figure out how to avoid doing so. For example, they could impose ceilings on taxable income, base pensions on salaries in the last few years (giving themselves an advantage because of their rising age-earnings profiles), and collect benefits for more years, given their longer expected lifetimes; these provisions are indeed found in most public plans today. Poor people are not likely to be in a superior position to manipulate messy systems or even to calculate how they are faring under them; in this regard, rich people are likely to have better access to expertise and political influence. The best check on this advantage is to make redistributions very transparent and allow wide discussion of the process.

It is true that low-income people have benefited from old-age security systems in the past and that old-age poverty has been substantially eliminated in most countries that have broad coverage. However, this poverty alleviation took place during the immature phase of current old-age security systems, when all members of the cohort received larger benefits than they had contributed in payroll taxes—a positive income transfer. High-income people were willing to allow low-income people to benefit from a system that also benefited themselves. This positive income transfer was made possible by a redistribution from future generations, who will get back less than they pay in. That is, for future generations the income transfer will become negative; there will be no surplus to share between rich and poor. Under these circumstances old-age systems will alleviate poverty among workers with low lifetime incomes only if financing of the public pillar becomes more progressive and benefits more targeted; but high-income people may be unwilling to redistribute when the game has become negative sum. Therefore, rather than keeping the system messy and nontransparent, it is essential to make it as efficient as possible so that the loss is minimized and the willingness to maintain the social safety net is maximized.

Closely related, it has been suggested that old-age security should continue to be financed by "contributions" instead of "taxes," because contributions meet with less political resistance and generate a stronger claim on benefits. In the period when benefits exceeded payments because of the intergenerational transfer described above, most people were quite willing to think of their payments as contributions that justified their benefits, even though these lifetime contributions were generally far less than the lifetime pensions that they received. However, in the coming era—when benefits will be less than lifetime payments, will have only a weak relationship to these payments, and could be increased if opting out of the system were permitted—most people will know that their mandatory payments are taxes, regardless of what professionals and academics choose to call them.

The study acknowledges the complexities and ambiguities of the impact of Social Security programs on savings. Although the evidence is inconclusive on the question of whether pay-as-you-go schemes have decreased national saving, it does show that full funding can be used to increase long-term saving, providing that certain conditions are met. One of these conditions is that the mandatory savings rate has to exceed the voluntary rate. A fully funded system that is voluntary, or a system that is mandatory but at a very low rate, will simply displace earlier voluntary saving or previously accumulated assets, so that national saving will not increase (although saving that is committed for the long term may increase). Relatedly, people should not be permitted to borrow against their retirement saving; if credit mechanisms develop that do permit this, aggregate saving may not increase. In general, it is necessary to convince people to consume less in order to increase saving. Contributing to an individual retirement saving account, over which that individual has some control, may be a politically more acceptable way to persuade people to postpone consumption than some other schemes (for example, higher taxes).

Another necessary condition for the positive savings effect is that the increased pension savings of households should not be offset by increased public dissaving. For example, if pension saving automatically becomes part of the public budget, or if it is used to purchase government bonds and thereby facilitate deficit finance, then the national saving available for private sector investment will not grow because the increased pension saving will be canceled out by the increased public dissaving. One of the reasons why the saving pillar should be privately managed is the greater probability that a privately managed fund will not be given exclusively to the government and used exclusively to finance increased public deficits. Therefore, such a fund would be more likely to increase national saving, to be invested in both public and private securities, and to lead to the best allocation of this saving.

Certainly the study does not profess to have a single blueprint that would suit every country in the world. It does present a general vision of the direction in which countries should move, but it necessarily leaves room for lots of individual variation. One way in which this individual variation can take place is in determining the nature of the public and private pillars. The public pillar could vary in size. It could be means-tested, or flat, or a minimum pension guaranty. The saving pillar could be based on occupational plans or on personal savings plans. Different countries will make different choices.

The division of responsibility between the two mandatory pillars can also be quite different, each varying between roughly one-third and two-thirds of the total. The funded pillar should be large enough to increase national savings, if that is one of the national objectives. And it should be large enough to justify the transactions costs involved, given substantial economies of scale. This means that a 2 or 3 percent contribution rate to the funded pillar is unlikely to be efficient because it will probably just crowd out other private savings, at a high incremental cost. However, the contribution rate could start at 3 percent, with a scheduled phase-in to a higher level over a period of years, as in Australia.

There will also be variation in the speed at which countries should approach this multipillar system. Most African countries, on the one hand, do not have either the regulatory or the financial market capacity to establish the funded pillar, so they should move very slowly. They should maintain a modest public pillar, designed to provide a social safety net, while developing the financial and regulatory capacities that are needed for the funded pillar and for economic development more broadly. Latin America, on the other hand, is going through a radical transition in the mid-1990s, stopping the clock on the old system, issuing recognition bonds for prior service credits earned, and instituting a new system for young workers and for middle-aged workers who choose to switch. And the East Asian countries have yet to decide how to proceed, although the solution will have to be quick, given their rapidly aging demographics.

Relevance to the United States and Other OECD Countries

Although the OECD countries, including the United States, were not the primary focus of the World Bank report, I outline four concerns about the current Social Security system in the United States and other OECD countries and explain how the approach described above would address these concerns.

First, as the proportion of retired people grows sharply over the next thirty years, the contribution and benefit schedules in the Social Security systems of all OECD countries will become financially unsustainable; either benefits will have to fall, or taxes will have to rise, or more likely, there will have to be some combination of the two. The questions that must be addressed are: What? When? And with how much political pain?

Second, people who are currently retired are receiving much more in benefits than they paid in as contributions (so Social Security is very popular among them), while their children and grandchildren will get back less than they paid in. Will future cohorts continue to support Social Security when they realize that it is decreasing their lifetime income?

Third, there are many low-wage workers in the United States and many unemployed workers in Europe. Incomes are becoming polarized, and a growing number of families with children are at the bottom end of the scale. This should be a concern for everyone, because it affects the balance between social harmony and unrest. Social Security taxes are contributing to poverty among the young. These taxes are much steeper than those their parents or grandparents had to pay and they are also much steeper as a proportion of total income for low- than for high-wage earners. In the past, old-age poverty was reduced by a massive windfall transfer to the old through Social Security, but in the future the windfall will become negative and poverty will not be eliminated unless the costs and benefits of the transfer become more targeted.

A fourth concern is a low rate of national saving and economic growth. This, of course, deepens the problems of poverty and income polarization. Current old-age systems are not helping this situation; indeed, they may be hindering it by creating disincentives to work and save.

To address these concerns, a rapid radical transition, as in Latin America, is indeed possible. But a gradual transition is also still feasible for most OECD countries, if started soon enough. This could be accomplished by the following measures:

—Reduce the financial pressures on current Social Security systems by raising the retirement age and lowering the pension rate.

—Make the benefit and financing structures more progressive to reduce poverty among young people as well as elderly people.

—Require people to save for their own old age.

RAISE AND INDEX THE RETIREMENT AGE. The retirement age is already scheduled to rise in the United States and several European countries, but this process should be accelerated and made continuous, to control costs. If a "standard" period of expected retirement—say fifteen years—was established, the normal retirement age could be raised automatically to maintain this standard period as longevity increases. In the past, governments have had to take the politically difficult step of raising the retirement age periodically as life expectancy has increased. Indexing the retirement age to longevity would take the onus off government. If people wanted to retire earlier, they could still do so, but they would receive a pension that was reduced in an actuarially equivalent manner. And conversely, those who chose to retire later than average would receive an actuarially increased pension, which should encourage their continued participation in the labor force.

REDUCE BENEFITS AT THE TOP. At the same time, the average benefit should gradually be reduced and the benefit structure flattened by bringing down the top end. Other countries have accomplished this through changes in the pensionable wage base, the credit granted per working year, or the indexation formula. The cut in benefits combined with the increase in retirement age should be calibrated to allow pensions to be paid to the growing number of old people without raising the payroll tax rate. (In some countries, where the payroll tax is already very high, promised benefits might be cut still further over time to reduce taxes needed for the public pillar.)

MAKE THE FINANCING STRUCTURE LESS REGRESSIVE. This could be done by raising the ceiling on taxable earnings while reducing the payroll tax rate for everyone, or by targeting tax cuts for a smaller group of low-income workers, in recognition of the fact that they tend to live and collect benefits for fewer years than high-income workers. This reduction of payroll taxes would increase take-home pay and hence keep low earners out of poverty. It would also encourage employers who so far have not been able to pass these costs on to workers to increase employment at the low end of the wage spectrum.

REQUIRE PEOPLE TO SAVE. At the same time changes are made in the Social Security system to reduce benefits, raise the retirement age, and make the structure more progressive, people should be required to save for their own old age, through privately managed defined contribution plans. In countries with high payroll taxes, some of these contributions might be diverted to the saving pillar, especially for young workers. In countries with relatively low tax rates, incremental contributions would be needed. The low costs of these countries were possible in the past only because they had few old people and many young people, so it did not cost much per worker to do the job in a pay-as-you-go system. The days of this free ride are now over. If people want to replace 40 percent or more of their last year's salary when they retire, if societies want to provide a safety net for low-income groups, and if survivors' and disability insurance are also included, contributions of 16 to 20 percent of payroll will eventually be required, even for a modest system. In effect, much of the fruits of future productivity growth would be used to finance pensions rather than wage growth. Still higher contributions will be needed if the system remains pay-as-you-go.[2] To minimize costs and maximize protection, the diverted and incremental contributions should go into the workers' own retirement savings accounts (such as IRAs) or employer-sponsored plans (such as 401[k]s) that

2. Indeed, in every OECD country except Canada and the United States, payroll tax plus general revenue finance of old-age security already exceeds 16 percent, in part because their populations have already aged and in part because their wage replacement rates are much higher than 40 percent. In most cases, the required tax rate for the next generation is projected to far exceed 30 percent, if current benefit schedules and financing methods are maintained.

are privately managed, with workers, or employers, or both controlling the choice of investment manager. For young and middle-aged workers, these savings would have to begin now if they were to be large enough when needed.

In sum, benefits in the public pillar would become flatter, more modest, and financed in a more progressive way, while the privately managed funded pillar would increase in size and take up part of the burden.

These reforms would protect elderly Americans while promoting economic growth. Social Security would be placed on a financially sound footing permanently. Putting incremental contributions into personal accounts would be more politically acceptable and less economically distorting than simply putting them into the old Social Security system, because they are more likely to be regarded as saving than taxation. Long-term national saving, and consequently productivity and growth, should increase as a result of the mandatory funded plans. The supply of experienced workers and their output would also increase, as a result of the change in retirement age and the elimination of rewards for early retirement or penalties for late retirement.

Low-income workers would be protected (both in their working and retirement years) by the more progressive public pillar. Middle- and high-income workers would fare better because the investment returns on their funded saving accounts would be greater than their rate of return from the old pay-as-you-go system. All workers would benefit from the greater diversification of their retirement income. Instead of depending only on a publicly managed program financed by a tax on wages, they would receive part of their pensions from a privately managed program financed by returns on capital.

A gradual transition of this sort is still feasible in the United States and other OECD countries, providing people begin to build their retirement savings now. It seems likely that, over time, demographic and economic pressures will force change in this direction. The sooner people act, the less disruptive and more growth-enhancing the transition path will be for everyone.

Conclusion

Although not all will agree with these recommendations for old-age income security systems in the United States and for the rest of the world, surely everyone recognizes that some change is necessary, that the public is not well informed, and that politicians are afraid to touch the issue. Therefore it is imperative to raise the level of public discourse, to put this topic on the political agenda, to make people aware of the problems and policy options, so that it becomes possible to move toward solutions.

Comment by Alicia H. Munnell

The World Bank study *Averting the Old Age Crisis* is very irritating; not because of the research or its presentation, both of which are commendable, but because of the recommendations that it provides. While it is very useful for finding out what is happening in pension systems around the world, the analysis is couched in a heavy-handed critique of pay-as-you-go pension systems. This approach is unwarranted, especially in the case of the U.S. Social Security system. This is one pension system that works well today and will continue to work well in the future.

The appeal of the three-pillar framework proposed by the World Bank is understandable because it seems so tidy, especially if all of the pillars do what they are supposed to do. In fact, it might not have been a bad idea to have used this approach back in 1935. However, given the present economic and political climate and the way in which attitudes toward the poor change, explicitly redistributive systems like this one are less plausible.

Anyone who cares about low-income people must value the U.S. Social Security system. It has been the country's best antipoverty program because it combines implicit redistribution with explicit redistribution. For while it is neat and tidy to separate out all of these functions into distinct pillars, real life is not neat and tidy. Under a system like the one proposed, vulnerable members of society would fare worse than they currently do under Social Security. Indeed, one reason for the success of Social Security is its flexibility—its ability to respond to the different needs of different people, some of whom may fall outside tightly prescribed pillars.

It is true that the first generation does well in a pay-as-you-go system. This is inevitable, unless the first generation is made ineligible for benefits. If a funded system is built up slowly, then there will be no free ride for the first generation. The decision to employ this type of system, however, must be made when the program is created. The United States made a different choice. This country opted for a system in which current workers pay for benefits given out to current retirees. To think about switching back now, in the second generation, involves huge transaction costs.

The study also tries to tidy up the issue of pensions and savings. This issue is not yet resolved even among economists. In terms of government-financed systems, it depends on what is happening in the non–Social Security part of the government. In terms of individuals, it is necessary to consider nonpension saving. No clear answer emerges as to the impact of Social Security on savings throughout the world.

Finally, I would recommend the study as a source of raw information. It does contain a lot of useful data. It does not, however, move the debate forward in terms of its policy prescriptions because it ignores the success of the U.S. system. There is no need to throw out pay-as-you-go social insurance programs when considering public pension systems in the international context.

Comment by Dalmer Hoskins

Estelle James and her staff and colleagues at the World Bank have made a very important contribution to the ongoing debate about pension policy in industrialized and developing countries. In taking advantage of this opportunity to discuss in detail some of the problems that I see in the study, my purpose it not to denigrate their work in any way; rather, I hope to advance the debate.

It is in the later chapters of the study, when it turns to policy recommendations, that the problems arise. Three stand out in particular. First, the study sets up an artificial dichotomy between public and private approaches to pension policy. This framework does not contribute to the debate or the dialogue needed about pension policy. Second, the study does not properly or sufficiently address the issue of governance—that is, the ability to deliver the product. In this case the product is social benefits. Third, the saving-and-investment issues need to be thought through more clearly. This topic is not only popular among economists, but it is much discussed in ministries of finance as well.

In regard to the public-private dichotomy, it is unfortunate that the three pillars have been trotted out once again. This concept has its strengths, but now it is being both overused and misused throughout the world. Everybody has a different idea of what these pillars are and what they stand for. In this particular instance more clarity is needed because the real world of Social Security is amazingly complex.

The numerous distinctions of the first tier, the second tier, and the third tier become very blurred when applied to real life. In the International Social Security Association (ISSA) membership, for example, there is an array of variations on the three-pillar theme. There are means-tested first pillars, income-tested first pillars. There are mandatory savings schemes. There are straightforward pay-as-you-go pension plans. There are combinations of social assistance and pay-as-you-go schemes. The variety of these approaches, while in some ways not so surprising, represents quite an achievement in the twentieth century, because it demonstrates that each country strives in a different way to reach the goal of providing income security. There is no simple formula to reach that objective. The World Bank report naively gives the impression that there is.

Also worrisome is the impression given by the report that public pay-as-you-go pension schemes are flawed and essentially out of date. This is not so. What is true is that every country with an advanced Social Security system is in the midst of debating how it will need to be changed, amended, and adjusted to ensure financial stability in the future. The very existence of this debate is a sign of the systems' health and vitality.

In this regard, the study criticizes the U.S. Social Security system for being politically flawed because its terms and conditions have been frequently changed, and because politicians are able to affect beneficiaries by changing eligibility or benefit provisions. This criticism is overblown. In fact, in most countries, including the United States, changes have been phased in over long periods of time, and there has always been an attempt to avoid hurting current beneficiaries. Many of the reforms that have been introduced in Japan, Germany, Switzerland, and France are scheduled to take twenty, thirty, or even forty years to be fully implemented, precisely so that the public will retain its trust in the system to which it has contributed.

Therefore the attachment of the public and of the political decision-makers to the current Social Security arrangements should not be underestimated because, in the western European countries at least, there still exists a broad consensus that these schemes are relevant and that they should continue to function into the future. In part this is a generational feeling. Twice in this century private arrangements were wiped out in places like Germany and Austria. Savings schemes, life insurance policies, thrift accounts, and bank accounts were completely obliterated by the economic disruptions of war and inflation. That is why such Social Security schemes have deep roots in these countries. Certainly the mix of income maintenance may change. There may be emphasis on one pillar or another pillar, on one approach or another approach; but the public pay-as-you-go structure still has strong and widespread public support.

The World Bank study gives the impression that the administration of these schemes is inefficient and costly. This is not necessarily true. One of the major achievements of the advanced Social Security systems over the past twenty years or so has been their efficiency and productivity gains. This has been partly driven by budgetary constraints. They have been compelled to cut their staffs and introduce modern management techniques. Many, including that of the United States, are running their programs with administrative costs of less than 1 percent. Unfortunately that is not the case in most of the developing countries of the world. The Chilean situation came about, in part, because of administrative problems and weak public confidence in the Social Security system. However, it is not evident that, as the World Bank study suggests, mandatory savings schemes or occupational pension schemes that are run in the private sector are immune from the mismanagement problems that face Social Security systems in much of the developing world.

This, in turn, relates to the issue of governance. The only sure way to ensure that private solutions would work better would be by means of an effective regulatory system. That is, there would have to be the regulatory capacity to ensure that the monies contributed to these systems would remain there and that a reasonable return on investment would be achieved. It is not clear that such regulatory systems are present in many countries of the world.

Not only do the administrators often lack necessary skills, but there is also a real danger of corruption when those who run the Social Security system are hired by people who have other designs on the money. This problem is indeed critical in many countries. And interference by the government can make it even more severe. Not only can a government avoid paying Social Security taxes as an employer, but many also dip into a system's reserves in order to finance current projects or mask the budgetary deficit.

Therefore, for both public and private Social Security systems, the real question is: What devices need to be in place to guarantee that the money will be in the trust funds when it is needed to pay out benefits? The World Bank should really focus its attention on this issue and explore how institutions like the tax system, the regulatory system, and the banking system are regulated, whether the approach is public or private.

Finally, the issue of saving warrants further discussion because among political decisionmakers and Social Security administrators there is much talk of using Social Security funds to increase both savings and capital for investment and greater productivity. There is nothing wrong with that, in theory. What is wrong with it in practice, though, is that it requires that people be very clear about their objectives. Most people in Singapore, for example, are willing to be quite frank about their objectives. Their system, with its huge provident fund, is not primarily a system for old-age protection. It was always intended as a method of building capital investment funds to be used for all kinds of purposes, of which old-age security was not first on the list. Similar situations exist in Malaysia and any number of countries that have provident funds. There is an increasing tendency for even the government representatives of these countries to admit that they are not first and foremost old-age income security schemes. But it is high time in every country to clearly map out the objectives of social security. Is it to provide old-age income security? Is it to promote savings? Is it a means of reducing employment? Is it a vehicle for supporting disabled people?

Mixing-up and blurring objectives may have certain advantages, but when talking about such huge sums of money in the national accounts, clarity of thinking is needed. This is what the World Bank study, unfortunately, does not provide.

Comment by Robert P. Hagemann

Possibly one of the most exciting activities undertaken at the International Monetary Fund is the provision of technical assistance in various fiscal fields, including Social Security reforms.[3] During the past several years, I have had the opportunity to advise governments of developing countries on ways of reforming the structure and institutional setup of their Social Security schemes in order to make them financially and administratively viable while at the same time achieving objectives that can be reasonably met. Context, that composite of social, political, and economic conditions, is a critical consideration in the shaping of recommendations. I would like to think that this experience has helped me to distinguish what is feasible from what is less so in different countries.

The World Bank study *Averting the Old Age Crisis* is a very impressive and useful piece of research. Thoughtful readers will inevitably come away better equipped to assess the relative merits of various policy options, based on the theoretical arguments and, importantly, on the country experiences that pepper the report. A gold mine of information on both general and specific issues, it is one of the few sources of information on policy issues related to old-age income security combined with country experiences and, whether one agrees with them or not, specific policy recommendations. A newcomer to the field can find extremely instructive introductory material on topics ranging from traditional approaches to parenting in Thailand to indexation options and the impact of population aging on pay-as-you-go financing. There is also an

3. These remarks do not necessarily reflect the views and opinions of the International Monetary Fund or those of its members.

abundance of cross-country comparative data that could prove invaluable to the interested reader.

The report is also forthright in its prescriptions. It is always refreshing when a report on a topic so potentially controversial as public pensions is unequivocal about the solutions it proposes. It is also the case that there is room in the world for much more variation than the report suggests.

I am actually quite an enthusiastic supporter of the multipillar approach to old-age income security. There is something appealing about combining the best of each approach into one system. Clearly, having separate tools designed to deal with separate policy objectives—redistribution, saving, insurance—is also attractive. It is like having separate instruments for the different targets in macroeconomic policy formulation. At the empirical level it is not terribly difficult to find examples of countries where the traditional defined benefit scheme, financed on a pay-as-you-go basis, has been unsuccessful, if not a dismal failure. The Italian and Brazilian situations, and the Chilean system before the introduction of the reform, show how unsustainable such schemes can become. Similarly, occupational pension schemes have occasionally proved to be less than fully funded even with strong regulation that, in the end, turned out to be poorly enforced. And recall the tenuous situation in the United States before passage of the Employee Retirement Income Security Act (ERISA), or the recent Maxwell disaster in the United Kingdom. As a general rule, the government would be the guarantor of last resort, at least if failures occurred on a sufficiently large scale, so that taxpayers would ultimately bear the risk of insuring the incomes of the elderly.

Thus it really does make sense to have a mix of tools. And given this, the most important question to emerge from the report is the relative size of the tiers. The report is sharp in its recommendations—namely, that the first tier should be very minimalist, possibly even means-tested, and financed on a pay-as-you-go basis out of general revenues; and that the second (a mandatory defined contribution scheme which is, by definition, funded) and the third tiers should together provide the bulk of the old-age pension. While the report offers several convincing arguments in favor of a first tier that will not crowd out the other tiers, there seems less reason to believe that every country should take the minimalist approach for the first tier and a maximalist approach for the second and third.

The first tier should preferably address more than basic old-age income protection and redistribution; it should have a contributory basis. The reason for this relates to concerns about the capacity of the second tier to provide a broad-based adequate income. It is well known that despite the increasing availability of indexed assets, defined contribution schemes provide poor protection against unanticipated inflation; a public defined benefit scheme, financed on a pay-as-you-go basis, is the only way of potentially protecting pensioners against unanticipated inflation after retirement. For this tier to have popular support and to make an adequate contribution to retirement income, it must be above the poverty line and linked to contributions. This does not preclude some limited redistribution, of course, although there are limits.

Pay-as-you-go financing does not, in and of itself, increase national saving; at best, it can leave it unchanged. In the worst case, it will reduce national saving. By contrast, defined contribution schemes could possibly increase the national saving rate, if the mandatory contributions were not offset by reductions in saving that would otherwise have taken place. It is worth emphasizing that the evidence is far from conclusive that the effect of mandatory retirement saving plans on national saving would be positive. However, in contrast to pay-as-you-go financing, it is highly unlikely to reduce national saving.

Regardless of the effect of mandatory retirement savings on national saving, the World Bank report is quite correct in suggesting that private management of such funds would reduce the risk that they might be invested in projects with a low social rate of return, as has so often been the case, especially in developing countries. This is, in fact, well documented in the report. It would therefore seem highly desirable to keep government intervention in such savings to a minimum. Although the report rightly emphasizes that government regulation is of paramount importance, it would have been useful if it had gone on to specify what would constitute a desirable regulatory framework for the successful implementation of a large defined contribution pillar. Moreover, the report also understates the fact that the other half of the regulatory story is strict enforcement. Many observers consider that the Maxwell disaster was not a consequence of lack of regulation but, rather, of weak enforcement.

These concerns, among others, are reflected and acknowledged in the report, and therefore it should not be assumed that the foregoing insights have been missed by the authors. Although mandatory defined contribution schemes should certainly be promoted, the report possibly places too much weight on the second tier. Instead, there should be greater balance between the first and second tiers. In turn, in order to minimize distortions, it is logical that the first tier be earnings-related, albeit with some redistribution. Although it is appropriate, where administratively feasible, to use general revenues to provide means-tested cash transfers as a social safety net, such a program should not be age-specific; a fiscally affordable antipoverty and social protection scheme should apply across the entire population.

There might also be reform proposals that suggest that the existing pay-as-you-go public schemes, although often in need of drastic adjustments, need not be tossed out entirely. It is well known that pay-as-you-go and funding are alternative ways of establishing claims on an economy's output. With full funding, the impacts of demographic transitions on the claims of retirees are, in a sense, endogenous and are borne by or accrue to the retirees. In a defined benefit scheme that is financed on a pay-as-you-go basis, when the dependency ratio rises the burden falls on contributors, barring adjustments to benefits. Although the World Bank report is right in calling for reforms of the public pillar in industrialized countries with mature defined benefit programs, it may not sufficiently recognize that with political will and sufficient foresight, countries can and do make adjustments that help to make such schemes more sustainable. To be sure, some countries seem to be waiting too long, like Italy. But many countries, including the United States, Japan, Sweden, Germany, and the United Kingdom, have taken bold steps to improve the long-run finances of their old-age pension programs. In those countries where disaster still looms, the problem lies more in the lack of political will and consensus-building, as well as in a shortage of unemotional public dialogue, than in the absence of viable solutions.

Comment by Jagadeesh Gokhale

The World Bank report *Averting the Old Age Crisis* warns about looming economic problems that many developed and developing countries will have to confront over the next several decades. The gradual increase in the proportion of old and retired individuals in relation to current workers will present a significant challenge to several nations. The primary economic task will be twofold: simultaneously to provide income security for a dilative older cohort and maintain, or even increase, rates of economic growth.

Unfortunately, these two objectives are incompatible. As populations age, maintaining the living standards of old and nonworking generations will require redistributing toward them an increasing share of total output. Because elderly persons consume more from their total resources than do younger persons, such redistribution is likely to depress rates of saving and investment. This, in turn, will reduce the capital available to future working generations, resulting in a decline in productivity, real wage, and output growth. Hence population aging is likely to intensify the long-standing debate about the appropriate trade-off between equity and growth. Now, however, the focus will be primarily on *inter*generational, rather than *intra*generational, equity.

The report correctly points out that current laws and institutions pertaining to old-age security, insurance provisions, and saving are unlikely to deliver good choices along this trade-off. A decline in saving is well documented in many developed countries. The United States is a case in point. Several decades of growth in public retirement and health support for elderly persons has improved their living standard considerably, but at the same time saving has plummeted. With the baby boom generation only a decade and a half away from retirement, reversing this trend may prove extremely difficult. For developing countries, the challenge of providing old-age security and increasing saving is complicated by the gradual disruption of informal family-based support systems, inadequate saving instruments, thin or nonexistent insurance and annuity markets, informational problems, and low tax bases, among other problems. Rapidly changing economic and social environments threaten to leave older generations in many of these countries exposed to economic and longevity risks.

To address these challenges, future policymakers will have to focus on four fundamental elements of fiscal policy:

—The distribution of resources within and across generations.

—Incentives for individuals to choose between consumption and saving and between work and leisure.

—The size and composition of public spending on goods and services.

—The provision of insurance against several types of economic risks.

Promoting better choices along each of these dimensions may require significant legal and institutional reforms.

The World Bank report focuses on the question: What types of policies will deliver the desired outcome of equitable distribution and robust economic growth for developed and developing countries? It also considers questions about institutional design at great length. Which features have the highest chance of success? Which features are needed to ensure the stability of the institutional structure? How can these elements be altered to suit the different economic circumstances of various economies? How can one ensure against inadequate performance by one or more components? In its discussion of these issues, the report presents an impressive array of information on the design features and operational experience of public and private retirement systems, insurance schemes, and fiscal saving incentives adopted in different nations.

Based on an anecdotal and comparative evaluation of alternative institutional arrangements, the report recommends setting up a three-pillar system for old-age income security and saving. The first pillar is a tax-financed scheme for redistributing resources toward poor elderly cohorts; the second is a mandatory and funded scheme to promote saving; the third consists of a voluntary scheme for supplementary saving by those who want additional resources and protection for their old age.

Appealing to past experience and adopting an eclectic approach to designing retirement systems cannot go very far in solving these problems. The most crucial issue, and one that must first be settled, pertains to the measurement of performance. The absence of a uniform set of principles for analyzing the impact of alternative policies on real economic outcomes leaves the report bereft of a meaningful way to communicate the desirability of alternative policies. As a result the report's recommendations are necessarily couched in general terms and relate more to the forms assumed by the institutions than to the stance of policy vis-à-vis intergenerational redistribution and saving.

Take, for example, a policy of extracting additional resources from younger generations (revenue) and giving them to older generations (expenditure) on an ongoing basis. All of the additional revenue could be called a tax, and all of the additional expenditure a transfer. If the policy were implemented in such a way that this tax was not distinguished from others and the transfer was included with preexisting ones, it might seem as though there were no social scheme at all—a zero-pillar scenario. Indeed, the expenditure could take the even more hidden form of a tax expenditure, or a reduction of existing taxes on older cohorts. Alternatively, by choosing explicitly to group one additional revenue and expenditure under the rubric of a social insurance scheme, it could be called a one-pillar system. Further, part of the extra revenue could be called a tax and the rest mandatory saving. Similarly, the additional expenditure could be broken down into a transfer and a return of principal with interest on the mandatory saving. This could be labeled a two-pillar system.

The transactions might be further divided into three components, the third revenue segment being retirement savings and the third expenditure segment public pension, to yield a three-pillar system. No matter how many such segments are created, the same underlying policy of reallocating a given amount of resources each period from younger to older generations could be preserved. Conversely, different fiscal policies could be followed even though institutional forms (that is, the number of pillars) remained the same.

Moreover, it would also be possible to construct what appeared to be a funded pillar for retirement saving, even though the underlying fiscal policy involved an intergenerational reallocation of resources. This argument indicates that the number of pillars, their status as a part of (or separate from) the rest of the government's budget, as well as their attributes of being funded or unfunded, are just veils and need not affect the implementation of any particular underlying fiscal policy.

Almost every fiscal policy that governments enact affect each of the four fundamental elements mentioned previously. A prerequisite for understanding the impact of any particular fiscal initiative on intergenerational wealth distribution is assessment of the stance of the entire fiscal setup vis-à-vis this distribution. That is, the contribution of fiscal operations as a whole to altering the cross-generational distribution of wealth must first be estimated. Research along these lines has recently been done for the United States and is being developed for OECD countries like Germany, Norway, Sweden, Japan, and Canada. Such an analysis helps in assessing how a change in any component of fiscal policy alters the distribution of wealth across generations.

Public and private retirement systems already redistribute resources from younger to older generations in many countries. Since population aging is likely to require additional resource transfers, it is important to know to what extent further reallocations are feasible. That is, it is necessary to evaluate the sustainability of current fiscal policy. Sustainability requires that current and projected purchases by the government be paid for out of the sum of current government wealth and contributions by current and future generations. An additional condition is that the projected burden on future generations should not be unrealistically large.

Assessing the sustainability of the current fiscal setup requires the collection of a substantial amount of data on the government's current net worth position, future demographic trends, budget projections, and the distribution of taxes and transfers among different generations. The organization of this data can then be used to evaluate directly the likely impact of demographic and policy changes on intergenerational wealth distribution and saving. The advantage of such a framework is that it imposes discipline on the analyst. First, no part of the fiscal setup is left out of the analysis. Second, every policy change has to be accompanied by an equal and opposite change in some other element in the sustainability constraint. Thus it forces the policymaker to confront the question: If more is to be redistributed toward elderly generations, how will this be financed? In addition, this framework may be combined with data on cohort-specific size, composition, and distribution of private wealth, to examine the likely impact of alternative policy changes on aggregate consumption and saving.

What criteria can such an analytical method provide for judging performance? Recent research in this area suggests estimating *lifetime net tax burdens* on living and future generations to assess the degree of imbalance embedded in current fiscal policy. The lifetime net tax burdens can be used to compute *lifetime net tax rates* as a measure of intergenerational equity and saving incentives facing different generations. It would also be possible to estimate the magnitude of fiscal policy changes necessary to achieve an equitable intergenerational wealth distribution.

To conclude, an analysis of alternatives should not be based on a piecemeal analysis of policies designed to provide social insurance. Concentrating on a particular policy without considering how the rest of the government's fiscal operations may neutralize (or enhance) its impact is not likely to be productive. The analysis should be based on an internally consistent analytical framework that takes the entire fiscal and demographic environment into account and generates a set of criteria for choosing between alternatives. This requires the collection and organization of a large amount of data for evaluating the sustainability and intergenerational stance of a country's fiscal policy. Such a research effort ought to be initiated on a global basis, and the World Bank would be the ideal organization for doing so.

References

World Bank. 1994. *Averting the Old Age Crisis: Policies to Protect the Old and Promote Growth.* Oxford University Press.

6

Social Security Reform in Chile: Two Views

THE PRIVATIZATION OF Social Security in Chile has attracted attention around the world. The Chilean example is the centerpiece of the analysis of the World Bank study that was the focus of chapter 5. In addition, Argentina, Colombia, and Peru have legislated reforms along similar lines. This chapter presents discussions of the Chilean reform by an actuary and an economist.

An Actuary's Perspective
Robert J. Myers

ONE OF THE BASIC principles of international consultants, whether in the social insurance field or in any other field, is not to say that whatever their own country is doing is the way that every other country ought to proceed. In other words, they would say that there is no perfect plan that will fit all nations because so much depends on political, demographic, sociological, and economic factors. Even for a given nation, no plan is the only one. Various plans might be as good or better, and often it is best to stay on the present course; or, as the saying goes, "If it ain't broke, don't fix it."

This principle is especially relevant when examining the pension plan recently developed in Chile. Although many things can be learned from a detailed study of the plan, caution is due when trying to apply those lessons to the situation in the United States. Chile's unique plan was developed in the early 1980s. In broad general principles, it is one that a number of people in the United States have proposed: privately administered individual retirement accounts instead of the traditional government-operated social insurance plan with a broad pooling of risk and only little individual equity. However, to understand the Chilean system, it is necessary to look at many of its details, and not just the broad principles. In essence, the Chilean system is a privatized defined contribution plan, although there are many elements that make it quite different from the pure concept of such a plan.

Why did Chile change from a standard social insurance plan after more than fifty years? The system as it existed in the 1970s and the early 1980s was a high-cost one, with a very high contribution rate, paid mostly by employers but with an employee contribution as well. One reason for the high costs was faulty benefit design. It paid benefits, in essence, on final earnings, and many people connived with their employers, deciding that there was no point to paying on their full salaries while they were young, since the pension payments would be based on the salaries of just the last few years of work. So disregarding the possibility that they might be disabled or die early, many people did not pay the contribution on their full salary, and others did not go into the system at all. There was very poor coverage compliance and coverage enforcement.

Another problem was that it was a fully funded system that would build up rather large reserves. However, severe inflation, particularly during the 1970s, made these reserves worthless. Because of these weaknesses, the system had great difficulty paying benefits, and this led to the creation of the current privatized pension plan.

Turning to the new Chilean plan and some of its rather unusual features, there are lessons for other countries to learn, if they look deeply. First, the system is based on a second type of money—a specially indexed currency that is also used for other purposes in Chile. In effect, this is the true basic currency of the country. But problems can arise when a country has two monetary systems. Chile is still experiencing very considerable inflation, although not as much as in the 1970s.

Coverage under the new system is such that all new employees after the initial effective date of 1981 have compulsory coverage, except for self-employed persons, who can come in voluntarily, and military personnel. (The plan was established by a military dictator.) Employees under the old system had the option of joining the new system, and some 90 to 95 percent did so. The question then arises whether there is a level playing field, or even if it was intended that there should be a level playing field? The answer is no. Several provisions of the old system were deliberalized, such as those for cost-of-living adjustments. They were thus real incentives for individuals to transfer to the new plan.

The very high contribution rate that, under the old system, had been borne largely by the employer, has been shifted to the employee. The new system is financed entirely by employee contributions—10 percent for pensions and about 3 to 3.5 percent for the disability and survivor benefits and for administrative expenses.

The initial impression is that this is unfair; the employer goes free and the employee pays all. But again, the entire picture must be taken into account. When the system was set up the government, having authoritarian powers, dictated that all employees would get a 17 percent increase in pay. So although the employees seem to be paying for the plan, the raise has actually given them a little net increase as well as meeting the new contribution rates.

There are special disability and survivor benefits. This is necessary in a defined contribution plan because if somebody dies or becomes disabled after a short period, he or she will not have built up much money in the account and will not be able to purchase anything significant in the way of disability or survivor benefits. So these benefits are bought separately, from insurance companies.

One very good feature of the system is that every four months, each participant receives a statement of how much is in her or his accumulation account. This is one reason for the popularity of the system among Chilean workers, because they see their bank accounts steadily growing in terms of pesos. But even though the accumulation account is in an indexed currency, how much will it be worth when they reach retirement age thirty or forty years later?

At retirement the accumulation account can be used to purchase an annuity from a life insurance company, or it can be drawn down (as can IRAs in the United States) and will possibly be exhausted. As for retirement benefits, there is one extremely important feature that many of the devotees of the Chilean approach either do not know about or do not recognize: prior service credits are granted, on a very generous basis, to people who were in the old system. This is one reason why so many people shifted over to the new system. The service credits are paid for entirely by the government and not at the time when the person enters the system, but when the person retires. So the government has huge general revenue obligations extending for decades from now.

Another highly significant element of general revenue financing in the Chilean system is the very generous minimum benefit provision. This minimum pension represents 85 percent of the legal minimum wage up to age seventy, and 90 percent thereafter. The government provides the difference between what is payable from the individual retirement accounts and this minimum benefit. The legal minimum wage is not indexed, but it is generally kept up-to-date by the legislature in one way or another and ranges from one-third to one-half of the average wage. Thus the minimum benefit is set at a substantial level and will incur high costs from general revenues into perpetuity.

Any country that is going to take lessons from the Chilean approach must realize that huge general revenue costs are involved; certainly, many countries, including the United States, do not have loose general revenues to spare. It so happens that Chile did. In the early 1980s Chile had a budget surplus, arising in part from the privatization of government-owned industries. Admittedly, it was paying out a large amount of money to support the deficit-ridden social insurance system. But there was also some laundering of the funds.

As to assets in the new system, each of the approximately twenty pension insurance companies can invest, under certain guidelines that the government sets up, in much the same way as insurance companies do in the United States. Because contributions and accumulations are in a special form of currency, the pension companies try to invest in securities that are also in this indexed currency. More than 40 percent of their investments, in fact, are in government bonds or government-guaranteed bonds. Most of the rest are in bank accounts that are also closely related to the government. Some of the money is invested in indexed mortgages and a small amount is in common stock. But the amount of money that is put directly into developing the economy is relatively small.

This is where funds are laundered. The government borrows money to pay the prior service credits and the minimum pensions, and then it issues this debt. Because the debt is bought by the pension insurance companies, the effect is similar to some social insurance systems—particularly pay-as-you-go ones— where the money coming in from current workers goes to pay current beneficiaries. In Chile this just happens indirectly.

There are several problems in the Chilean system, both actual and potential. One problem is coverage compliance. Coverage is compulsory, except for certain groups mentioned above. Possibly no more than 75 percent of the labor force is actually in the system. Moreover, it seems logical to suppose that, as lower-income workers realize that the minimum pension will ultimately override the amount derived from their accumulation and this is all that they will receive, they will decide to contribute only the very tiny amount necessary to get credit for coverage. Thus there will be increasing coverage noncompliance, as low-paid employees realize that it is possible to get the same benefit by contributing less, and their employers will cooperate with them by sending smaller amounts to the pension insurance company.

Another problem concerns how all this money will be used. There will not be enough investments in Chile. There is discussion about investing a considerable amount abroad, but some people who do not like the idea say that the money ought to be spent within the country. As these huge amounts keep coming in year after year, will there be new sources of investment, other than government bonds? Or will the availability of so much money result in very loose loans and poor investments? There could be defaults, and even thievery. It is a problem of having too much money.

Yet another problem is the system's high administrative expense. Currently administrative costs for the retirement benefits alone account for 12 or 13 percent of contributions; in the future, it is likely that the cost will be considerably higher when monthly retirement benefits are paid, either by the pension companies or when the accounts are annuitized by purchasing annuities from insurance companies. Even without considering the equivalent expenses for the separate disability and survivor benefits, that is a fairly heavy cut out of contributions, as compared to a social insurance system that can operate on administrative costs of 1 to 3 percent of contributions.

Another problem is that the system's planners think that the 10 percent contributions will provide adequate pensions, on the order of 50 to 70 percent of final salary. This is based on the assumption that there will be a 7 percent real rate of return. Up until now the experience has been very favorable. In most years there has been a 12 or 13 percent real rate of return. However, over the long run, it is unrealistic to expect a real return of 7 percent.

There is also the problem of increasing longevity. Although these levels of benefits may possibly be maintained under existing mortality conditions, it is not clear what will happen as mortality rates improve. As with any defined contribution plan, there is no guarantee of the amount of pension that will be received in the end.

Furthermore, the system is quite young. Fifteen years is a short time in the life of any pension plan or social insurance system. It is still too early to say that the Chilean system is a great success and that every other country in the world ought to follow it.

In conclusion, what was done in Chile was very good for that country, considering its condition at the time. It was not the only solution, and there are certain problems that might arise in the future. On the other hand, this approach would be highly undesirable for the United States. This country does not have the general revenues to put a system like the Chilean one into effect. The problems of transition would be tremendous. The U.S. system is not broken and does not need to be discarded, although some adjustments are needed. As to other countries, each one ought to study the Chilean system and learn from it. It should not be accepted as a model simply on the general assumption that individual equity will prevail and, thus, everybody will get their money's worth.

An Economist's Perspective
Peter A. Diamond

THE 1981 REFORM of social security in Chile has received a great deal of comment, attention, and imitation.[1] There has been similar legis-

---

1. This discussion draws very heavily on Diamond and Valdes-Prieto (1994). Salvador Valdes-Prieto's coauthorship was essential in the development of that analysis. Naturally, he does not

lation in Argentina, Colombia, Mexico, and Peru, and consideration of its implementation in other Latin American countries. In contrast with the central role of the benefit formula in a traditional social security system, the central concept in the Chilean system is the contribution rate. The conceptual starting place of a Social Security system has powerful effects in shaping the details that follow. Indeed, the distinction between contribution and benefit base is more illuminating than the distinction between privatized and government-run systems, for various pieces of either type of system can be privatized.

In the final analysis, the Chilean approach gets high marks for defending the system from political risk. The Chilean approach gets low marks for the provision of insurance and for administrative cost. It also gets high marks for its effects on capital accumulation and on the functioning of the capital market, provided the implementation is done as it was in Chile, including a government budget surplus running at 4 percent of GDP as part of overall policy. In addition, the Chilean capital markets were not well developed at the start of the implementation process, so social security reform and capital market reform have gone hand in hand.

Overview of Chilean Reform

Chile established its social insurance system in 1924. By the 1970s the system had developed a pattern that is not uncommon. There were separate defined benefit systems for different industries and occupations. Since these were not unified, benefit structures and levels varied across sectors. It was inefficient to have multiple bureaucracies. The benefit formulas were not well designed for providing economic incentives. The political determination of benefit levels had resulted in very high contribution rates, which (including health) were in the range of 51 to 59 percent in 1975. Government financial support to health, pensions, and contributions for government employees represented 20.5 percent of total government expenditure. A major problem was the tendency of the politicians to raise benefits when short-run financing was available because of immaturity of a particular benefit system. In light of these issues, planning for Social Security reform was begun under the Pinochet government in the 1970s and, after a significant fiscal surplus had been built up, implementation began in 1981.

The heart of the reform is a privatized mandatory savings plan, with a market for indexed annuities. It is important to recognize that a mandatory

necessarily agree with everything in the present discussion, a longer version of which has been published as Diamond (1994).

savings system needs some mechanism for converting accumulations into retirement income flows. In Chile all covered workers must place 10 percent of monthly earnings in a savings account with an approved and highly regulated intermediary, an Administradora de Fondos de Pensiones (AFP). Each AFP manages a single fund, allocating the complete return on the fund to the individual accounts. The AFP also provides disability and survivors insurance, according to rules set down by the government. Workers must pay a commission to the AFP, in addition to the mandatory 10 percent savings, to finance disability and survivors insurance and to cover the costs and profits of the AFPs. The commission rates are set by the competing AFPs; the government regulates their structure, but not their level. Workers are free to select any AFP and to switch among them. On becoming eligible to receive pension benefits, a worker can choose between a sequence of phased withdrawals or a real annuity. The annuity option involves switching financial intermediaries, as the annuity must be purchased from an insurance company. The fact that Chile has a long history of using indexed debt has made it easy for the annuity option to be restricted to indexed annuities. It is worth noting that the private providers of Social Security are closely regulated; there has not been reliance on unregulated market forces. In addition to this privatized system, there is a sizable guaranteed minimum pension. Unlike the purchased annuities, the minimum pension is not indexed, but it is adjusted by the government from time to time.

Cost

Privatization has come to be seen as a route to greater efficiency and lower costs. Thus perhaps the most surprising aspect of the Chilean reform is the cost of running a privatized Social Security system, which is as high as the "inefficient" system that it replaced. Possibly this high cost should not have been surprising, for Beveridge noted the "markedly lower cost of administration in most forms of State Insurance."[2]

The administrative costs of the new system include both those of the AFPs that manage the mandatory accumulation and those of the insurance companies that produce disability insurance, life insurance, and annuities. Salvador Valdes-Prieto has estimated that the average administrative charge per effective affiliate while active (assuming purchase of an annuity) is U.S.$89.10 per year, which represents 2.94 percent of average taxable earnings.[3] This comprises over 20 percent of the 13 percent of earnings paid for the program. The

2. Beveridge (1942, p. 286).
3. Valdes-Prieto (1994). The estimates quoted are for 1991.

cost per person is not far from costs observed in other privately managed pension systems, such as defined benefit private pensions in the United States. However, it compares unfavorably with administrative costs in well-run, unified, government managed systems. For example, the U.S. Social Security Administration (SSA) reports a cost of U.S.$18.70 per person per year on the same basis. Admittedly, this figure includes only a small charge made to the SSA by the Internal Revenue Service (IRS) for the collection of payroll taxes and is limited in its ability to measure capital costs. As a guess, the U.S. system probably costs less than twice what it reports, although any specific number is dependent on the arbitrary allocation of IRS overhead costs between the different taxes that it collects.

Because the costs of running a pension system are unlikely to be either proportional to average wages or independent of average wages in the economy, it is not obvious exactly how to compare costs across countries in the absence of an estimated cost function. Comparing the United States and Chile, the answer probably lies somewhere between the 2.5-to-1 and 12.5-to-1 cost ratios on these two bases. The issue here is the administrative efficiency of relying on the private market to satisfy a mandate that is placed on individual workers. The extent to which the costs depend on the particulars of the implementation in Chile is discussed briefly below, and the evidence will soon be supplemented when we have evidence from other countries that choose different regulations.[4]

For example, in the United States the life insurance industry has costs of 12 to 14 percent of annual benefits. In contrast, the SSA reports administrative costs that are less than 1 percent of annual benefits; even if these costs were doubled, they would still be well below the private market cost.

Valdes-Prieto's estimate includes the costs of running the annuities market. High costs here are in line with the common perception that individual annuity markets do not work very well. Although many countries have a well-functioning group annuities market, Chile relies on individual annuities with no provision for group formation for annuity purchase.

A number of elements lie behind this cost differential between private insurance markets and compulsory government systems. One is the economies of scale that come with a single compulsory system without choice. A second is the costs that arise from competitive attempts to attract more customers in the market, such as advertising, and sales personnel. For example, in Chile in June 1994 there were 11,500 salespeople employed by the AFPs relative to 3.5 million workers who had contributed at least once in the previous twelve

---

4. On annuity costs in the United States, see Friedman and Warshawsky (1990).

months. This is a ratio of nearly 3.5 salespeople per 1,000 contributors. The same ratio in the United States would imply 450,000 salespeople. The third element is the fact that in actual markets demand is much less sensitive to price variation than in idealized competitive markets. This implies that firms will exercise what market power they do have and, in turn, the positive markups allow room for slack and inefficiency and serve as an incentive for sales efforts to attract more customers.

These elements apply to many products other than insurance, although the feature of the infrequent purchase of a product that is difficult for consumers to evaluate, and the presence of adverse selection probably contributes to higher costs in this market. Also, the low demand for insurance, which is one rationale for having a mandatory program in the first place, probably raises costs as well.

It is also necessary to consider the conditions affecting the administrative costs of public supply. The collection of contributions and delivery of cash benefits probably represents the kind of well-defined task that lends itself to efficient public supply.[5] Moreover, the limited effort to vary products with consumer preferences (associated with the limited consumer understanding and demand for insurance) also makes the government's task easier and less costly.

These high administrative costs of private markets raise two questions. One question is the extent to which a system with many small accounts is desirable, because compulsory savings are less attractive when costs are eating up a large fraction of these savings (even if costs are similarly high for voluntary savings). A low mandatory savings rate, as considered by the Entitlements Commission, would also generate many small accounts. A second question is whether there are alternative designs, with more government involvement or more employer involvement, that would keep costs down. For example, the Chilean approach of limiting the role of government (without eliminating it) has left collecting monthly payments to the market, despite this being a natural monopoly. The institution for collection could have been organized, even if not run, by the government.

The Chilean approach focuses on individual choice. As a general proposition, group choice is considerably cheaper than individual choice. For example, in the United States mutual funds directed toward individuals are, on average, roughly three times as expensive (measured relative to assets) as mutual funds handling large accounts and so directed toward groups. Thus allowing employers to select a single AFP for all their workers would be likely to generate cost

---

5. For a discussion of the variety in bureaucratic responses to alternative tasks, see Wilson (1989).

savings. In a recent paper Valdes-Prieto and two Australian economists, Hazel Bateman and John Piggott, compare marketing expenses in Chile with those in Australia, where the retirement savings mandate is placed on employers, not workers.[6] In Chile 35.7 percent of the accounting costs of AFPs are attributed to marketing, while in Australia this proportion varies between 3.2 and 6.4 percent across funds. How much of the difference is due to the location of the mandate on employers rather than workers and how much is due to the nature of the regulation of charges in Chile is hard to tell. In Australia employers are allowed to set up and run multiemployer funds, without necessarily employing financial firms.

Capital Market

The combination of a steady flow of contributions together with very high real rates of return (an average of 14.5 percent from July 1981 to July 1992) has meant a large accumulation of funds invested in the Chilean economy.[7] As of June 1992, the total accumulations were equal to 35 percent of 1992 GDP; equity holdings by pension funds were 9.6 percent of the value of the Santiago stock exchange (with life insurance companies holding another 1 percent); and pension funds held 61.1 percent of registered corporate bond issues outstanding (with life insurance companies holding close to another 30 percent). On the other hand, at that time close to 40 percent of pension fund assets were in public debt. The high rates of return, and implied rapid accumulation, are the result of generally high rates of return in the Chilean economy, not of particularly astute investment choices by private fund management. No doubt these high rates of return have contributed to the popularity of the reform with Chilean workers.

Together with this accumulation, the regulation of the markets in which these funds are invested has been evolving to create a set of capital markets that function far better than they did before the reform. The regulation of capital markets is not easy and requires continuous adjustment as new ways of causing difficulties develop; Chile has had repeated adjustments. Thus the careful regulation of capital markets is both a necessary part of a successful privatization of Social Security and a significant benefit of successfully accomplishing such a privatization.

---

6. See Bateman, Piggott, and Valdes-Prieto (1995).

7. Although these figures are slightly out of date, I have been told by Chilean colleagues that there has been little change in the basic picture of the effects of the Chilean reform since.

In Chile, the privatization of fund management has been combined with individual choice of fund. This is not a necessary combination. There could be a system where individual accounts were kept by the government, and shares earned their return from their proportion of a single fund that was privately invested; that is, there can be privatization of fund management without individual choice of fund. This combination would have lower costs. Insofar as people do not understand risk-return trade-offs, the removal of choice may have little or no welfare significance. However, such a structure would require a new institution with the independence of a central bank, and would also require transparent transactions between the institution picking the private fund managers and the managers themselves. This combination may not be possible in many places, but it may be useful to recognize that many of the pieces of the Chilean model could be combined with other, alternative pieces.

If individuals held shares in a single, privately managed fund, it would be straightforward to expand the system to two or more funds, so that individuals could choose the proportions of their accounts that went into the different funds. Thus younger people might choose proportions bearing higher risk, while older people, closer to retirement, might choose proportions with lower risk.

At present in Chile, each AFP has a single fund. Thus while workers can choose an AFP, they are restricted in the range of funds because of the incentives for different AFPs to have similar funds. In the absence of regulation, the pattern of risk-to-expected return points offered is understandably somewhat limited in a setting where each AFP has a single fund. In addition, there is regulation guaranteeing that no fund will perform too much worse than the average of all funds.[8] This creates an incentive for fund portfolios not to differ too much from the average fund, since the AFP bears some of the down risk and receives none of the up risk (except through increased enrollments). Thus allowing AFPs to offer a choice of funds in a way that significantly expanded the range of alternatives available would require a change in the guarantee structure. The inexperience of many small investors suggests that some form of guarantee is important, especially in the early stages of this type of reform.

Financing the Transition

During the transition of a reform like that in Chile, mandatory savings flow into new individual accounts rather than directly paying pensions owed by the

---

8. The guarantee is the lower of half the average return and the average return less 2 percent.

existing, mature, pay-as-you-go social insurance system. This leaves a large fiscal cost on the government budget. This could be financed either by explicit debt or by taxes. In Chile there has been little issue of new (explicit) public debt to finance the benefits being paid under the old system. Active workers who switched to the new system have received explicit government debt, called recognition bonds, on account of past contributions. The maturities of these bonds correspond to the retirement dates of the recipients. This financing decision has meant an increase in fiscal saving. Indeed, the decision to avoid debt financing implied an improvement in the primary fiscal balance of 3.5 to 4 percent of GDP each year in the 1980s and early 1990s. It is anticipated that the level of needed fiscal saving will remain roughly constant for the rest of the 1990s, and will gradually decrease thereafter. Before the start of the pension reform, the government built a primary surplus of 5.5 percent of GDP with a view to avoiding debt financing for its implementation. Thus most of the transition deficit—the deficit in the old pension system—has been financed out of a primary surplus. In addition, a simultaneous increase in the age of retirement under the old system significantly decreased the implicit liabilities of the government.[9]

The Chilean privatization could have been accomplished without the buildup of a surplus to finance the transition. Such a course would not have produced the level of additional capital accumulation that is associated with a simultaneous improvement in the government fiscal balance. It is sometimes suggested that privatization is a tool that will help to press a government with a chronic deficit into doing something about it. There would seem to be serious political risk associated with such an approach. If there were a sizable government deficit, there would be considerable political incentive to channel the privatized mandatory savings into government debt. If there were large government debt holdings by the intermediaries and a large continuing deficit, there would be a strong incentive to pay low interest rates on this debt in order to lower the deficit. Indeed, in the Philippines below-market interest rates have been paid on government debt held by pension funds. The combination of primarily government debt and politically determined interest rates defeats much of the purpose of privatization. Rather than privatization being a cure for a chronic deficit, it may be the case that a surplus is an important condition for a successful privatization.

---

9. Minor portions of this deficit were financed by the sale of shares in formerly state-owned utilities (some of which were purchased by pension funds) and, over the business cycle, by the issue of debt.

Redistribution and Political Risk

Benefit-based systems seem to result in more redistribution to and among the current elderly than do contribution-based systems. A country like Chile, which had multiple Social Security systems, is particularly prone to the risk that well-off elderly people will receive a disproportionate share of such redistribution. This difference in outcomes is interesting since there is little in one system that, on average, could not be accomplished by the other.[10] Yet adding amounts to individual accounts seems a much more difficult measure, politically, than choosing a benefit formula that results in much higher returns on taxes for some workers. Individual accounts seem to require identification of the source of any funds to be added to those accounts. This is different from redistribution to the current elderly from a benefit structure that leaves the cost vaguely to the future. In other words, from a political perspective, handing out explicit debt is different from handing out implicit debt.

Because legislating a benefit formula can easily lead to a program that is not viable in the long run, individual accounts have real appeal as insulation from political actions to increase benefits without direct financing. The Chilean system gets high marks on this dimension, although it is not clear what other aspects of the Chilean reforms, beyond individual accounts, are needed to keep this sort of political action in check.

There are further political issues stemming from the choice of basic design. Redistribution within the mandatory savings pillar is not part of the Chilean system, and the annuities purchased from these accounts must be indexed. In contrast, the Chilean minimum pension is financed out of general revenues and is not indexed for inflation, but adjusted from time to time. At a quick glance, this combination appears to be an example of the aphorism that "a program for poor people is a poor program." Fluctuations in real benefits, depending on the state of the government budget and the party in power, would place risk on the poor elderly that many would find difficult to bear. It is legitimate to ask whether pensions that flow through the government budget should fluctuate more than pensions that do not. But there is no apparent reason for one sort of pension to fluctuate more than the other. Although it is unfortunate that the minimum pension is not similarly protected, the political insulation of benefits from mandatory savings inherent in the Chilean system does seem very attractive. It is interesting to note that Chile did freeze the cost of living adjustment (COLA) for pensions received under the old system, in 1985. Because COLAs

---

10. For example, Boskin, Kotlikoff, and Shoven (1988) have proposed a system with individual accounts and annual redistributions.

paid by private insurance companies do not directly affect the government budget, it is not likely that the government would freeze pensions paid under the new system in the event of some future budget squeeze.

Social Risk and Aggregate Change

Examining the actuarial forecasts of Social Security systems, it is clear that they are subject to large aggregate risks. These include the rate of growth of real wages, the real rate of return, mortality factors, and in pay-as-you-go systems, the growth of the labor force. In addition, some economies, including Chile, are projecting significant aging of their populations.

Different pension systems have different degrees of need to adapt to changes in basic economic and demographic parameters. The Chilean system is sensitive to interest rate and mortality changes since these affect the adequacy of retirement income relative to prior earnings. Pay-as-you-go systems have more concern with population factors. Commonly, Social Security systems are subject to political gridlock as they attempt to adapt to significantly changed circumstances. The Chilean system can be left on automatic pilot, in the sense that the system remains viable and the magnitude of cost from nonoptimal parameters would probably not be too large. This is in contrast with systems that become nonviable if they do not adapt when circumstances change. While pay-as-you-go systems could be put on automatic pilot, such that taxes, or benefits, or a combination of both would adjust automatically, in practice they are not.

Insurance

Labor market efficiency is affected by Social Security systems, depending on how well the law balances redistribution, insurance, and disincentives. Some disincentives are a necessary part of redistribution and insurance. It is common for benefit-based systems to have poorly designed labor market incentives. The Chilean reform avoids these by basing eligibility for benefits on age (and eligibility for early benefits on the size of accumulation), not on employment or earnings. But one price of this strategy is the absence of insurance for varying length of working life, an important risk for many workers. In addition, the government guaranteed minimum pension provides significant disincentives for work in the covered sector and for payment of the mandatory contributions. Any redistribution has disincentives. The Chilean approach of a guaranteed minimum and no other redistribution may not be a good structure for balancing redistribution and disincentives.

The Chilean system gives workers of retirement age a choice between purchasing an indexed annuity and making a series of phased withdrawals from their account, subject to a maximum allowable rate of withdrawal. This rate varies with age and recent interest earnings on the funds. Without such a limit, some people would have a powerful incentive to withdraw rapidly in order to tap into the minimum pension. Widespread use of phased withdrawals rather than annuities may reflect incomplete understanding of the risks of long life. However, removing this option would cut against the idea that individuals control these funds. Moreover, reducing the set of alternatives would probably decrease the price sensitivity of demand for annuities, resulting in higher markups.

A benefit-based system normally relates benefits to earnings history using a formula that does not recognize differences in life expectancy for different retirees. If allowed to do so, a private market will use different annuity conversion factors for different people, reflecting estimates of different life expectancies for different groups, different markups by different firms, and varying interest rates. In the Chilean system funds are accumulated until retirement age is reached, when an annuity may be purchased. Accumulations of workers who die before retirement go to their estates, not to finance higher benefits for those surviving until retirement age. Some workers would prefer a system where estates are smaller and retirement benefits are larger. A traditional benefit-based system does this automatically. Similarly, a worker contemplating the future purchase of an annuity has no way to insure the rate at which the annuity will be quoted. A benefit-based system also provides this insurance automatically.

Conversely, if varying life tables are not allowed in the private market, selection problems arise as insurance companies compete to attract the groups who will be most profitable. This would probably add to the costs of competition.

Conclusions

Chile provides a fascinating example to observe. Other countries can do worse than to imitate Chile (and many have). As has been shown, countries choosing to privatize can do better by recognizing that the private market is an expensive institution, and so trying to hold down the cost of using it. Group choice, rather than individual choice, often represents a good trade-off of lower costs against fewer options.

It is also important to recognize that it is not easy to imitate Chile—it requires strict regulation and political discipline so that the reform does not unravel into either private or public raids on accumulated funds. The insulation from political risk and the development of capital markets, which are the major benefits of the Chilean approach, do not follow automatically—they require skill and discipline. Moreover, some countries need this capital market development and the political insulation more than others. Thus whether to go the Chilean route and how closely to imitate the Chilean details are questions best answered separately, on a country-by-country basis.

References

Bateman, Hazel, John Piggott, and Salvador Valdes-Prieto. 1995. "Australia y Chile: Prevision Privada con Normas Diferentes Comparacion de Regulaciones y de Comisiones de Administración." Documento de Trabajo 176. Pontificia Universidad Católica de Chile.

Beveridge, W. H. 1942. *Social Insurance and Allied Services.* Cmd 6404. London: HMSO.

Boskin, Michael J., Laurence J. Kotlikoff, and John B. Shoven. 1988. "Personal Security Accounts: A Proposal for Fundamental Social Security Reform." In *Social Security and Private Pensions,* edited by Susan M. Wachter. Lexington, Mass.: Lexington Books.

Diamond, Peter A. 1994. "Privatization of Social Security: Lessons from Chile." *Revista de Analisis Económico* 9: 21–34.

Diamond, Peter A., and Salvador Valdes-Prieto. 1994. "Social Security Reforms." In *The Chilean Economy: Policy Lessons and Challenges,* edited by Barry Bosworth, Rudiger Dornbusch, and Raul Laban. Brookings.

Friedman, Benjamin M., and Mark J. Warshawsky. 1990. "The Cost of Annuities: Implications for Saving Behavior and Bequests." *Quarterly Journal of Economics* 105(1): 135–54.

Valdes-Prieto, Salvador. 1994. "Administrative Charges in Pensions in Chile, Malaysia, Zambia and the United States," Policy Research Working Paper 1372. Washington: World Bank.

Wilson, James Q. 1989. *Bureaucracy: What Government Agencies Do and Why They Do It.* Basic Books.

7

The Future of Social Security

Peter A. Diamond

THE RELEASE of the 1995 annual reports of the trustees of Medicare and Social Security did not receive much news coverage even though the trustees project that Medicare will run out of money in 2002 and that the cash benefits part of Social Security—Old-Age, Survivors, and Disability Insurance—will run out in 2030. This was hardly news because everyone already knew that there was a problem. Also, the problem was slightly less severe than had been projected the year before—both dates had receded by one year. It also was hardly news because public confidence in the future of Social Security was already quite low. Indeed, the fraction of people reporting themselves very or somewhat confident in Social Security is only around 40 percent.[1] This response should be taken with a grain of salt, however, since the same surveys show that over 90 percent of the interviewees are expecting to receive Social Security benefits, commonly as a major source of income.

How serious are these two problems? Briefly, the Medicare problem is very serious, but the problem in Social Security (that is, OASDI) is not so severe. Indeed, if the politicians would address the latter soon, it could be fixed in a satisfactory way without too much pain.

First, it is important to recognize the big difference between these two problems. Not only will the Medicare fund reach zero sooner than the Social Security fund, but more important, Social Security is a program that promises money according to a formula that is controlled by Congress, while Medicare

An earlier version of this section was given as the Erwin Plein Nemmers Prize Visiting Professor Inaugural Lecture, Northwestern University, April 19, 1995.

1. Survey done by American Viewpoint Inc. for the 1991 Advisory Council on Social Security. Robert B. Friedland, "When Support and Confidence are at Odds: The Public's Understanding of the Social Security Program," National Academy of Social Insurance, Washington, May 1994, p. 23.

is a program that promises to pay for medical expenses despite having limited ability to control what medical care will cost. That is, in addition to needing to decide how much to spend on this program, Medicare has the additional problem of trying to affect the choice of medical services that result from its spending decisions. Uncertainty about medical technology and organization makes it difficult to know how future spending levels will translate into the provision of medical care, or to fully understand the links between decisions about what services are covered by health insurance and the cost of Medicare. By having a directly controlled benefit formula, and then a simple link that money spent is money received by beneficiaries, OASDI presents a problem that is much easier to solve.

Both funds are going to be hit by the aging of the population—in particular, the retirement of the baby boom generation. But the Medicare fund is scheduled to reach zero well before that happens. It is precisely because medical costs have been rising more rapidly than other costs, and more rapidly than incomes, that this problem is so big and so hard to deal with, both in the United States and in other advanced countries. While there has been a slowdown in the trend growth of medical expenses in the last couple of years, it seems all too likely that this is merely temporary. Slowing medical cost increases permanently would require some mechanism to undertake the extremely unpleasant task of deciding what medical services are simply too expensive for society to buy collectively. This problem arises both with very expensive medical treatments for some of the sick, and also with diagnostic tests that are expensive when performed on a large fraction of the population but detect only a small number of people who can be helped. It is too expensive to do everything that is medically useful, and therefore it is necessary, somehow, to decide what medical services are worth the cost, just as with other expenditures. But that is a very difficult decision to make well.

On the other hand, the Social Security problem is easily manageable. I will describe how big the problem is, describe the importance of addressing it sooner rather than later, and discuss a number of different approaches to addressing the problem.

The law governing Social Security is in two parts. One part determines benefits: who will get them and how much. The other part of the law determines revenues, mostly the payroll tax, but also the income taxation of part of benefits and the interest earned on the trust funds. Each year, the Office of the Actuary of the Social Security Administration projects Social Security for the next seventy-five years and calculates whether there is actuarial balance for the seventy-five-year period. At present, the system is not in balance; the imbalance is a little more than 2 percentage points of payroll. That is, if the payroll tax were to be raised immediately by 2.17 percentage points, in addition to the current 12.4 percentage points, balance would be restored for the seventy-five-year period. Unfortunately, it would slip a little out of balance the next year, as the seventy-five-year evaluation period moves one year into the future.

A second way to see the size of the problem is to ask how big the payroll tax would have to become if, each year, just enough money was collected to pay that year's benefits (net of the revenue from income taxation of benefits that goes to OASDI). As the population ages, this number will get steadily bigger. Seventy-five years from now it would be roughly 18 percent. That is, if nothing were done to hold down benefit growth, a payroll tax that grew steadily to 18 percent would deal with the Social Security problem. This is much higher than at present, but not a crippling rate. Many countries function perfectly well with high payroll taxes.[2]

At the present time, the country does not seem to have much taste for tax increases in general. Yet polls asking about tax increases just for Social Security find the population solidly behind such measures. In a recent poll, 64 percent of respondents favored raising taxes now to lessen tax increases in the future, while only 28 percent preferred not increasing taxes before 2010. A majority opposed (15 percent) or strongly opposed (38 percent) decreasing benefits by 10 to 20 percent for those born after 1960 in order to avoid a tax increase.[3] Since the message of such polls is always ambiguous, and government by opinion poll is not desirable, this should be viewed as a sampling of mood, not as the basis for a policy recommendation.

If the country was not willing to raise taxes and the shortfall was balanced completely by cutting benefits, how great would the impact on benefits be? This would depend critically on when the benefit cuts began. To take three examples: if benefits were cut for everyone turning age sixty-two in 2002 or later, then a 20.5 percent cut would suffice; by waiting until 2012, a 25.5 percent cut would be needed; by waiting until 2022, a 33.5 percent cut would be needed.[4] Again, this is not a recommendation for such a sharp break in

---

2. Another way to see the difference in size between the Medicare and Social Security problems is to compare expenditures to GDP. OASDI is now 4.8 percent of GDP. In seventy-five years it is projected to grow to 6.8 percent. In contrast, Medicare (hospital insurance [HI] and supplemental medical insurance [SMI]) is now 2.5 percent of GDP and is projected to grow to 8.75 percent, a much larger difference.

3. Gallup, Inc., and Employee Benefit Research Institute, "Public Attitudes on Social Security, 1995," Gallup-EBRI Report G-62, 1995, p. 23.

4. These estimates were made by the Office of the Actuary of the Social Security Administration for the Technical Panel on Income and Retirement Security appointed by the Advisory Council on Social Security and are based on the assumptions and projection period used for the 1994 trustees' report.

legislated benefits, but it gives a sense of the importance of addressing the problem sooner rather than later.

There are two approaches to addressing this problem. One is to muddle through in the traditional way, legislating a few changes in parameters of the system in order to restore balance, as did the last major Social Security legislation, in 1983. This is better done now than when the problem is more severe and more imminent. The second approach is to consider larger structural changes, including privatization.

Congress does not like to admit that it is cutting benefits, even when it is doing so. In order to avoid the vocabulary of benefit cuts, therefore, Congress looks for actions that do reduce benefits, but can be described in different words. The 1983 legislation included a one-time delay in cost-of-living adjustments (COLAs). From an economist's perspective, this is just another way of cutting benefits, but Congress preferred delaying COLAs to explicitly making an identical cut in benefits. Similarly, the legislation phased in a delay in the normal retirement age. This is scheduled to rise from its current level of age sixty-five to age sixty-seven in a long series of slow steps. What does it mean to delay the normal retirement age? As legislated in 1983, it does not change the age at which people can first claim retirement benefits; any insured worker over sixty-two can retire and start receiving benefits. But the amount of benefits received at age sixty-two, or at any other age, is made smaller if the normal retirement age is higher. Thus it is yet another way to reduce benefits without stating that they are being cut. Indeed, there is nothing inherently wrong with this pattern of benefit cuts, apart from the euphemisms. On the other hand, whether the early entitlement age of sixty-two should be changed is a complex question to analyze.

Proposals to muddle through the current imbalance generally include some benefit cuts in this form. Some people propose delaying the normal retirement age beyond the age of sixty-seven that has been legislated; perhaps to sixty-eight, or as late as seventy. A common suggestion is to speed up the phasing of the already legislated delay. Some proposals include a change in the way that benefits are calculated. Currently, benefits are based on the best thirty-five years of a worker's indexed earnings. One proposal is to expand this averaging period to thirty-eight years, reducing average lifetime earnings and thus the level of benefits. Again, this is a reasonable way to make a benefit cut. A critical question to consider is the distribution of these cuts among people of different ages. It would seem fair to spread cuts across many generations without exempting any cohort, and not concentrate the cuts on the younger workers of today.

Proposals to muddle through frequently would extend Social Security to the last large set of workers who are not covered. This comprises some state and local government employees who are currently allowed to remain outside the system. Including these workers in Social Security would help with the financing, in part because they would begin paying taxes soon, but would only receive the resulting benefits later on.

Alan Greenspan, chairman of the Federal Reserve, recently received considerable coverage for his statement that the rate of inflation is overstated. Since this rate is used to calculate COLAs for Social Security, any reduction in measured inflation will save the system money. Measurement of the consumer price index (CPI) probably does overstate inflation, although there is considerable dispute about the magnitude of the discrepancy; consequently, the measurement of the CPI should be reviewed and steps taken to make it as accurate as possible. However, speculation that inflation is inaccurately measured should not be used to reduce COLAs by a legislatively chosen amount. Inflation should b_____ _____ _____ Shrinking real benefits should not be inflicted on re_____ _____ _____ _____ inflation. Poverty among the o_____ _____ _____ who live a long time, p_____ _____ _____ not to make arbitrary ad_____ _____ _____ and reduce benefits fo_____ _____ _____ of those who study Soci_____ _____ _____ efits for this population_____

The p_____ _____ _____ h the sort of modifica_____ _____ _____ over the years. They co_____ _____ _____ ase, to restore actuaria_____ _____ _____ em. Two other changes_____ _____ _____ anges in Social Securit_____ _____ _____ rivate economy, in stoc_____ _____ _____ ls completely in Treasu_____ _____ _____ lividual workers control over the in_____ _____ _____ nefits received by a retired worker would depend on the succ_____ _____ ual's own investment.

A proposal to put part of the trust fund into private investments would once have been seen as socialism, as increasing government control in the private economy. Such arguments are not heard any more, for a variety of reasons. One is that the arrival of socialism seems less likely now than previously. The second is the massive change that has taken place in the nature of financial markets. It is now straightforward for an investor, even one as large as Social

[handwritten note on attached slip:] reduce COLA to INFL - 1%? increase normal retire age to 68 to 70?

Security, to invest while having little say about the allocation of capital in the economy. The innovation that is central for this possibility is the growth of mutual funds, particularly index funds. Index funds hold a fraction of the shares of all the firms that make up some index, such as the Dow-Jones average, the Standard and Poors index, or, for that matter, all the firms traded in a particular stock exchange. No one seems to think that the Social Security trustees should be picking good investments. Rather, passive investment into indexes is considered to be both prudent fiduciary behavior for the trustees, and the government behavior desired by people fearing poor investment policies.

Such investment looks very attractive at a time of actuarial imbalance since, on average, private bonds and equities have greater rates of return than do treasury bonds. Therefore the actuaries would project a higher rate of return for Social Security if the funds were privately invested than otherwise. This would contribute to an overall projection that looked better and indeed was better. However, it is necessary to consider why the average rate of return is higher in the private economy. There are two possible reasons. One is that the risks are higher, and the higher average returns are an appropriate return for taking risks. But is it appropriate for Social Security to take on such risks?

To address this, the first question is what it would mean for Social Security to take on these risks. Would poor stock market returns in some year or decade affect future beneficiaries, future payroll tax payers, or possibly, general revenues? There is no clear answer. The legislative process is one of periodic change, and no one can be sure what a future legislature might do in the face of a larger shortfall than would have resulted if the funds were all in treasury bonds. It is probable that Social Security as a whole is a reasonably adequate risk bearer, since the risk can be spread over time, using the portion of the funds that is still in treasury bonds as a cushion for spreading this risk. Moreover, with sufficiently rapid inflation (which is unlikely but not impossible) an investment in treasury bonds would be very risky. In some countries, inflation removed most of the value of their Social Security trust funds.

A second view is that the average return in the private economy is higher than on treasury bonds because investors do not have an accurate picture of the alternative risks. Thus there is a higher return available without as much increased risk as might be feared. Also, there may be a premium for the higher liquidity in treasury bonds—a liquidity that the Social Security Administration does not need because its cash needs are relatively predictable. It is difficult to assess these two views without a very long time series of returns. Either way, such investment seems a fairly good idea, or at least not a bad one.

A still more radical change, as was discussed by the Entitlements Commission in the fall of 1994, would be to shrink Social Security by enough to permit

Proposals to muddle through frequently would extend Social Security to the last large set of workers who are not covered. This comprises some state and local government employees who are currently allowed to remain outside the system. Including these workers in Social Security would help with the financing, in part because they would begin paying taxes soon, but would only receive the resulting benefits later on.

Alan Greenspan, chairman of the Federal Reserve, recently received considerable coverage for his statement that the rate of inflation is overstated. Since this rate is used to calculate COLAs for Social Security, any reduction in measured inflation will save the system money. Measurement of the consumer price index (CPI) probably does overstate inflation, although there is considerable dispute about the magnitude of the discrepancy; consequently, the measurement of the CPI should be reviewed and steps taken to make it as accurate as possible. However, speculation that inflation is inaccurately measured should not be used to reduce COLAs by a legislatively chosen amount. Inflation should be measured correctly. Shrinking real benefits should not be inflicted on retirees if policymakers guess wrongly about inflation. Poverty among the over-sixty-five population is concentrated among those who live a long time, particularly elderly widows. Therefore it is imperative not to make arbitrary adjustments in COLAs that would compound over time and reduce benefits for this vulnerable population especially. Indeed, many of those who study Social Security advocate making changes to increase benefits for this population.

The potential changes described above are in keeping with the sort of modifications of Social Security that have been implemented over the years. They could be designed, with or without a payroll tax increase, to restore actuarial balance without massively changing the present system. Two other changes currently under discussion represent major style changes in Social Security. One would be to invest part of the trust funds in the private economy, in stocks and corporate bonds, rather than keeping the funds completely in Treasury bonds. The second change would be to give individual workers control over the investment of part of the funds, so that the benefits received by a retired worker would depend on the success of the individual's own investment.

A proposal to put part of the trust fund into private investments would once have been seen as socialism, as increasing government control in the private economy. Such arguments are not heard any more, for a variety of reasons. One is that the arrival of socialism seems less likely now than previously. The second is the massive change that has taken place in the nature of financial markets. It is now straightforward for an investor, even one as large as Social

Security, to invest while having little say about the allocation of capital in the economy. The innovation that is central for this possibility is the growth of mutual funds, particularly index funds. Index funds hold a fraction of the shares of all the firms that make up some index, such as the Dow-Jones average, the Standard and Poors index, or, for that matter, all the firms traded in a particular stock exchange. No one seems to think that the Social Security trustees should be picking good investments. Rather, passive investment into indexes is considered to be both prudent fiduciary behavior for the trustees, and the government behavior desired by people fearing poor investment policies.

Such investment looks very attractive at a time of actuarial imbalance since, on average, private bonds and equities have greater rates of return than do treasury bonds. Therefore the actuaries would project a higher rate of return for Social Security if the funds were privately invested than otherwise. This would contribute to an overall projection that looked better and indeed was better. However, it is necessary to consider why the average rate of return is higher in the private economy. There are two possible reasons. One is that the risks are higher, and the higher average returns are an appropriate return for taking risks. But is it appropriate for Social Security to take on such risks?

To address this, the first question is what it would mean for Social Security to take on these risks. Would poor stock market returns in some year or decade affect future beneficiaries, future payroll tax payers, or possibly, general revenues? There is no clear answer. The legislative process is one of periodic change, and no one can be sure what a future legislature might do in the face of a larger shortfall than would have resulted if the funds were all in treasury bonds. It is probable that Social Security as a whole is a reasonably adequate risk bearer, since the risk can be spread over time, using the portion of the funds that is still in treasury bonds as a cushion for spreading this risk. Moreover, with sufficiently rapid inflation (which is unlikely but not impossible) an investment in treasury bonds would be very risky. In some countries, inflation removed most of the value of their Social Security trust funds.

A second view is that the average return in the private economy is higher than on treasury bonds because investors do not have an accurate picture of the alternative risks. Thus there is a higher return available without as much increased risk as might be feared. Also, there may be a premium for the higher liquidity in treasury bonds—a liquidity that the Social Security Administration does not need because its cash needs are relatively predictable. It is difficult to assess these two views without a very long time series of returns. Either way, such investment seems a fairly good idea, or at least not a bad one.

A still more radical change, as was discussed by the Entitlements Commission in the fall of 1994, would be to shrink Social Security by enough to permit part of the payroll tax to be put into individual accounts, like IRAs and 401(k)s, and let individuals control the accumulation until they reached retirement age. Note that this proposal requires generating additional net revenue to free up payroll tax revenue for such investment and still reach actuarial balance. That is, if part of the payroll tax goes to individual accounts instead of to the Social Security trust funds, then the funds need an additional source of revenue, or smaller benefit commitments, to be able to maintain actuarial balance.

There are a variety of economic and political questions about this sort of proposal. The source of its popularity is the Chilean privatization of social security. Chile privatized its social security system in 1981, beginning with a slow phase-out of its existing system. Workers in Chile must save 10 percent of their earnings in individual mutual fund accounts. They also pay for survivor and disability insurance, and for the costs and profits of the mutual funds. On average, they pay 13 percent of earnings in order to save 10 percent and have this insurance. The Chilean economy has grown quite well since 1981, although not without some setbacks. The funds have had very high returns—a real return of roughly 14 percent. It is natural to hope that high returns and a rapidly growing economy are the fruit of privatizing social security, and that this fruit can be reaped by imitating the privatization. The real story, of course, is more complicated. The rapid growth and the high interest rates in the Chilean economy have caused the high returns on individual accounts. Indeed almost all of the money was invested in government debt in the early days, and a great deal still is. But the privatization has also contributed to the growth in two ways.

One is that the government vastly increased the regulation of the capital markets because the mandated social security savings were being invested there. This has improved the Santiago stock exchange and has resulted in the development of a corporate bond market.

The other is that the government has financed the phase-out of the old system by running consistent surpluses of roughly 4 percent of GDP on the government budget. This sustained pattern of surpluses has contributed to capital accumulation and so, to economic growth. Furthermore, improved efficiency in the capital market also helps economic growth.

However, there are two drawbacks to the Chilean system. For retirement income purposes, the most desirable form of benefit is generally an annuity, not an accumulated lump sum. Like everyone else, the Chileans have not been successful at organizing an efficient annuity market based on individual choice. As a result, many retirees choose not to purchase annuities, preferring instead to risk outliving their money, and to fall back on the government-provided minimum pension. Those who have bought annuities have found them very expensive.

In addition to the high cost of annuities, the accumulation process using individual accounts has been expensive, especially as compared to the very low costs of U.S. Social Security, which is a highly efficient operation. Some of these costs are a result of the particular way in which Chile has organized the market for allocating and accumulating mandated savings, and some of these costs seem to be inherent in a situation of individual accumulations with many small accounts.[5]

What does the Chilean experience suggest about the advantages and disadvantages of having a system based on individual accounts in the United States? It seems all too likely that the bad features of the Chilean system would carry over more easily than the good ones.[6] In particular, there would be additional costs. The level of these costs would depend on the method of organization. There is a real possibility of holding down much of the cost if the accounts were organized by the government, while the investments were managed by private companies. However, the large selling costs incurred as mutual funds tried to attract customers, seem almost impossible to avoid. Second, the United States would also have a difficulty in annuitization, unless the government plays a major role in organizing this market. Private, (relatively) unregulated annuity markets based on individual choice do not work well. One source of difficulty is the issue of adverse selection: insurance companies are particularly eager to sell annuities to some people, but they want to avoid others. This problem is familiar from the health insurance market, where it is much more severe. Reliance on the private market would require a mechanism that allowed private insurance companies to provide indexed annuities, such as CPI-indexed treasury bonds. In addition, if the market is to be efficient, the government would have to organize it around group annuity purchase, rather than individual purchase. One way to avoid adverse selection would be for the government to supply the annuities.

As to the positive features, the United States already has a well organized set of capital markets; it would not reap the economic benefits, as Chile did, of moving from poorly organized and nonexistent markets to well-organized ones. Second, the capital accumulation advantage would only be realized if Congress were to vote for extra tax revenue (or decreases in other spending) in order to replace the lost Social Security revenue that would go into individual

5. Two further issues that lie beyong the scope of the present discussion are the allocation of risk inherent in the retirement income system and the implications for the politics of retirement income.

6. Having individual accounts, rather than benefit formulas, greatly reduces the tendency to give large benefits to early generations of retirees. For better or for worse, this has already happened in the United States and is not undone by changing the system.

accounts. If the government were to increase its borrowing to offset the loss of payroll tax revenue, capital accumulation would not increase because some funds would flow to individual accounts. In Chile the phaseout of the old Social Security system took place at a time when there was already a large government surplus to finance the process. In the United States some people think that creating further demands on the budget would result in Congress, which is already unable to deal with a sizable deficit, being somehow better able to deal with an even larger one. This seems unlikely. Indeed, recent history and the discussion around the balanced budget amendment suggest that the budget process today is driven primarily by the difficulty of cutting expenditures. Budget measures are set up to facilitate politically plausible levels of deficit reduction; they do not drive expenditure cuts. Thus some Republicans have said that they would favor the balanced budget amendment if the Social Security surpluses were included in the accounting for the amendment, but not if they were excluded from it. This reflects a recognition of the kind of deficit reduction that is politically plausible.

The bottom line is that small, mandated, individual accounts would be expensive and would be poor providers of retirement income. They would contribute little or nothing to capital accumulation beyond what could be accomplished by investing part of the trust funds in the private economy. Fortunately, such institutional changes are not needed to balance Social Security. Compared with this, muddling through seems a good approach.